Mapping the Journey
Case Studies in Strategy and Action toward Sustainable Development

Lorinda R. Rowledge, PhD
Russell S. Barton, PhD
Kevin S. Brady

in collaboration with

James A. Fava, PhD
Cynthia L. Figge
Konrad Saur, PhD
Steven B. Young, PhD

Sustainable business practices are the foundation for current and future business success. Through the collection and presentation of case studies, the authors of *Mapping the Journey* have created a framework for both thought and action concerning the implementation of sustainable development. The change, actions and leadership described in this book present exciting potential to use sustainable practices to benefit customers, employees, shareholders and society.

Kip Smith, President and CEO, Ballard Power Systems Inc.

Although many of the companies profiled in this book of case studies have already been recognised for their environmental and/or social achievements, they are not—and most would not claim to be—anywhere near their final destination. We have yet to see a genuinely sustainable enterprise in most sectors of the economy. But the case studies do provide useful clues to some of the competences and leadership skills required. In short, they provide elements of a road map that will help today's pathfinders—and tomorrow's would-be pioneers—to understand both the market and political challenges they will face and the tools and behaviours that will help them on their way.

John Elkington, Chairman, SustainAbility Ltd

The road to corporate sustainability is fraught with many twists, turns and potholes. The wonderful case studies detailed in this book provide much-needed signage and guideposts for the journey.

Stuart Hart, Kenan-Flagler Business School, University of North Carolina

---

Re-inventing our industrial system is a critical necessity if we are to have a sustainable global society on the earth. This useful book documents the beginnings of that change— voluntary first steps by a number of leading companies toward a more environmentally benign business model. Such path-breaking examples bear close scrutiny, because the strategies they suggest may soon become a necessity for virtually all companies.

Allen Hammond, Senior Scientist at the World Resources Institute; author of Which World: Scenarios for the 21st Century

---

In *Mapping the Journey* the authors have captured the three essential elements of the journey of learning of companies that have chosen sustainable development as the context for achieving their vision: first, the focus on knowledge—from innovation in strategy and action as well as from the remembering and building upon past wisdom; second, the journey as a collaboration in community with employees and stakeholders; third, and above all, the action that produces the results and knowledge that energises and supports the next stage of the journey.

Jim Leslie, President, International Institute for Sustainable Development (IISD) Business Trust

The authors of **Mapping the Journey** have done an outstanding job of describing the current threats to global sustainability and providing many excellent examples of innovative industry responses. I have no doubt that this text will become a 'must read' for anyone interested in advancing the case for sustainable development in their organisations.

Cliff Bast, Global Product Stewardship Manager, Hewlett-Packard Company

---

The social, economic and environmental consequences of 'business as usual' will affect everyone. Any company planning to be in profitable business in fifty years' time needs to be building sustainability into their strategic thinking today. This book offers some practical and encouraging examples of such foresight.

Chris Tuppen, Corporate Social and Environmental Programmes, British Telecom

---

The authors of **Mapping the Journey** have provided a critically important investigation of the development and implementation of corporate strategies toward sustainability. Through extensive case studies of actual company experiences, this book provides extraordinary insight and guidance to these new developments and provides directions to all companies as they consider their responses to social and environmental impacts and issues. This is essential reading for all managers.

Marc J. Epstein, Research Professor of Management, Rice University; author of Measuring Corporate Environmental Performance

---

The path toward sustainability is requisite travel for all companies that expect to survive and thrive in the years ahead. **Mapping the Journey** identifies valuable insights from seasoned travellers on the road to sustainable business solutions. It provides concrete examples of organisations that have developed the strategic decision-making and innovative capacity to turn the challenge of sustainability into opportunities for both short- and long-term success.

Ronald J. Bergin, Director, Office of the Auditor General of Canada; Commissioner of the Environment and Sustainable Development

---

The efforts of these public and private organisations in pursuing sustainability are case studies in enlightened and heroic leadership. Their examples will lead and inspire those who seek to build enduring institutions.

Susan Mecklenburg, Director, Environmental and Community Affairs, Starbucks Coffee Company

---

As leading companies find themselves on the verge of the Second Industrial Revolution, and as resource efficiency, life-cycle management, dematerialisation and sustainability become the buzzwords of the new millennium business ethic, **Mapping the Journey** both sets the scene and offers practical examples to others wishing to start the journey to corporate sustainability. An excellent read, full of inspiring examples of corporate engagement in the sustainability debate.

Mark Barthel, Head of Sustainability Group and Director of Strategic Development, British Standards Institution

Mapping the Journey uncovers the old but often buried truth that environment and economy are but two sides of the same coin. More importantly, these case studies provide excellent real-world examples of the strategies and tools required by organisations to improve their environmental and economic performance.

Prof. Dr-Ing Peter Eyerer, Chair of Material Science, University of Stuttgart; Managing Director, FraunHofer Institute for Chemical Technology

---

Mapping the Journey is an excellent compendium of strategies and managerial tools applied by organisations leading the way in the sustainability journey. The book offers a practical analysis of sustainable development. It demonstrates how we can enhance economic development while at the same time address the environmental challenge that is on the horizon for all of us. In reading this book, I found a clear message. This is a strategic business issue, so fundamental to enlightened managers and yet still so subtle to many . . . an essential message for all business leaders and business schools.

Georges Michaud, Director, Environment, Business Strategy, Corporate Environmental Services, Nortel Networks

---

Successful companies in the next millennium will be those that understand and practise sustainability. *Mapping the Journey* provides excellent insight through very well-documented case histories of companies that not only drive the sustainable development agenda forward but are also economically successful. Don't miss this book; it is inspiring to read.

Manfred Wirth, Director, Wirth Sustainable Business Consulting

---

Mapping the Journey provides an excellent description of how leading-edge companies have learned to make gold from green. These information-packed stories will both educate and spur others to action.

Robert W. Slater, Senior Assistant Deputy Minister, Environment Canada

---

Since the Rio Summit, more and more enterprises have been talking about sustainable development and how this most ambitious goal may be reached. In *Mapping the Journey* we find an impressive collection of examples from companies that not only talk about sustainable development but are also firmly committed to working towards its achievement.

Dr Manfred Marsmann, Product Stewardship, Bayer AG

Mapping the Journey offers a rare combination: ecological conscience and smart business sense. Every industry can benefit from this examination of sustainable-business success stories, with industrial systems designed to offer profits beyond the bottom line.

Susan I. Marvin, President, Marvin Windows & Doors

Mapping the Journey

Case Studies in Strategy and Action toward Sustainable Development

Lorinda R. Rowledge PhD, Russell S. Barton PhD and Kevin S. Brady

in collaboration with
James A. Fava PhD, Cynthia L. Figge, Konrad Saur PhD and Steven B. Young PhD

Greenleaf
PUBLISHING

1 9 9 9

To our children:
Mackenzie, Taisha, Logan
Shonagh, Liam, Duncan
Andrea and Evan
Jessica, Ross
Reid, Bronwyn, Deirdre

Published by Greenleaf Publishing
Aizlewood Business Centre
Aizlewood's Mill
Nursery Street
Sheffield S3 8GG
UK

Typeset by Greenleaf Publishing Limited and printed on environmentally friendly, acid-free paper from managed forests by Bookcraft, Midsomer Norton, UK.

British Library Cataloguing in Publication Data:
    Rowledge, Lorinda R.
        Mapping the journey : case studies in strategy and action
        toward sustainable development

        1. Social responsibility of business - Case studies
        2. Industries - Environmental aspects - Case studies
        3. Sustainable development - Case studies
        I. Title   II. Barton, Russell S.   III. Brady, Kevin S.   IV Fava,
        James A.
        658.4'08

        ISBN 187471925X Hbk
        ISBN 1874719268 Pbk

CONTENTS

Acknowledgements 9
Foreword 13
Preface 15
Introduction 19

THE CASE STUDIES

Case 1: Volvo
Strategic action toward sustainable mobility for society 40

Case 2: Suncor
Taking stakeholder relations to a new level 67

Case 3: AssiDomän
Foresters integrating dual goals of economy and environment 87

Case 4: Patagonia
First ascents: finding the way toward quality of life and work 95

Case 5: Interface Flooring Systems
Driving industrial standards higher 123

Case 6: Sony
Operationalising the slogan 'Entertaining the world: caring for the environment' 129

Case 7: ASG
Trailblazing toward sustainable logistics and transport 151

Case 8: SC Johnson
Eco-Efficiency and Beyond 165

Case 9: DaimlerChrysler
Redefining cost   179

Case 10: Center for Technology Assessment
Pursuing regional approaches to qualitative growth and sustainability   185

Case 11: Henkel
Traditional values and ecological leadership   201

Case 12: SJ Rail
Turnaround to sustainable transport for the 21st century   219

Case 13: TransAlta
New terrain: reducing greenhouse gas emissions   237

Case 14: The Netherlands National Environmental Policy Plan
Developing sustainable industrial strategy   259

Closing comments   275
About the authors   278
Index   281

ACKNOWLEDGEMENTS

This book would not have been possible without the significant contribution of time and ideas from the many people who so generously shared with us their journeys, hopes and challenges. More so than in any other type of publication, writers of case studies reflect the insights and wisdom of those they interview. We have made every attempt to be true to the information as it was presented to us, and apologise for any misinterpretations.

A sincere thank you to the dedicated managers of ASG, AssiDomän, Daimler-Chrysler, Center for Technology Assessment (CTA), The Dutch National Policy Plan (NEPP), Henkel, Interface Flooring, Patagonia, SC Johnson & Sons, Inc., SJ Rail, TransAlta, Sony, Suncor and Volvo, listed by name below.

This book is an extension of a report originally written by several of the authors for the Canadian Office of the Commissioner of Environment and Sustainable Development. A special thanks is owed to the originator of that initial study, Ron Bergin. The book is also an outgrowth of Executive Study Missions to Europe on Business-Driven Sustainability led by EKOS International and sponsored by Boeing, Lynx, Monsanto, Nike, Ontario Hydro, Step-by-Step and the Canadian Ministry of Environment. We would like to acknowledge Tatum Nolan who served as a research assistant in the initial stages of the project, Gil Friend and Timothy O'Shea, who supported the study missions, and Joy Cordell for translating documents from Swedish to English. A special thank-you to the managers, companies and organisations that provided great insights during those study missions, including Per Grunewald and Henrik Troberg of Electrolux, Ernst Ulrich von Weizsäcker, Wolfgang Sachs, Christa Liedtke and Hartmut Stiller of the Wuppertal Institute, and Karl Henrik Robèrt, John Holmberg and others from The Natural Step office, Sweden. Finally, we would like to express our great appreciation to John Stuart, Dean Bargh and the staff of Greenleaf Publishing who provided gracious and thorough editorial support and went more than the extra mile to bring this project over the finish line.

ASG
Magnus Swahn, Environmental Manager
Johan Saarm, Controller

AssiDomän
Nippe Hylander, Senior Vice-President,
    Development and Environment
Nina Haglund, Senior Advisor, Packaging
    Development
Jonas Jacobsson, Director, Forest
    Management
Katarina Lindel, Development and
    Environment
Professor Jan-Erik Lundmark, Senior
    Ecologist
Lars Ströberg, Co-ordinator of
    Environmental Affairs, Development
    and Environment

Center for Technology Assessment (CTA)
Professor Ortwin Renn, PhD, Director and
    Professor of Environmental Sociology
Hans Kastenholz, PhD, Technology,
    Society, Environmental Economics
Diethard Schade, PhD, Director of CTA

DaimlerChrysler
Robert Kainz, Senior Manager, Pollution
    Prevention and Life Cycle Programmes

Henkel
Michael Bahn, Corporate Safety, Health
    and Environmental Quality
Rüdifger Wagner, Environmental
    Protection and Safety
Hans-Jürgen Klüppel, Process and
    Environmental Management

Interface Flooring Systems
Rahumathulla Marikkar, Manager,
    Technical and Environmental,
    Belleville Plant

The Dutch Policy Plan (NEPP)
Jans Suurland, Directorate General for
    Environmental Protection, Ministry of
    Housing, Spatial Planning and the
    Environment
Henk Wijens, Directorate General for
    Environmental Protection, Ministry of
    Housing, Spatial Planning and the
    Environment

Patagonia
David Olsen, CEO
Lu Setnicka, Director of Public Affairs
Randy Harward, Director of Fabric
    Development, Quality and
    Environmental R&D
Kevin Sweeney, Director of
    Communications
Gary Eckwortzel, Team Leader, Hardgoods
Neil Edwards, Director of Finance
Mike Brown, Environmental Assessment
Eric Wilmanns, Environmental Assessment
Julie Ringler, Production
Geoff Cline, In-House Counsel
Adrienne Moser, Team Leader, Kids'
Roger McDivitt, Director of Contract
    Management
Karyn Barsa, Director of Operations
Terri Wolfe, Director of Human Resources
Bruce Barbour, Team Leader, Watersports

SC Johnson
Ken Alston, Director of Sustainable
    Product Innovation
Greg Anderegg, Manager, Community
    Relations Worldwide
Tom Benson, Environmental Actions
    Manager, North America
F.H. 'Chip' Brewer, Director of Worldwide
    Government Relations
Armin Clobes, Platform Leader, Indoor
    Environmental Science
Ed Eeg, Senior Packaging Engineer
    (Retired)
Lew Falbo, Director, Worldwide Safety,
    Health and Environment Operations
Cynthia Georgeson, Director, Corporate
    Pubic Affairs Worldwide
Brenda Gieszler, Department Manager,
    Packaging Development
Patrick Guiney, PhD, Senior Section
    Manager, Product Safety
Reva Holmes, Vice-President, Secretary
    and Trustee of SC Johnson Wax Fund
    (Retired)
Jane Hutterly, Senior Vice-President,
    Worldwide Corporate Affairs
Robert Israel, PhD, Director, Regulatory
    Affairs and Product Safety, SC Johnson
    Professional
Darcy Massey, Senior Vice-President,
    Research, Development and
    Engineering

David Sanders, President and Chief Operating Officer, SC Johnson Polymer, Worldwide

Craig Shiesley, Senior Brand Manager, Home Cleaning

Judy Zaunbrecher, Director, Global Home Cleaning, Research, Development and Engineering

SJ Rail

Daniel Johannesson, Director General and Group CEO of SJ Rail

Karin Jansson, SJ Communications

Anders Lundberg, Senior Vice-President, Director of Corporate Planning and Strategic Development

Gunnel Sundbom, Senior Vice-President, Director of Communications

Johan Trouve, MSc, Policy Officer Environment/R&D

Sony

Jürgen Günther, Senior Manager, Mechanical Engineering

Oliver von Quast, PhD, Project Manager, Environmental Center Europe

Christian Ridder, Project Manager, Environmental Center Europe

Y. Sasagawa, Assistant General Manager in Corporate Environmental Affairs, Japan

Karl Sturm, Manager, Environmental Center Europe

Dietrich Wienke, PhD, Project Manager, Environmental Center Europe

Suncor

Eric Axford, Director of Strategy and Planning

Mark Shaw, Director of Sustainable Development, Oil Sands

Ron Shewchuk, Corporate Manager of External Communications

Gordon Lambert, Corporate Director of Environment, Health and Safety

TransAlta

Jim Leslie, Consultant (former Senior Vice-President), Sustainable Development

Robert Page, PhD, Vice-President, Sustainable Development

John A. Tapics, PEng, Vice-President, Generation, TransAlta Utilities Corporation

Paul Vickers, PEng, Manager Sustainable Development Operations

Don Wharton, Manager of Business Integration, Sustainable Development

Volvo

Jan Blennius, Vice-President, Corporate Strategy

Torsten Dahlberg, Managing Director, Volvo Mobility Systems

Bo Egerdal, Vice-President, Industry and Trade Policy

Ulla-Britt Fräjdin Hellqvist, Director, Competence Center, Environment

Lena Gevert, Director, Environmental Affairs

Inge Horkeby, MSc, Director, Corporate Environmental Auditing

Agneta Wendel, Environmental Manager, Product Development Process, Volvo Car Corporation

FOREWORD

John Elkington

Chairman, SustainAbility Ltd; Member, EU Consultative Forum
on Sustainable Development; author, Cannibals with Forks:
The Triple Bottom Line of 21st-Century Business *(Capstone Publishing, 1999)*

You can often tell a great deal about what people are really thinking by listening to the language they use. Companies considering the sustainable development agenda frequently talk in terms of a 'journey' towards sustainability, of 'crossroads', 'milestones' and 'road maps'. Some, it has to be said, talk of the journey as a way of putting off the evil day when they have to set out on the hard road, but others embrace the challenge—and are eager to be off. This book is heavily skewed towards the second group, and their accounts make fascinating reading.

The agenda tends to evolve in spasms. There have been two big waves of environmental pressure on industry, peaking in 1969–73 and 1988–91, followed by two great downwaves (1974–87 and 1992–98). At SustainAbility, we have for some time predicted a third wave, but cautioned that it would be nothing like the previous two.

We expected the drivers to be different, with the social and economic fallout from globalisation likely to be a more powerful driver than climate change (which is far harder for ordinary citizens to respond to than ozone depletion was in the last wave) and the millennial watershed. The evidence suggests that the third wave has indeed started to roll, with the travails of companies such as Shell and Nike suggesting that the implications for business are likely to be on a very different scale.

Both of these companies are among those now talking about their planned transitions towards sustainable development. They are also reviewing their performance against what some call the 'three pillars' of sustainable development—but which I and my colleagues prefer to call the 'triple bottom line'. This requires companies to manage, account for and report on their performance in terms of their net contributions to economic prosperity, environmental quality and social equity. Already, we are hearing leading companies beginning to talk in terms of the value they add in all three dimensions.

Companies committed to integrating the sustainability agenda into their businesses tend to display all of the following features:

▷ A clear and focused strategic perspective on how sustainability relates to the company, its value chains, markets, products and operations

▷ Management systems that enable the company to monitor and manage environmental and social issues and integrate them into core business decisions

▷ Stakeholder dialogue processes that ensure that internal and external concerns are heard early and effectively addressed

▷ Product development processes that integrate triple-bottom-line thinking into the design process and account for impacts throughout the life-cycle

▷ Open, transparent, quantified and verified communication of their triple-bottom-line performance, with growing numbers of companies signing up to the Global Reporting Initiative (GRI) reporting guidelines

▷ Innovative supply-chain management approaches, where the environmental and social performance of a company's suppliers is seen as an important part of that company's overall performance

▷ A toolbox that includes life-cycle assessment, design for the environment and life-cycle costing methodologies that internalise what were previously external environmental costs

▷ And a range of tailored communications activities designed to carry the message through to key market actors, particularly consumers and customers (in terms of performance and quality messages) and financial markets (in terms of various measures of return on investment)

Although many of the companies profiled in this book of case studies have already been recognised for their environmental and/or social achievements, they are not—and most would not claim to be—anywhere near their final destination. We have yet to see a genuinely sustainable enterprise in most sectors of the economy. But the case studies do provide useful clues to some of the competences and leadership skills required. In short, they provide elements of a road map that will help today's pathfinders—and tomorrow's would-be pioneers—to understand both the market and political challenges they will face and the tools and behaviours that will help them on their way.

A number of years ago, I took one of the most memorable journeys of my life: a 250-mile rafting trip down the Colorado River through the magnificent Grand Canyon. It was a stunning experience on a number of levels. One, in particular, is relevant to this book.

Often our small group would huddle around the campfire in the fading light, listening to the ominous sound and vivid descriptions of the rapids that would face us the following mornings: 'Crystal', 'Sockdolager', 'Granite', 'Hans', 'Lava Falls'. Interspersed in our echoing commentary, read by firelight, were excerpts from the diaries of John Wesley Powell, the undisputed first purposeful explorer of the Colorado River in 1869. As terrified and exhilarated as we were by the tremendous hydraulics and threatening cavities created by the confluence of river, rock, volcanoes, flash floods and gravity, I couldn't help but reflect on the fact that our group had detailed river maps, experienced comrades, and equipment with the latest in technology. What must it have been like for those first explorers, charting an unknown course through those raging torrents? What vision, courage, team spirit and strength of character sustained them through the hardships?

This book features—and honours—people and organisations charting unknown paths in a different, yet equally challenging, landscape. These pathfinders are mapping the unknown territory, finding the hidden trails, and gaining the critical knowledge for **creating a sustainable industrial system**. Clearly, the entire path is not yet visible. Nor has any individual company or a society as a whole reached the destination (as members of these companies will quickly attest). Yet, just as any journey is defined as **'travel or passage from one place to another . . . an often extended experience that provides new information or knowledge beyond that which one might normally acquire'** (*Webster's Dictionary*), these companies are challenging old assumptions, creating a new world-view, and blazing a trail that will guide others through a wilderness or unknown country. They, like Powell, are proving that it can be done.

Mapping the Journey is a book of case studies. It illuminates leading examples of significant progress on the journey toward sustainable development in both private and public organisations worldwide: the companies Sony, Volvo, TransAlta, SC Johnson, ASG, Patagonia, SJ Rail, Interface, Henkel, Suncor, AssiDomän and DaimlerChrysler; the Center for Technology Assessment in Germany (CTA); and the Dutch National Environment Policy Plan. Research for the book involved numerous interviews with key managers, site visits, reviewing internal and external publications, and examining relevant literature. *Mapping the Journey* summarises the business rationale, strategic decisions, product design features and process changes made by these leading companies and organisations as they proactively and seriously address the ever-increasing requirement to lessen the environmental burden of our products and production processes. Many companies and governments are taking steps in this direction. What differentiates those featured here is that they are moving beyond compliance to proactive integration; beyond environmental management toward sustainability; beyond process to product; beyond end-of-pipe controls to design innovations; beyond eco-efficiencies toward creation of value. In our analysis, they are on a fundamentally different trajectory.

A primary objective of this book is to illustrate not only what is being done, but *how* it is being accomplished. To this end, we have endeavoured to describe the implementation steps followed, the specific management processes created, and the personal viewpoints and leadership contributed by each organisation on its journey of implementing strategies and practices for more sustainable development.

My fellow authors and I have the fortune—good and bad!—of seeing the complex, systemic nature of the sustainability dilemma. We understand the pressures on business to remain competitive, keep costs down, satisfy customers and create shareholder value. Simultaneously, we recognise the environmental and societal price being exacted as a result of existing global industrial paradigms and practices. Our corporations and society are a long way from the end-point of an environmentally and socially sustainable industrial system. We deeply understand the shortcomings of industry, even those companies described here as being exemplary. We see the fatal flaws in our current system of commerce, the cultural *zeitgeist*, and the societal metabolism in which today's organisations are embedded. Also, though, we see the inherent need for a system for the production and distribution of goods; for a means of creating and distributing wealth; for an economic infrastructure that contributes to human prosperity. And, we believe, business will be a key institution providing leadership to a new, more sustainable economy. The answer for the future is in the innovative *integration* of economic, environmental and social system goals and requirements. The organisations described in *Mapping the Journey* are taking initial steps toward solving this tripartite equation.

We have chosen to highlight the positive, proactive steps being taken as these organisations break new ground, in full recognition that there could be many criticisms of these companies, and any company for that matter, against a pure definition of sustainability. Also, this book focuses primarily on the accomplishments of leading companies and organisations in the arena of *environmental* sustainability. For the most part, organisations are further along the environmental sustainability journey, even though many of the companies included in this book have solid social sustainability programmes in place. We have left for another book a more thorough illustration of the topic of social responsibility and management in service of human prosperity, as well as an extensive development of the strategic and moral rationale for pursuing sustainable development.

No one company is doing it all. Each company must proceed within the context of their particular circumstance, business conditions and culture. Yet it is extremely valuable to examine the principles and strategies underlying specific practices. By taking an active learning stance, and putting aside critique as to where these organisations may yet make progress, one is able to slowly construct a powerful multi-dimensional map, complete with guidelines, milestones, targets, measures of success, tools and techniques, and valuable wisdom about travelling toward a prosperous, sustainable future.

Lorinda R. Rowledge, PhD
EKOS International
Seattle, 6 September 1999

Preview of the book—and the future

Embodied in the present is prescience of the future:

▷ **Volvo** added environment to its core values of quality and safety and views it as an integral part of company strategy for competitive advantage. Changes were targeted at three areas of highest leverage: (1) **product design** based on reducing environmental impact over the entire product life-cycle; (2) **business development**—for example, market access in Asia and a new company 'Volvo Mobility Systems' aimed at providing products and solutions for the design of safer and more environmentally benign transportation systems; and (3) tough **procurement** standards for suppliers regarding environmental management and materials. All of this has been supported by clear messages from the boardroom to the shop floor regarding the business relevance of environmental issues, and by extensive education of engineers, employees, suppliers, customers and stakeholders.

▷ **Sony**, one of the world leaders in brand strength and innovative product development, has extended its world-class management and technological innovation to include environment, requiring that **all Sony products incorporate environmental issues as part of product development**, employing **rigorous environmental management systems** nearing 100% ISO 14001 or EMAS certification of manufacturing sites, and focusing **R&D on technologies to reduce environmental impact**.

▷ **Patagonia**, a leading US designer and distributor of speciality outdoor clothing, has declared its fundamental purpose as 'inspiring and implementing solutions to the environmental crisis', backed by breakthrough commitments to **using entirely organic cotton** in products, **contracting for 100% renewable (wind) energy** in all 14 California facilities, developing core product lines with **fleece fabric made from postconsumer recycled soda bottles**, and phasing out all PVC in travel bags. Environmental performance has clearly become a critical element of Patagonia's definition of style.

▷ **Suncor**, a Canadian energy company, has a stated goal to become a **'sustainable energy company'**. This objective presents a significant challenge as we enter the carbon-constrained world of the 21st century. Suncor has stepped away from the pack within its sector, acknowledging the immense challenge of climate change and developing an action plan to aggressively address this issue. Additionally, Suncor has redefined **stakeholder relations** to such an extent that it has been able to vault ahead of the regulatory process and add significant value to the company.

▷ **Interface Flooring Systems**, following the lead of Interface, Inc. CEO Ray Anderson to 'build the world's first **sustainable and eventually restorative enterprise'**, has become the company leader in **elimination and management of toxic substances**, and follows a strategic approach to *intensify* government standards.

▷ **The Netherlands**, in the third phase of its **National Environment Policy Plan**, focuses on 'absolute decoupling of economic growth and environmental pressure and on the **sustainable use of natural resources'**. To achieve this ambitious objective, it has forged new alliances with industry and is pursuing a **sustainable industrial strategy** at the national level. The wide array of **integrated environmental planning, policies and programmes** has produced tangible results toward the breakthrough goal of sustainability by 2010.

▷ **Henkel** has merged traditional business values and ethics with an outstanding **integrated management system** in which quality, safety, health and environment are addressed simultaneously. For Henkel there are no niche or 'green' products; **all products must be environmentally sound** and the company has established the systems and product development processes required to meet this objective.

▷ **The Center for Technology Assessment (CTA)**, a government-funded think-tank institute, is working intensively with industry and other stakeholders to implement **sustainable economic development policies and programmes** at a regional level in Germany's highly industrialised Baden-Württemberg area, where total exports top US$70 billion.

These organisations, together with the others described in this book, are taking a radically different approach to environmental pressures inherent in traditional products and production processes. 'Sustainable development' is seen as central to strategic positioning and competitive advantage—a key component in future economic success and market value.

Sustainable development

Currently we are in the midst of a paradigm shift with respect to how society views the environmental, social and economic implications of participating and surviving in the modern world. The shift is away from an industrial model in which environmental activity is viewed as a cost, resources are viewed as a free good, and the social implications of industrial policy are an afterthought. Leading decision-makers and thought leaders in academia, industry, government and non-governmental organisations are now embracing a new model in which economic, environmental and social considerations are highly integrated. In this model, industrial environmental activity is viewed as an opportunity for cost reduction, product innovation and increased shareholder value; understanding the social implications of decision-making is seen as a platform for the long-term prosperity of organisations. Rather than being an add-on, the economic viability of a national economy or an organisation is predicated on understanding and integrating environmental and social considerations into core decision-making processes.

The term most often used to describe this shift, 'sustainable development', has its roots in *Our Common Future*, the 1987 report of the World Commission on Environment and Development (commonly known as the 'Brundtland Report'; WCED 1987), and in the 1992 United Nations Conference on Environment and Development (UNCED) held in Rio de Janeiro. Based on an unprecedented global consultation process, *Our Common Future* set out a vision for sustainable development that integrated economic, social and environmental concerns. The UNCED conference further translated this vision into a series of actions for governments around the world. At UNCED, governments made a formal commitment to develop and promote more sustainable forms of consumption and production.

The definition of sustainable development offered in *Our Common Future*— development that 'meets the needs of the present without compromising the ability of future generations to meet their own needs' (WCED 1987)—has become widely used globally.

Since 1987, sustainable development has emerged as a concept, and now a movement, disentangling economic growth or progress from material resource use. The prominent economist and author, Herman Daly, who spent six years at The World Bank, clarified the critical concept that our economic system is

▷ Waste elimination and reduction: zero waste

▷ Reduction of toxic dispersion: zero emissions

▷ Enhanced resource productivity: Factor 4, Factor 10

▷ Clean production: processes, technologies, products

▷ Increased energy efficiency

▷ Closed loops: re-use, remanufacturing, recycling

▷ Design for X: design for recyclability, disassembly, environment added to design for manufacturability and assembly, serviceability, repairability

▷ Extended product durability, functionality, flexibility

▷ Dematerialisation: shift from product to service or information

▷ Product stewardship: taking environmental responsibility for products throughout the life-cycle

▷ Transparency: environmental and social corporate reporting, and performance measurement

▷ Ethical production: human rights, workplace conditions and practices, safety, living wages

Box 1: Strategic industry responses to sustainability

necessarily a subsystem of the ecosystem, and that we must substitute goals of 'growth' for those of 'development', where increase in human prosperity is achieved without overshooting the carrying capacity (resources *and* sinks) of the earth:

> The demands of these (human economic activities) on the containing ecosystem for regeneration of raw material 'inputs' and absorption of waste 'outputs' must be kept at ecologically sustainable levels as a condition of sustainable development. This change in vision involves replacing the economic norm of quantitative expansion (growth) with that of qualitative improvement (development) as the path of the future progresses . . . 'Growth' is an increase in size through material accretion while 'development' is the realization of fuller and greater potential—so sustainable development is progressive social betterment without growing beyond ecological carrying capacity (Daly 1996).

Partly in response to—but in many cases ahead of—governments, industry has also taken up the mantle of sustainability. Individual companies, and organisations such as the World Business Council for Sustainable Development, have been developing a number of industrial responses to the need to move toward more sustainable production. Some of these responses are outlined in Box 1.

This governmental and industrial shift toward a sustainability paradigm is taking place on a planet that is, in the minds of many leading thinkers and decision-makers, already reaching ecological limits in critical areas such as food production, fresh-water supply, ozone layer depletion and climate change. The challenge, for industry, governments and individuals, will be to ensure that continued economic development and social wellbeing are compatible with ecological support systems. *Mapping the Journey* is an exploration of this challenge, documenting how organisations that have made a commitment to move toward sustainability are progressing.

Sustainability as a central strategic issue

▷ What critical insights can guide managers and governments as they make strategic decisions to position for the emerging economy?

▷ What will be the business context of the next decade?

▷ What innovations in business design and technology will redefine the future competitive landscape?

▷ What shifts in market demand will drive new requirements and expectations for winning customer loyalty?

▷ How can corporate policies and strategies be translated and implemented in multinational companies with very diverse product lines?

▷ What competences and practices from leading global companies and governments could inform our business strategies and practices?

▷ What is the key to achieving sustainable competitive advantage and value?

▷ By what measure should we determine success?

The principles of sustainability—perspectives and processes for redesigning our industrial system and practices and our social culture and metabolism (industrial throughput) to achieve sustainable development—offer critical insights for developing the answers to these strategic questions. The organisations in this book are using sustainability in forming strategic plans to:

▷ Position for the new economy

▷ Anticipate critical elements of the emerging business context

▷ Meet shifting customer requirements

▷ Build customer loyalty and brand

▷ Stimulate innovations in business design and technology

▷ Develop new competences

▷ Achieve competitive advantage,

▷ Increase value

▷ Redefine measures of corporate, community, and national success

There is a fundamental shift occurring in mainstream business, moving environmental and social sustainability into the forefront of strategic planning and positioning.

For the past many decades, these so-called 'corporate responsibility' pressures have been largely viewed as a thorn in the side of management: an additional cost to be endured. Consequently, these issues have often been shunted to environment and public affairs departments, far from the core strategic decision-making and product and service development of the company. With the exception of a few niche 'green' product manufacturers, corporate response to environmental pressures has largely been constrained to compliance with legislative requirements in production sites and promoting paper recycling in office facilities. On a parallel stream in the public sector, policy-makers have often felt squeezed between constituents' voiced concern for the environment and the pressing need for jobs, community and regional economic development, and the financial support of corporations with strong vested interests. Rhetoric was often hollow and laws sporadically enforced when faced with 'real-world' needs to boost employment, support economic growth, and gain campaign finances. Today, the business context is changing dramatically and, with it, the corporate and public policy strategic response.

As a society, we are increasingly aware of the environmental impacts and degradation that result from our industrial activity.

There is a mountain of evidence and growing consensus that our industrial system is on a collision course with the realities of the resources and sinks of the natural system on which it depends, at a significant cost to the health and wellbeing of humans and other species inhabiting the planet today and in the future. The more effective our corporations are at transforming raw materials into products to be distributed worldwide, and the more effective our communities and nations are at stimulating economic development, the more 'effectively' we contribute to the environmental degradation and social disruption which are the unintended consequences of our current industrial system. Data on the ramifications, or 'underbelly', of our current industrial system, living habits, and consumption patterns are summarised in Box 2.

WORLDWATCH INSTITUTE'S *STATE OF THE WORLD: 1998*
REPORTS ENVIRONMENTAL DEGRADATION.

▷ **Climate change** from greenhouse gas emissions. Carbon dioxide (CO_2), at the highest concentrations for 160,000 years, due to the six billion tonnes currently released annually, has seemingly contributed to 14 of the warmest years ever recorded, which have all occurred since 1980, with collateral damage to grain harvest due to heat, flooding and storms.

▷ **Ozone depletion**: the 'hole' in the ozone above Antarctica is larger than North America.

▷ **Toxic build-up and dispersion**, linked to a dramatic rise in birth defects, cancers (one in eight women now die of breast cancer) and other illnesses. Of the 100,000+ widely used chemicals reported by the National Academy of Science, we have enough information to assess the human health effects of only 5%.

▷ Massive **extinction and loss of biodiversity**, whereby 25% of all mammal species, 33% of all fish species, 20% of reptiles, 25% of all amphibians and 14% of all known plant species are officially endangered—an extinction rate of 1,000 a year, compared to a natural background extinction rate of 1–3 species a year.

▷ **Forest loss**, whereby 80% of all large intact natural forests have vanished worldwide, while 50% of landfill waste is wood and paper.

▷ Dramatic **decline in fisheries,** with 70% of all ocean fish species in decline, 11 of the 15 major fishing areas worldwide officially over-exploited, and 60% of all coral reefs endangered.

▷ **Scarcity of fresh-water**, with water tables falling on every continent, many rivers no longer reaching the sea, and 57% of all US watersheds declared by the US EPA to have 'serious' water quality problems.

WORLDWATCH REPORTS PARALLEL STRESSES IN HUMAN SYSTEMS.

▷ Gross **inequities in resource use**, whereby the richest 20% of the world consume 86% of the world's production output; yet the poorest 20% consume only 1.3%.

▷ Massive **poverty**, whereby 1.3 billion people live in what The World Bank calls 'absolute poverty' of income lower than $1 a day; 1.2 billion people have no access to clean water; 3 billion have no sanitation services; and 100 million are homeless in the industrialised nations.

▷ **Poor health** seven million children die annually from malnutrition; India records 2.5 million deaths from air pollution; and cancer of all types, age adjusted, is up 60% in the US from 1950 to 1998.

▷ **Violence and conflict** leading to death, physical and emotional trauma, and 70 million refugees.

Box 2: Snapshot of the 'State of the World'

Source: Summary of data presented in Brown *et al.* 1998

Further, Wackernagel and Rees (1996), using their 'Ecological Footprint Analysis', vividly demonstrate that, if the entire world population were to enjoy North American standards which require about 4.5 hectares (11 acres) per person, we would need an additional two planet earths to accommodate the increased ecological load, even of the people alive today! The trajectory of the 'ecological footprint' requirements of our current North American industrial metabolism, with global economic development and projected population growth, portends the requirement of five additional earths in the next century.

Pressures resulting from these environmental and social impacts are increasingly significant drivers of business and policy.

Both corporate customer and end-use consumer expectations regarding environmental performance of products, social responsibility and transparency are rising, as are legislative requirements and supplier qualification 'hoops' such as ISO 14001 certification. Nations, urban centres and individual corporations are planning their response to the Kyoto agreements on climate change. Varying by geographic region, there is a general trend towards increased costs for waste disposal, landfill and hazardous waste treatment. Some organisations are vulnerable to scarcity and increasing costs of resources. And, finally, investor expectations are changing, driven by both economic and social goals.

Concurrently, there is mounting evidence that our 'old-world' 'trade-off' paradigm, pitting economic success against environmental and social goals, is seriously flawed.

Both research studies and practical experience have demonstrated that improved environmental and social responsibility *increase* value to shareholders, customers, employees and society (rather than adding costs). Improving environmental and social performance in fact leads to enhanced profitability and value: cost reduc-

Box 3: Environmental performance and shareholder value

In 1997 the WBCSD convened a working group of 40 business and financial experts to examine the relationship between environmental performance and shareholder value (WBCSD 1997). Among their findings:

▷ Environmental drivers can provide competitive advantage to any company.

▷ Environmental issues can drive financial performance.

▷ The quality of a company's environmental management is a good indicator of the overall quality of its business management.

A recent book by Gretchen Daily (1997) quantifies in the trillions the ecosystem services provided by nature:

> *generation and renewal of soil and soil fertility, pollination of crops and natural vegetation, control of the vast majority of potential agricultural pests, dispersal of seeds and translocation of nutrients, maintenance of biodiversity, from which humanity has derived key elements of its agricultural, medicinal and industrial enterprise, protection from the sun's harmful ultraviolet rays, partial stabilisation of climate, moderation of temperature extremes and the force of winds and water, support of diverse human cultures, providing of aesthetic beauty and intellectual stimulation that lift the human spirit.*

While exposing the difficulties of assigning valuations to these services, the contributors convincingly argue that our policies and decision-making grossly undervalue the multitude of ways in which we are dependent on the biosphere, to the tune of trillions of dollars of services contributed annually, and that 'safeguarding ecosystem services represents one of the wisest economic investments society could make'.

Box 4: Valuing nature's services to society

tions from eco-efficiencies, waste reductions and process improvements; price premiums, especially for those first to market; enhanced brand equity and customer loyalty; lowered cost of capital due to reduced liability and risk; increased revenue from new products, markets and even new businesses; and enhanced asset management.

Electrolux provides a tangible example:

> It has become more and more evident that our long-term, holistic approach was the right way to go. We are aiming towards both sustainability and to create shareholder value . . . In one key product area, for example, the products with the best environmental performance . . . have a 3.5 percentage points higher [profit] margin than the average.
>
> *Per Grunewald, Senior Vice-President,*
> *Group Environmental Affairs, Electrolux* (Electrolux 1997: 3)

Superior environmental and social performance has also been found to lead to intangible benefits: higher employee job satisfaction and commitment, increased innovation and creativity, and motivation from a sense of higher purpose. Additionally, at a societal level, we are coming to understand the economic value of natural-system services, which a recent estimate has placed in the trillions of US dollars per year (Daily 1997). Box 4 provides more details.

Model for a sustainable future economy

▷ In the coming decades, what will be the context defining corporate and managerial success?

▷ What will shape economic stability and evolution toward more liveable and prosperous communities?

Pressures are enormous on those formulating strategies and building competences for survival, let alone success, in this future marketplace. Most managers are well aware of dramatic discontinuous changes driven by the information revolution, technological innovations, massive consolidations, and structural shifts from vertical to horizontal integration that are redefining the competitive arena in industry after industry. Furthermore, the previous high bar for success—world-class performance in parts per million quality, rapid cycle times, superb customer service and low costs—has moved a notch higher, now requiring rapid time-to-market, mass customisation, customer intimacy, agility in strategy and production capability, and knowledge management.

What many managers are less aware of is that there is a parallel shift, or discontinuity, at the magnitude of the 'Next Industrial Revolution', which is creating new customer requirements, reshaping corporate strategy and business models, and changing the fundamental value proposition of companies. It is also expanding product design requirements, redesigning and systematising production and distribution processes, and stimulating new forms of stakeholder relationships. This sleeper discontinuity—sustainable development—is reframing the very nature of how value is created. After working over $1\frac{1}{2}$ decades with state-of-the-art management technology and leading two extensive executive study missions visiting dozens of leading organisations in Europe implementing business-driven sustainability, our overriding conclusion is that understanding sustainability as a central strategic issue is one of the key aspects of the transformation to a post-industrial age.

Current industrial practices are exerting extreme pressures on every major natural system, from sea (devastated fisheries) to sky (climate change from greenhouse gas emissions, ozone depletion, urban air pollution); from plants and animals (massive loss of biodiversity) to soil and water (acidification and toxic build-up, falling water tables on every continent). Given that the requirements for sustainable industry are driven by the physical limitations on resources and sinks—which dramatically affect health and quality of life—the question is not if, but when, the requirements will take effect. Claude Fussler, in his book *Driving Eco-Innovation* (Fussler with James 1996), cautioned:

> The irresistible forces of population growth and consumer aspirations
> are meeting the fragility of our planetary systems and resources. The only

> solution is radical shifts in values, technologies, and patterns of consumption and production. This will mean the 'sunset' of unsustainable products and processes. It will also create boundless opportunities for the entrepreneurs who can match cost-effective capabilities with the needs for cleaner products and processes.

Sustainable development *will* be a defining element of the future economy: a central element of future value creation and prosperity. The breakthrough paradigm is seeing the goal as integrating, rather than trading off or balancing, the three goals of: economic development; environmental protection and restoration; and social equity and wellbeing. Visually and conceptually, progress toward 'sustainability' is optimally attained through strategies and actions at the intersection of three converging circles (see Fig. 1). This illustrates graphically that sustainability is achieved at the nexus of excellent managerial and production systems, in alignment with and restorative to natural systems, in optimal service of human prosperity and development (EKOS 1997).

Tremendous opportunities exist for those corporations that take the lead in transforming our pervasive industrial-age model to align with natural-system requirements, in higher service of human development and prosperity. This book describes the new ways of thinking and acting employed by organisations, both private and public, proceeding on this path.

Figure 1: **A model for sustainability: the nexus of economic/manufacturing, natural and human systems**

Source: EKOS 1997

SUSTAINABILITY: NEXUS OF INNOVATION AND VALUE

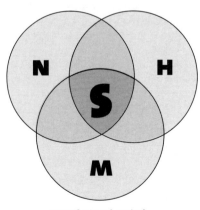

Natural capital
Integrative and restorative interaction with natural ecosystem constraints and resources

Human prosperity
Optimal contribution to employees, customers, community, global society

Manufactured capital
World-class strategy and execution, excellent business design, product and service design, production capability, core competence development

Overview of the book

Mapping the Journey consists of 11 in-depth case studies and three short vignettes. The full case studies document the historical journey the company has taken. This approach allows for a fuller story and hopefully gives some insight into the organisational transformation that occurred. The vignettes highlight examples of best practice on particular issues (for example, measurement in AssiDomän and management of toxic substances in Interface Flooring Systems and Daimler-Chrysler). Table 1 presents a summary of the exemplary practices of each organisation, in the order they appear in the book. As these leading organisations so clearly show, sustainable development has moved from the fringes to the mainstream of strategy and decision-making. Box 5 summarises the new approach to sustainability presented in this Introduction.

ORGANISATION	HIGHLIGHTS AND EXEMPLARY PRACTICES TOWARD SUSTAINABLE DEVELOPMENT
Volvo	▷ Sustainable development is an integral part of business strategy for competitive advantage and business development.
	▷ Design for Environment (DfE) is embedded in engineering guidelines, procurement, engineering education and manuals, and stage gate reviews in the product development process.
	▷ Life-cycle assessment is enabled by over 15 years' worth of data collected within the entire supply chain, and by the Environmental Priorities Strategies (EPS) software tool which aids designers in assessing 'Environmental Load Unit' impact on natural resources, human health, biodiversity, aesthetics and biological production.
	▷ The model 'Dialogue on the Environment' education programme has been delivered to over 40,000 (and this number will increase) employees, suppliers and dealers, with expected follow-up implementation action.
	▷ Supplier guidelines are in place, including: early involvement in product development; 'black list' and 'grey list' of prohibited materials; environmental management system requirements; and materials use expectations.
Suncor	▷ Goal to become a 'sustainable energy company'
	▷ Recognised leader in environmental management and stakeholder relations
	▷ Initiated one of the world's first greenhouse gas emissions trades
	▷ Established a climate change action plan that differentiated itself from many of its competitors in the energy sector
	▷ Is developing alternative energy sources in conjunction with its Oil Sands business

Table 1: **Highlights and exemplary practices toward sustainable development**
(continued opposite)

ORGANISATION	HIGHLIGHTS AND EXEMPLARY PRACTICES TOWARD SUSTAINABLE DEVELOPMENT
AssiDomän	▷ Dual and equal goals of production and ecological values ▷ A long-term perspective to strengthen the company's profitability ▷ The 'Ecological Balance Sheet' measures progress on forest ecology objectives. ▷ Two weeks' training per year for loggers on forest ecology
Patagonia	▷ A revolutionary purpose 'to inspire and implement solutions to the environmental crisis' ▷ The company is clearly driven by 'the right thing to do'. ▷ A commitment to 100% organic cotton; the 'Synchilla' fleece fabric made from post-consumer recycled soda bottles; an infant 'pre-cycling' line cut from scraps of adult clothing lines; and elimination of PVC in travel bags ▷ The integration of environment as a part of quality definition and quality management in the entire supply stream
Interface Flooring Systems	▷ The CEO has led the expedition to 'build the world's first sustainable and eventually restorative enterprise'. ▷ The Belleville plant is the company leader in the elimination and management of toxic substances, which includes the systematic elimination of zinc borate, decabromodiphenyloxide (DBDPO), antimony oxide, molybdenum dioxide, lead, cadmium, barium, dispersing agents with formaldehyde, and silica products. Traditional solvent-based adhesives have been replaced by water-based products. ▷ A strategic approach to intensify government standards, to communicate the environmental attributes of products to customers, to emphasise the health connection, and to lead the industry ▷ Active work with suppliers ▷ Employee bonuses are linked to environmental improvement through 'eco-points'.
Sony	▷ A top management-driven comprehensive approach integrates environmental improvement goals into product design, technology development, production processes, facilities design and operation, and procurement management. ▷ 'Greenplus 2000' requires all Sony products to incorporate environmental issues as part of the product development process by 2000. ▷ 90% of worldwide manufacturing sites are ISO 14001-certified as of 5 July 1999. (100% of manufacturing sites in Japan and Europe are ISO 14001-certified.) ▷ 'End-of-life' is addressed in product design, technology development, procurement, industry-wide collaboration on R&D, and relations with dealers and customers.

Table 1: **Highlights and exemplary practices toward sustainable development**

(from previous page; continued over)

ORGANISATION	HIGHLIGHTS AND EXEMPLARY PRACTICES TOWARD SUSTAINABLE DEVELOPMENT
ASG	▷ There is a worldwide infrastructure for driving, co-ordinating and disseminating learning. The executive management-led Environmental Conservation Committees (ECCs) at headquarters and in each of four major markets serve as a local–global forum for determining strategy, setting and monitoring improvement goals, and diffusing innovation. ▷ There is a clear strategic rationale that environmental performance leads to increased shareholder value and 'option value' (or right to operate in the future). ▷ Positioning to move toward sustainable logistics ▷ Extremely specific operational implementation objectives for group environmental work, complete with targets, measures and monitoring ▷ The environment viewed as a key element of the brand.
SC Johnson	▷ Eco-efficiency breakthroughs in packaging and chemical formulas ▷ A software support system for creating new chemical formulas to reduce or eliminate chemicals that are toxic or on any watch list of any constituency in the world ▷ Knowledge management ▷ Community and civic responsibility
DaimlerChrysler	▷ Systematic integration of environmental, health and safety considerations into the product development process ▷ Documentation of the full life-cycle costs of hazardous substances ▷ Demonstrating that the environmentally sound option is the less-cost option
Center for Technology Assessment (CTA)	▷ A unique focus on 'regional sustainability' in Germany's largest industrial export area (over US$70 billion) ▷ The organisational structure ensures multi-stakeholder representation and participation. ▷ A collective deliberative process composed of citizens' panels informed by experts and stakeholders which makes policy recommendations ▷ A working definition of sustainable development and 'qualitative growth', defined evolution and phases, and development of regional indicators ▷ Government-funded research that crosses sectors and disciplines
Henkel	▷ A comprehensive safety, health and environment plus quality management system ▷ Shifting from products to services ▷ Establishing an environmental standard of excellence for all products ▷ Building brand image through actions and strategic communication

Table 1: Highlights and exemplary practices toward sustainable development
(from previous page; continued opposite)

ORGANISATION	HIGHLIGHTS AND EXEMPLARY PRACTICES TOWARD SUSTAINABLE DEVELOPMENT
SJ Rail	▷ Competitive positioning and marketing based on the superior environmental performance of rail as the most sustainable transport option succeeds in capturing market share ▷ A branded transportation service called 'Green Cargo' ▷ An innovative communication plan galvanised the corporate turnaround. ▷ On-line software enables customers to calculate and compare the environmental impacts of various modes of transport and logistics plans.
TransAlta	▷ Structural changes have elevated attention to environmental issues in corporate decision-making and business development. The Senior Vice-President of Sustainable Development position is staffed by an expert in ecology and there is also a position of Manager of Business Integration, Sustainable Development. ▷ The company is ahead of schedule in meeting its greenhouse gas emissions goals, stabilising to 1990 levels through improved efficiencies internally and with customers, through offset and joint implementation, and through displacement from co-generation. ▷ Environmental performance is playing an increasing role in winning bids globally. ▷ Nine out of ten employees have been educated in the 'Environmental Citizenship Initiative'.
Netherlands: National Environmental Policy Plan (NEPP)	▷ The NEPP goal is to achieve sustainable development in the Netherlands within one generation. The goal in NEPP 3 is to decouple economic growth and environmental pressure and ensure the sustainable use of natural resources. ▷ Sectors and media frameworks for public policy have been replaced by a scientific-driven focus on eight key environmental themes with well-defined targets: climate change, acidification, eutrophication, toxic pollutants, contaminated land, waste disposal, groundwater depletion, and resource dissipation. ▷ The environmental programme is focused on the integration of the environment into land use planning, internationalisation of policy, biodiversity, sustainable economic development, sustainable consumption and production, and self-regulation. ▷ A 'covenants' system of agreements increases flexibility and moves away from the regulatory toward a partnership approach to achieve long-term breakthrough results.

Table 1: **Highlights and exemplary practices toward sustainable development**

(from previous page)

▷ There is increasing understanding and endorsement among leading businesses and public-sector organisations around the globe that our industrial products and practices must be fundamentally redesigned in alignment with the environment on which they depend—that we must have 'sustainable development'.

▷ Sustainable development has been defined as 'meeting the needs of the present generation without compromising the ability of future generations to meet their own needs' (WCED 1987), or as 'the realisation of fuller and greater potential . . . or progressive social betterment without growing beyond ecological carrying capacity' (Daly 1996). Sustainable development requires the 'dematerialisation' of our economy by decoupling economic growth from growth in material resource inputs and waste 'outputs', designing more equitable and socially beneficial industrial practices, and replacing quantitative growth with qualitative development.

▷ Leading organisations are moving beyond compliance and even eco-efficiency, proactively incorporating environmental and social sustainability considerations into their core business strategy for competitive advantage and value creation.

▷ Sustainability is not shunted off into an environment department; instead, leading companies are integrating environmental and social sustainability into strategic planning, product design, process design and management, facilities design, relationships with customers, and employee relations.

▷ Environmental concern is no longer constrained to production processes: the focus of concern is increasingly on the product itself throughout the entire life-cycle.

▷ It is sexy (well, sort of)! Sustainability is driving innovation, stimulating redefinition of the value proposition to customers, leading to entirely new business models that redefine the competitive playing field, spurring the substitution of knowledge for material, and coalescing new partnerships and deepened relationships around a deeper value.

▷ In practice, in corporations, increased sustainability is achieved through: innovations that inject environmental performance goals and engineering guidelines into product design and review procedures; production process redesign to reduce resource consumption, emissions and unsafe procedures; environmental management in operations modelled after quality assurance systems; supplier management; and distribution.

▷ For those who make a threshold level of commitment to more sustainable management of the public sector and private industry, benefits accrue in the form of competitive advantage, increased customer loyalty, lowered cost of capital, new product and business lines, new markets, decreased operating costs, increased margins, and improved employee recruitment, commitment and retention.

Box 5: **Summary of the new approach to sustainability**

Alternative world-view

Decades ago, Joseph Juran, one of the 'founding fathers' of the Total Quality movement, noted that change required first a revolution in Thinking, and then Knowledge, before one could attain a revolution in Action (Juran 1964). So, too, with sustainability.

The strategies and actions of the organisations featured in *Mapping the Journey* are inextricably embedded in a world-view made up of assumptions and theories about goals, paths to achieving goals, and principles and processes with which to operate. There are a number of essential components of the higher-order paradigm overlying the strategies and actions:

1. Simultaneous solutions to economic, environmental and social goals: integrative nexus rather than trade-off

2. Life-cycle thinking, responsibility and management (based on the concept and tool of life-cycle assessment [LCA])

3. Closed loop internally and in industrial ecology

4. Prevention and design as leverage

5. Beyond environmental management to full-scale integration into all aspects of the organisation

6. Shifting focus toward product as much or more than process

7. Total-cost management and asset management over the entire product/ service life-cycle

8. Decoupling industrial economic growth from environmental resource use: qualitative growth, optimising resource use, and dematerialisation

9. Intellectual capital and social capital as central

10. Continuum of value creation: level of commitment and action on the continuum 'traditional–reactive–proactive–integrative–transcendent' correlated with return from sustainability.

Note to reader: conflicts and caveats

Current debates on sustainability are marked by a large degree of confusion with respect to issues such as terminology and what constitutes best practice. What does it mean to claim that an organisation is moving toward sustainability? How is this measured? There is even confusion over the fundamental concept, with many people querying whether sustainability is a destination or a journey. Some people lament this confusing state of affairs, but in a sense it is typical of any paradigm shift. The explosion of tools and the overlapping terms and concepts (industrial ecology, eco-efficiency, life-cycle management, design for environment, cleaner production, etc.) are indicative of the creative forces that are at work to understand and address the challenge of moving society toward more sustainable forms of production and consumption. This challenge is accelerating and becoming more focused as decision-makers begin to comprehend the reality of a world that must provide a reasonable quality of life not just to today's population of six billion but to a total of somewhere between seven and ten billion more people in the next half-century (Fussler with James 1996).

It is also important to note that, as authors, we have not undertaken to criticise the selected companies, but rather have focused on highlighting interesting approaches and practices. The reader is asked to keep in mind that these case studies profile organisations that have agreed to publicly share their journey. We have deliberately focused on solutions—in some cases putting aside, for now, more challenging questions about weaknesses yet to be corrected. There are interesting and difficult discussions and decisions many of these organisations will face as they continue to proactively incorporate principles of sustainability. For example, what are the major systemic shifts required in energy and transport systems in the future, and where are the companies in relation to this future desired state?

In addition, the case studies presented here probably represent the state of the art with respect to the environmental aspects of sustainability. Sustainable development, however, also demands consideration of the social aspects of the industrial system, both internally and externally. In some cases (for example, Patagonia and SC Johnson), these companies have exemplary social practices. In general, though, while many companies are dealing effectively with the economic and environmental aspects of their operations and products, very few have started the more difficult task of fully addressing the social dimension of their business. There are, however, clear indications that social issues are gaining importance and companies are increasingly paying attention to this 'third leg' of sustainable development. In future case studies, more examples of social innovations will be required to complete the picture.

There are no easy solutions with respect to sustainability, and to speak about a 'sustainable company' is in some measure ridiculous. But it is also clear that, given current population and ecological trends, patterns of production and consumption must change. The good news is that there are innovators and leaders experimenting with new strategies, concepts and tools that promise to contribute to sustainability. The organisations documented in this book of case studies provide examples of the 'practice of sustainability'. These examples of practice are perhaps best viewed as pieces of a puzzle that we are trying to bring together to provide a more complete picture of the breadth and depth of actions that can be undertaken to move an organisation forward with respect to sustainability. These actions include:

▷ Innovative stakeholder engagement processes (Suncor)

▷ Long-term strategic planning processes focused on environmental and social considerations (Dutch government)

▷ The development of tools to evaluate the environmental implications of products and services (Volvo)

▷ Product development processes that are geared to meet a changing marketplace where the environmental attributes of products will be considered on an equal footing with cost, quality and performance (DaimlerChrysler)

▷ Corporate policy that requires all products to incorporate environmental issues as part of the product development process (Sony)

▷ Vivid demonstrations of the life-cycle impacts of products to educate and engage suppliers in considering environment as a key part of quality (Patagonia)

▷ Branded 'green' service with contemporary marketing campaign (lime green ties on businessmen!) (SJ Rail)

▷ Internal market exchange for CO_2 emissions to increase awareness and stimulate action (TransAlta)

Individually, the case studies illustrate what in real terms is being done to move each organisation forward into a new century in which the rules of the game or the paradigm will be very different. Collectively, the case studies provide an overview of the opportunity sustainability can provide in terms of enhanced economic and environmental performance. The case studies demonstrate that, for companies, this opportunity leads to tangible benefits:

▷ Reductions in operating costs

▷ Production and process improvements

▷ Reduced liability and risk

▷ Enhanced brand image

▷ Increased employee morale

▷ Increased opportunity for innovation

▷ Increased opportunity for revenue generation, including new products, markets and businesses

> ▷ Better supply-chain management

> ▷ Deeper, more meaningful relationships with customers

For public-sector organisations, benefits include progress toward societal goals with respect to the environment, the development of more robust industry that is better prepared to meet the challenge of the next century and a better return on investment with respect to environmental expenditure of tax dollars. The greatest contribution, though, may be that these advances of first explorers into the realm of sustainability have provided tangible models and 'proof of concept'—it can be done!

References

Brown, L.R., *et al.* (1998) *State of the World 1998: A Worldwatch Institute Report on Progress toward a Sustainable Society* (New York: W.W. Norton).

Daily, G. (1997) *Nature's Services: Societal Dependence on Natural Ecosystems* (Washington, DC: Island Press).

Daly, H.E. (1996) *Beyond Growth: The Economics of Sustainable Development* (Boston, MA: Beacon Press).

EKOS (1997) *Sustainable Competitive Advantage: Summary Report of the June 1997 Study Mission to Germany, Sweden, and Switzerland* (internal document; Seattle, WA: EKOS International).

Electrolux (1997) *Electrolux Environmental Report* (Stockholm: Electrolux Group Environmental Affairs).

Fussler, C., with P. James (1996) *Driving Eco-Innovation: A Breakthrough Discipline for Innovation and Sustainability* (London: Financial Times/Pitman).

Juran, J.M. (1964) *Managerial Breakthrough: A New Concept of the Manager's Job* (New York: McGraw–Hill).

Wackernagel, M., and W. Rees (1996) *Our Ecological Footprint: Reducing Human Impact on Earth* (Gabriola Island, BC, Canada: New Society Publishers).

WBCSD (World Business Council for Sustainable Development) (1997) *Environmental Performance and Shareholder Value* (Geneva: WBCSD).

WCED (World Commission on Environment and Development) (1987) *Our Common Future* ('The Brundtland Report'; Oxford, UK: Oxford University Press).

THE
CASE
STUDIES

As this book was being written in January 1999, Ford Motor Company announced its intention to purchase the car division of Volvo for US$6.45 billion. Jac Nasser, Ford's CEO, stated in a Ford press release that 'Volvo has a world-class reputation for safety, quality, durability, and environmental responsibility'.

Ford will leverage Volvo's brand name, access to loyal customers, and substantial investment into the S80 platform (engineering structure) for related models. The upscale Volvo series cars will fill a market segment gap in Ford's product line. Ford's economies of scale will reduce production and distribution costs. Volvo, freed of the prohibitive cost and limited profitability in the car corporation, is expected to use the capital generated by the divestiture for acquisitions aimed at gaining dominance in speciality vehicles (trucks, buses and construction equipment).

It remains to be seen how Volvo Car Corporation's strategic, production and design initiatives will be integrated within those of Ford, and how the remaining Volvo Group divisions will evolve. Like all major auto manufacturers, Ford has joined the 'Enviro-car' race. Faced with public concerns about the industry's contribution to global warming, regulatory pressure to meet tough new emissions standards in California and Europe (particularly for its Sports Utility Vehicle) and competitive pressure to match products such as Toyota's Prius gasoline–electric hybrid and Honda's 'VV' hybrid and Civic GX natural gas vehicle, Ford has joined other auto-makers in accelerated efforts to create more environmentally benign vehicles. Ford is also attempting to strengthen its brand as an environmentally responsible company. It has certified all manufacturing plants worldwide under ISO 14001; acquired Volvo Cars, at least in part for its environmental proactivity; developed the Ford P2000 LSR (a hybrid diesel–electric engine system that achieves about 60 mpg); and increased advertising to raise awareness about its recycling efforts.

Critical to Ford's evolution toward more sustainable products and production processes will be the leadership of self-proclaimed environmentalist Chairman William Clay Ford Jr. Harking back to legacy of his great-grandfather—company founder Henry Ford—Bill Ford has gained positive press ('Does Bill have a better idea', *Newsweek*, 23 November 1998; 'Ford's Clean Revolution', *Tomorrow*, September/October 1999) for his pro-environmental convictions. *Tomorrow* quoted Bill Ford's speech in Germany attended by Chancellor Gerhard Schröder: 'While my great-grandfather was a leader in the first industrial revolution, I want Ford Motor Company to be a leader in the second industrial revolution—the Clean Revolution.' Ford will have a tough job maintaining profitability and share value while working to lessen the considerable environmental impact of his best-selling products.

Even more significant is Ford's substantial investment in the development of fundamentally different technologies for the future. In a global alliance formed in April 1998 with DaimlerChrysler and Ballard Power Systems Inc., Ford and its partners initiated the leading commitment to fuel-cell-powered diesel trains and components for cars, trucks and buses. Ford invested $420 million in Ballard, the world leader in the development of the proton exchange membrane fuel-cell power system. This investment positions Ford as a leader in technologies considered to be key components in sustainable transport solutions for the next century.

Volvo's likely evolution might be projected from the directions, competences and new business concepts such as 'Volvo Mobility Systems' described below. It is clearly focused on developing not only products, but solutions for sustainable mobility in the future.

For simplicity, we have left the text as it was originally written, so the term and descriptions of 'Volvo' here refer to the entire Volvo Group prior to the divestiture of the Volvo Car Corporation to Ford. Most principles and strategies are relevant whether in Volvo, Ford or another industry.

VOLVO

Strategic action toward sustainable mobility for society

1. *The lie of the land*

a. *Corporate overview*

AB Volvo, at year-end 1998, is the largest industrial group in Scandinavia, with over 79,000 employees and 55 production plants in 26 countries. Sales in 1998 were SEK 212,936 million (US$25 billion). The Volvo Group's products include cars, large trucks, buses, aircraft engines, construction equipment, and drive systems for marine and industrial applications. About 88% of Volvo sales are outside Sweden, primarily in Western Europe and North America.

To students of management, Volvo gained recognition over 20 years ago for challenging the traditional approach to assembly-line production processes by designing production work around intact teams with 'whole tasks'. Volvo's innovative work redesign, which considered the 'social-system' in addition to the technical system, set the standard for creating self-managing work teams and improving 'Quality of Worklife'.

In the last decade, this strength in high-performance work teams has been augmented by an impressive implementation of lean production methods such as Just-in-Time (JIT) manufacturing, waste reduction, flexible manufacturing, and concurrent engineering, to shorten time-to-market. Volvo now manufactures using a 'pull' production system, produces cars to individual customer specifications, and has inventory turns of about four hours in its car assembly plants.

To this powerful production capability and team synergy—driven by market demand, legislative requirements and a visionary strategy—Volvo has added a rigorous effort to reduce the negative environmental impact of its products. Based on a deep understanding of the entire life-cycle impacts of the automotive and transport industries, Volvo has integrated its value for 'Environmental Care' into design of products and services, production process design and management, product end-of-life handling, customer and employee education, supplier management, and new business services and products.

b. *Preview*

What perceptions does the 'Volvo' brand generate? Historically, it has been associated with safety and a commitment to high quality. More recently, it has acquired associations of environmental excellence.

To the car-buying public, Volvo is well known for the core values of safety and quality related to all aspects of product concept, design, engineering, production and service. Now, as an extension of its established commitment to high-quality, safe transportation, Volvo has for the first time since 1927 added a third core corporate value: 'Environmental Care'. Adding environment to the brand identity of Volvo in this way represents an important component of Volvo's overall strategic platform. The company has determined that brand image is critical to its future strategic positioning, so placing environment as such a central attribute of its corporate brand sends a strong message both internally and externally.

Volvo's expectation is that its comprehensive and aggressive strategy for integrating environmental considerations into all aspects of business will be increasingly crucial to achieving customer satisfaction and meeting legislative demands in the future. President and CEO of AB Volvo, Leif Johansson, views environmental issues as playing a key role in Volvo's strategy for growth: 'I am convinced that we can create new business opportunities and long-term competitive gains through aggressive, dedicated and comprehensive [environmental] action programmes.'

Although most automotive companies have been working on improvements to reduce the environmental impact of their products, Volvo's comprehensive approach and leadership in a number of key areas can provide a valuable model for other corporations in their journey toward more sustainable industrial practices. Described in this chapter are Volvo's pioneering work in the following areas:

▷ Integration of environment at a strategic level, including new business development

▷ Development of a structure for implementing environment into design engineering

▷ Development and use of information and databases regarding life-cycle impacts

▷ Education of employees, suppliers and dealers

▷ Supplier management, including education, expectations and requirements

▷ Product declaration and measurement

Box 1: Sustainable development in Volvo today

▷ Volvo's strategy for sustainable development is an integral part of their wider competitive business strategy, and environment has been added as one of three core underlying values of the company.

▷ There is alignment on environmental strategies and objectives, and their relevance to the business, from the board of directors to the shop floor.

▷ By 31 December 1998, over 49,000 employees, suppliers and dealers will have been educated about the basic functioning of nature and conditions of life, the key environmental issues facing our society today (e.g. climate change, ozone depletion, loss of biodiversity), the environmental aspects and impacts of energy and transportation, and the company's environmental objectives and programmes.

▷ About 350 people from almost 60 European suppliers have received environmental education and clear performance expectations regarding establishment of an environmental management system, environmental impact improvements, data exchange for life-cycle assessments, 'black lists' and 'grey lists' of chemicals, optimised handling of waste and packaging, and materials recyclability.

▷ Improvements have been made in **production processes**, where emissions (particularly from solvents) have been reduced substantially with the result that Volvo estimates it is achieving savings of US$2.50 per car directly to the bottom line simply from its improvements in waste sorting.

▷ Volvo has implemented **product design** changes. For example:
  1. Design changes focus on reduction of environmental impact 'in use' by providing: greater fuel efficiency; buses as alternative modes of transportation (one-third of the Volvo buses sold in Sweden in 1996 were designed to burn alternative fuels, and 21 natural gas buses were supplied to the UK in 1997); mobile data communication systems; and products with alternative fuels such as natural gas, biofuel, alcohol and electricity.
  2. The degree of recycled materials in cars is increasing—with rising levels of economic viability. Today the average recycling percentage of cars is around 75%, and of heavy trucks over 90% (by weight higher than cars, given the higher metal content).

▷ Volvo has developed a **new company**, 'Volvo Mobility Systems', to provide products and solutions for the design of safer and more environmentally benign transportation systems globally. (For example, Volvo has partnered in developing a more sustainable transportation system based on bus systems which provide service and environmental impact equivalent to light rail systems—at a $1/_{100}$th of the cost.)

▷ Volvo's platform car S80 (May 1998) is the first car in the world with an 'Environmental Product Declaration' certified by a third party and based on life-cycle assessment.

Volvo's major accomplishments in managing for environmental sustainability are summarised in Box 1.

Before examining the specifics of Volvo's exemplary progress in strategy, design, data, education and supplier management, the business context and events that converged to propel Volvo along this path will be examined.

c. *The business context*

Today's automotive industry is experiencing unprecedented competitive pressure and massive structural shifts. Automobile manufacturers are facing constrained new car sales (due to high saturation in North American, European and Japanese markets and economic turmoil in Asian, Eastern European and Latin American markets); estimated 25%–30% excess production capacity worldwide; globalisation of markets and production; and increasingly demanding requirements from sophisticated customers. These trends are driving tremendous cost/price pressures, new investment requirements and rapid consolidation in the industry. There has also been an industry restructuring trend toward horizontal rather than vertical integration (as in the computer industry). The Daimler-Benz–Chrysler merger exemplifies a consolidation to increase financial power, distribute development costs across multiple platforms, and increase economies of scale for sourcing, components, distribution and services.

Volvo's other major business segment, the commercial products industry, is expected to remain a growing sector globally, spurred by the requirements in developing nations for transportation systems infrastructure and the demand in industrialised areas for efficient urban mobility.

Public, consumer and regulatory pressure regarding the poor environmental profile of transportation is intensifying—primarily due to greenhouse gas and other toxic emissions. Environmental performance is increasingly a differentiating factor in competitive posturing. These and other drivers toward sustainability are described in more detail below.

Up until the early 1990s, Volvo enjoyed a long-standing reputation for its caring attitude, and had demonstrated leadership in environmental issues by becoming one of the first companies in the world to publish an environmental policy in 1972, and by introducing the three-way catalytic converter in 1976, reducing emissions by about 90%. In the early '90s, however, events were to unfold that put Volvo's environmental agenda on a whole new plane.

d. *A new direction: bringing the outside in*

This story begins with an ending. After several years and a monumental effort to merge the operations of its companies, the 'marriage' between Volvo and Renault was called off. In 1993, after this arrangement had collapsed, Volvo underwent a major reorganisation of its board of directors, and substantially reoriented its company direction. This new board met every two to three weeks for four months, listening to experts from the outside world, and then defining Volvo's new strategy for the future. The board of directors, together with company strategists and management, made great efforts to listen to these experts—understanding shareholder mentality, defining customer needs and trends, drawing on research on macro-economic and political trends, examining the thinking of leading theorists and managers, analysing the company's competitive position, examining technological advances, and looking at general business environment intelligence.

Coming out of this process, Volvo developed a comprehensive strategic effort to increase its competitiveness and profitability, based on its core values. The strategy included:

▷ Refocusing on its core automotive products and services

▷ Divesting all non-automotive interests (SEK 46 billion [US$5.4 billion] sold in three years)

▷ Achieving greater efficiencies and economies of scale from basic improvements in its industrial system and joint ventures

▷ Positioning as one of the leading automotive manufacturers in the area of sustainability

▷ Accelerating new product development

▷ Developing an external focus

▷ Developing and leveraging its brand identity

Volvo's consolidation of focus and de-merger with Renault led to a doubling of its share value in the three years following. Sustainability-related initiatives are seen as having contributed to this increase. Volvo managers have stated that environmental management has been shown to be correlated with good management in general, that it differentiates their product brand, and has increased market share (and therefore increased profits and share value) in Volvo Truck Corporation. So, although it is difficult to demonstrate a direct relationship, it is likely that improved environmental performance has contributed to increased margins, profits and share value.

e. Key drivers of sustainability strategies

Volvo's evolution toward sustainability has been influenced by a number of key market drivers: increasing customer demand, competitive pressures, stringent regulatory requirements and new business opportunities. Additionally, Volvo's high-integrity, holistic, life-cycle approach to understanding customer requirements, business value management and environmental impacts has radiated into all elements of their business management.

Market demand. Volvo is experiencing increasing market demand in certain segments in many countries. Industrial customers, fleet owners, leasing customers, 'authorities' and community sectors (e.g. city transport, airports) are intensifying their purchasing requirements, information requests and concerns about the environmental impact of their transportation choices. The ripple effect that is cascading through the supply chain, especially in northern Europe, is affecting Volvo. As any one corporation seeks to improve its environmental profile, it of course looks to lessen the negative impacts within its supply chain and transportation activities. So, for example, as Baxter Europe or Eastman Kodak communicated their environmental improvement expectations and goals to their transport company, ASG, this spurred ASG to be more selective in its choice of transport vehicles. Volvo's work in the development of fuel-efficient trucks, alternative fuels and other environmental performance attributes positioned it well for this business. There is growing demand for efficient and environmentally friendly transport solutions.

Legislative pressures. The transport industry faces increasingly rigorous legislative standards regarding emissions (led by California's 2003 zero emissions law, and a plethora of European Union emissions standards for cars, trucks and buses which will be introduced from 2000 onwards, recycling (e.g. Sweden's June 1996 legislation which established producer responsibility for scrap cars, mandating that, by 2002, 85% of the vehicle weight must be recovered for re-use, material recycling or energy recovery), waste handling, reduction of noise and traffic congestion, and packaging (e.g. the 1994 legislation in Sweden establishing producer liability for packaging requiring that manufacturers facilitate the sorting and re-use, recycling or energy recovery of all packaging made of glass, corrugated board, paper or cardboard, metal, and plastic). More stringent controls on diesel-powered buses and trucks are on the docket in the US (1998), Japan (2000) and the EU (2001). Many of the regulations have parallels in other countries, and the overall expectation is that these provisions will continue to be tightened in the future. For example, in July 1999, the EU approved 'End-of-Life Vehicle' (ELV) legislation requiring take-back for new cars from 2001 and for all cars by 2006. By the later date, manufacturers must recycle or re-use 80% of vehicle weight (this legislation is awaiting ratification by the European Parliament). Volvo is working actively to promote harmonisation of regulations at an international level. (Overall, there has been exponential growth in the number of legislative restrictions on industry, and the expectation is that this trend will continue.) Legislative requirements related to environment facing the automotive and transport equipment industry are summarised in Box 2.

▷ California has the toughest emissions legislation, where the mandate for a 'zero-emission vehicle' is expected to come into force in 2003. EU standards on car, truck and bus emissions tighten in 2000, 2005 and 2008.

▷ Greenhouse gas reduction goals in Europe require 25% reduction of 1995 levels of carbon dioxide emissions by 2008.

▷ Sweden legally requires producer liability for 'End-of-Life Vehicles' as of 1998, and at least 85% by weight of a vehicle will have to be recovered for re-use, recycling or energy recovery, increasing to 95% in 2015.

▷ The EU has approved a similar measure on end-of-life vehicles (awaiting ratification by the European Parliament) which will require manufacturers to take back new cars for recycling and re-use by 2001 and all cars by 2006.

Box 2: **Current and pending legislative requirements impacting transport equipment and transportation industry**

Life-cycle perspective. Another key driver of Volvo's journey toward sustainability stems from approaching strategy and decisions from its high-integrity, holistic, integrated life-cycle perspective, which stimulates powerful insights into customer requirements, generating and managing value, and reducing environmental impacts and effects.

A holistic, life-cycle perspective based on facts and data has permeated Volvo's planning and decision-making at all levels within the organisation, from strategic planning efforts that examine Volvo's strategic positioning within the value chain to improvements in design and production to attain environmental efficiencies. Volvo managers have remarked that life-cycle thinking is a natural consequence of focusing on the environment, and that it has been dramatically reflected in priority-setting moving to a product (rather than production process) focus. Life-cycle analysis is now part of the basic public dialogue internally in Volvo, within its value stream, and in Europe more generally.

Genuine caring. Volvo managers are quick to point out that their interest in environment is not only externally driven. Since 1927, a deeply held concern for people has been a central underpinning of the Volvo company culture, so current efforts toward sustainability are not 'trendy', ancillary or superficial. Rather, it builds on a long-standing tradition in Volvo of commitment to supporting human safety in transport.

2. *Trailblazing: exemplary systems and practices toward sustainable development*

This section looks more deeply into Volvo's efforts over the last ten years in six key areas:

1. Integration of environment at a strategic level, including new business development

2. Development of a structure for implementing environment into design engineering

3. Development and use of information and databases regarding life-cycle impacts

4. Education of employees, suppliers, and dealers

5. Supplier management including education, expectations and requirements

6. Product declaration and measurement

a. *Integration of environment at a strategic level, including new business development*

Vision of sustainable mobility

As a response to the drivers listed above, and as a part of its overall strategic reorientation, Volvo has redefined its mission to explicitly include environmental care as a key element, and begun initiatives to achieve what it sees as its fundamental challenge: to create sustainable mobility for society.

Volvo is not abandoning its core business; instead, it has posed a challenge to itself to discover and develop 'sustainable mobility'—to fulfil the transport requirements of people and goods through transportation systems that are simultaneously safe, secure, environmentally acceptable, cost-efficient and user-focused. Volvo sees sustainable mobility as a critical component of achieving sustainable industry, a subset of a broader goal to achieve a sustainable society. A question for the future is whether Volvo's version of 'sustainable mobility' is adequate to achieve this broader goal and, even if it is, whether Volvo will push it fast enough—not only in order to maintain competitive advantage, but also to promote truly sustainable industrial and social practices.

Integrated strategy

At first, we tended to ask, 'Where is your sustainable development strategy?'—but then it became clear that Volvo is on the road to a truly integrated position. There are specific environmental performance and environmental management system goals, but, at the highest level, both environmental and social sustainability are integrated into the mainstream business strategy. Sustainability is embedded into the core image and brand of the company, models of thinking, choices regarding business opportunities and strategic alliances, design of products and services, selection and management of suppliers, and so on. Progress toward sustainability is seen as an inseparable part of future business profitability and competitiveness.

Volvo's vision of environmental positioning has clearly moved beyond a compliance orientation in response to environmental regulation toward integrating consideration for sustainability into core business plans, products and operations. The most important thing about this evolution is that it is soundly based on prudent strategic analysis and business planning. Rather than approaching environmental issues with an 'end-of-pipe' mentality, Volvo instead addresses environmental considerations upstream in product and process design. Further, Volvo expects and realises much more return on its investment than simply liability cost avoidance and eco-efficiencies; rather, its leading environmental performance is seen as a path to increased competitive advantage, market share, access to new markets, and new business opportunities. For example, when Volvo introduced the new FH truck series, the superior fuel-efficiency and lower emissions were widely publicised. In the four years after its introduction, Volvo's European market share grew by 35%, and the contribution of truck operations to the company's operating income rose from 30% to 56%, an 83% increase, with operating margins of 9.9% (WBCSD 1997).

Volvo's vision for the future and strategic decision-making are anchored in a sophisticated understanding of customer needs, current and projected market demand, legislative conditions and trends, rich competitive and industry analysis, substantive models of societal mobility, and projections of 21st-century demographics. The extensive strategy development work done at the board of directors level has been outlined above.

New business

Volvo has identified its strategic strengths and capabilities within the context of more environmentally sustainable industrial practices. It is well positioned to take advantage of emerging business opportunities created by the need for more sustainable transport systems through their action programmes of: supplying natural gas and biogas buses; providing integrated rapid transit system design services; addressing concern about pollution levels and emissions in emerging markets; assuring production facilities have strong environmental management systems; and providing transport and logistics information services. In some cases, these competences already existed; in others, Volvo is investing heavily in technology, process and human resource development to build them.

A major signal that a company is moving toward sustainable development is its willingness to fundamentally incorporate different products, services and business

Volvo used innovative but simple technology to support the Brazilian city of Curitiba in creating a bus line that rivals the efficiency of light rail or subways, at a fraction of the construction cost and disturbance. Typically, a 12 m bus normally carries 1,000 passengers per day. By incorporating double-articulated buses each with a capacity of 270, exclusive bus lanes, timed traffic signals for peak times, and tube stations for prepaid fares, these larger buses can each carry 4,000 passengers per day along the main busway.

The 900 km network transports 23,000 passengers per peak hour, approximately the same number as on the Rio de Janeiro Metro. The double-articulated buses operate at 20 kmh, only 5–12 kmh slower than the New York City Subway. Although subways and light rail systems have a slight advantage if they have been previously established, Curitiba's transit system presents many advantages for cities that have not yet developed rail systems. The primary advantage is cost: Volvo's Curitiba system cost $200,000 per km, only $1/300$ of the cost of subway construction. Construction time is also $1/4$–$1/10$ that of rail.

This unsubsidised system carrying 800,000 passengers per day has been proven effective by those using it. Although Curitiba has the highest rate of car ownership in Brazil (one in three), it also has the highest rate of use of public transit: 75% of all commuters take the bus. In addition, 28% of car owners regularly take the bus. As a result, fuel consumption per capita is 30% less than in other Brazilian cities. Traffic has declined by 30% since 1974, while population has doubled.

Box 3: **Volvo's Curitiba story**

designs. The theoretical underpinning of this redesign is often a move toward dematerialisation. Industry, overall, is moving toward becoming solution suppliers rather than simply product suppliers. Volvo is actively working to be part of this. Although the company's primary focus is certainly still on production of transportation equipment, it is taking initial steps to lay the groundwork for an alternative business design as a provider of transportation system technology products and services, rather than simply manufacturing.

A major success for Volvo in this area involves its collaboration with the city of Curitiba, Brazil, to develop an attractive, cost-effective, environmentally sensitive mass transport system. The system is based on buses, and was implemented quickly at significantly lower costs than light rail alternatives. This is described in Box 3.

Based on value creation opportunities revealed by Volvo's experience in assisting Curitiba and other cities design transportation systems, in 1998 Volvo established Volvo Mobility Systems (VMS) as a new company. The history behind the Executive Committee's deliberations in forming VMS, and its vision for the company, are described in Box 4. Volvo Mobility Systems is intended to: 'Create value by providing efficient, clean, and safe mobility systems for goods and people to demanding customers, primarily in metropolitan areas'.

In Volvo's 1998 *Environmental Report*, President and CEO Leif Johansson explains the purpose and potential of the new company as follows:

During 1997 and 1998, the Volvo Group Executive Committee held many discussions and meetings centred around exploring the future role of Volvo in a society that was required to be much more sustainable. Top managers deliberated the implications of 'sustainable development' for Volvo's technology, brand and strategy. These discussions culminated in a 36-hour 'seminar' outside of Gothenburg, where top management, together with mid-management and representatives of The World Bank, the Organisation for Economic Co-operation and Development (OECD) and the European Union examined the future demands of the external world for supply and development of transport systems. The outcome was a document summarising guidelines of sustainable mobility for Volvo in the future. Volvo would:

▷ Work with and supply the development of environmentally sensitive mobility solutions

▷ Develop alternative power sources and fuels

▷ Actively develop sustainable transportation systems

▷ Operate in the forefront of mobility systems, thus becoming known as a credible partner

▷ Assist in the development of inter-modal transport systems that managed the seamless transition between different modes of transport

▷ Leverage information technology to support transport

Based on this vision, in April 1998 the Executive Committee decided to establish Volvo Mobility Systems. Torsten Dahlberg, a 32-year veteran with wide Volvo experience, accepted the challenge of leading the development and execution of a business plan for operationalising this vision.

Box 4: The establishment of Volvo Mobility Systems (VMS)

Source: Personal communication with Torsten Dahlberg

. . . developing new transport systems which will contribute to the alleviation of the acute atmospheric pollution and traffic congestion problems currently affecting cities around the globe. All of this will open doors to new markets with significant potential . . . The new unit's mission is to act as a working partner to urban and regional authorities around the world, assisting in the development and construction of safe, clean and efficient transport systems by contributing know-how and products. Volvo Mobility Systems is more than a vehicle for exploiting new business opportunities; it also demonstrates Volvo's intention of making a responsible and meaningful contribution to mankind's need for transport and freedom of mobility in the long term (*Environmental Report* 1998).

Torsten Dahlberg and his team gained strong support for their business plan for Volvo Mobility Systems. To summarise, VMS is focused on creating value for customers and shareholders by working closely with Volvo corporate units and external partners to provide a total product and service package for urban mobility systems. This total package includes both complete vehicle systems (equipment, financing, parts supply, etc.) and infrastructure development, recognising the interdependence of transport goods and people from a customer's perspective.

Volvo Mobility Systems will build on and continue to develop competences gained with Curitiba, Gothenburg, and other urban transport projects completed by Volvo in the past. They plan to start small, with a great deal of respect for the different players, and, in Torsten Dahlberg's words, 'Walk, then soon run.' What this humble statement translates into is that Volvo plans to have this business running at full scale in three years.

Torsten Dahlberg commented that the vision and mission of Volvo Mobility Systems has captured the energy and excitement of the younger (aged 30–35) Volvo employees. President and CEO Leif Johansson's above-mentioned description of Volvo's framing of this business reflects the deeper purpose and vision seen in many companies leading the way in sustainable development.

It would be a mistake to consider this move on Volvo's part within the same realm solely as a sophisticated strategic positioning to meet an emerging market demand. It is no doubt that. But, more significantly, it represents a willingness to reconceptualise the fundamental business that Volvo is in—from product manufacturers to solution suppliers, from players in the industrial system of the 20th century to leaders in the transition to a sustainable industrial system of the 21st century.

Anticipating the market

Volvo managers were clear that their strategy was to go beyond compliance, to exceed expectations. One manager commented that 'market demand in fact has progressed more slowly than I had personally expected. We still have the vision but are less sure of the speed. It depends on what happens. If there is an environmental catastrophe, *market demands can change in a day!*' Another commented: 'Maybe we are doing it in a time when we have the planning in our own hands. If not, it is more costly and the planning is difficult. This is something we use to our advantage.' Volvo is clearly ahead of the demand curve in building the competences and technology it anticipates will be required for the future.

b. Development of a structure for implementing environment into design engineering

It is often difficult to persuade the modest Swedes to admit they are extremely accomplished, so one should take heed when Volvo manager Agneta Wendel, a Volvo engineer for 15 years, responsible for strategic sustainability design in the product planning department, credits Volvo as the likely world leader in developing a structure for implementing environment into design engineering. (This was communicated with the expected caveats of 'from what my colleagues tell me . . .' and 'as far as I know . . .'.)

The single greatest leverage point for influencing the environmental impact of a product is typically design. Volvo has spent over ten years understanding and creating the strategic rationale, systems, education, knowledge, life-cycle data and information, tools, relationships and widely held motivation needed to actualise Design for the Environment (DfE). Energy is directed towards new products not yet in production, especially into the platform designs that will serve as the foundation for a family of new products.

Volvo's approach has been to view environment as a validated 'property', like reliability or strength, with a set of defined aspects, such as fuel-efficiency or material intensity, to be carefully targeted, monitored and improved at each stage of the product development process. Its aim is to have environmental considerations as ingrained in people's thinking as cost—in the sense that no new idea is considered without determining how much it will cost. Progress towards meeting environmental goals is a required element of each 'stage gate' of the product development process, and design engineers must report on progress toward targets. Design engineers responsible for different components must demonstrate efforts they have made and report against a 'measure of possibilities'. Targets are determined as a combination of external pressures from customers, competitors and the market, with an internal assessment of what it is possible to achieve.

Volvo starts with the big picture of what it is trying to 'safeguard': resources, human health, biodiversity, aesthetics and biological production. It then takes an 'applied environmental holistic view' which includes energy and materials use and emissions releases to air, water and soil, in all phases of product development, including transport. Volvo's holistic view assumes that the responsibility of product development is expanded from the traditional view of including only assembly and use to include all phases of production (from raw materials extraction, vehicle in use and end-of-life; see Fig. 1).

Design engineers are provided with education and manuals on how to design for environment. This manual provides guidelines and design rules in the following areas:

▷ Volvo's environmental policy: strategy, continuous improvement, technology development, and efficient use of resources

▷ Minimising the total burden on the environment

▷ Selecting materials: plastics, metals, leathers (see Table 1)

▷ Planning to reduce resource use in manufacturing processes (waste reduction)

▷ Designing for lower fuel consumption

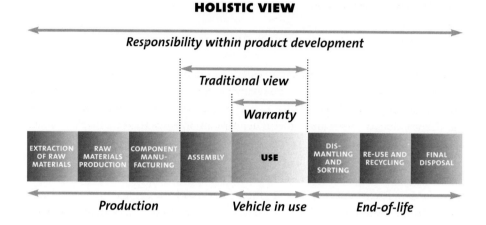

Figure 1: Volvo's holistic view of product development responsibility

	Burden on the environment (ELU/kg)*	Weight savings reduction (compared to base of steel)	Environmental toxins	Recycling material and energy
Aluminium				
Lead				
Glue				
Glass				
Copper				
Polycarbonate				
Acrylic plastic				

* ELU (environmental load units)/kg is the pressure on the environment generated by 1 kg of the pure element while under production, based on typical use of 200,000 km.

Table 1: Sample from Volvo's materials selection design guidelines

 ▷ Designing for lower emissions

 ▷ Designing for recycling

 ▷ Working with suppliers

Failure Mode and Effect Analysis (FMEA), a proven quality improvement tool, has been applied to the analysis of environmental impacts and hazards as part of product development. This E FMEA, as it is called, supports preventative action in the design phase, and assists in the determination of need for fuller life-cycle assessment.

An additional tool used by Volvo designers is to compare what they call the 'reference car' (the one they would like to build)—with the 'requested car' (the car with features the customer is asking for), and then generate strategies to reduce the environmental impact of the requested car to or below that of their reference car, resulting in what they call the 'vision car'. The thinking is that this vision car meets the customer's feature and functionality requirements, but, inspired by the standard of Volvo's reference car, can be designed with lower environmental impacts.

An additional powerful information and analysis tool developed to support DfE by determining the life-cycle impacts of products is described below.

c. Development and use of information and database regarding life-cycle impacts

Volvo, in collaboration with the Swedish Environmental Research Institute, the Federation of Swedish Industries, Chalmers University of Technology and other enterprises, has developed a computerised 'Environmental Priority Strategies' (EPS) tool, to enable life-cycle assessment (LCA) to evaluate the environmental impact of components at every stage of their life-cycles, from raw materials extraction to end-of-life waste disposal, recycling or re-use. This tool was designed to aid designers in assessing the environmental impact value in environmental load units (ELUs) of product designs, enabling comparison of different products. Results reflect the degree of impact on the five key 'safeguard areas' of natural resources (land use as well as metals, fuel, etc., valued according to scarcity or availability), human health (using World Health Organisation standards), biodiversity, aesthetics and biological production (foods, forests, etc.). Volvo's goal is that each element of the calculation of total environmental impact is transparent and reproducible.

Internally, 4–5 specialists in life-cycle analysis support product development departments in each business area (added to them are environmental co-ordinators at the product development departments acting as facilitators). A simple LCA screen is used at the first decision gate of product/component development; at the second gate a more full-scale analysis may be conducted. Volvo's central LCA specialist group conducted about 60 LCAs in 1998. These LCAs are used for valuation or validation of one aspect toward another, not simply inventories.

The development of this database and software demonstrates not only Volvo's commitment to life-cycle analysis, but also an expansion of partnerships with suppliers, external agencies and stakeholders that is characteristic of sustainability-driven strategies.

d. *Education of employees, suppliers and dealers*

Volvo has successfully employed **widespread education and communication** throughout its organisation, dealers and supplier base. Based on a goal of a common language and understanding ('It's too important for just a few specialists . . .'), Volvo created a six-hour environmental training programme called 'Dialogue on the Environment', for all 79,000 employees and dealers, and a modified version, 'The Environmental Dialogue', for suppliers and contractors.

The 'Dialogue on the Environment' course provides: (1) a broad description of the ecological context of nature, state of the globe given current practices, and conditions of life; (2) a group discussion of energy, transport and the environment; and (3) Volvo car programmes, performance and the environment. In Volvo Car Corporation (VCC), this 'overview' training course is expected to be followed by implementation of each section's own environmental management and improvement system, capitalising on the momentum that this has produced.

This environmental training for over 70,000 participants started in June 1995, and had been delivered to 35,000 employees by year-end 1998, including almost all Asian-market countries and production facilities; 250 in-house trainers have been certified to lead these discussions. The course is delivered in seven languages, including Thai.

Most importantly, in order to maintain the momentum, within six months of the education, each area in VCC must initiate work on its own environmental management system. Managers report that this education has been extremely powerful in those areas where it was followed with immediate implementation.

Volvo managers reported that, three years ago, it was a struggle convincing people to conduct the education, eliciting the reaction that all this was 'green not business'. Now, internal concern about environmental issues matches high national concern, and the relevance of sustainability to business success is clearly understood and accepted.

e. *Supplier management, including education, expectations and requirements*

Volvo has fully engaged its suppliers in achieving environmental improvements with regard to life-cycle assessment. Suppliers are viewed as development partners, and involved early in product development. They are expected to be expert in the environmental impact of their products or components, and use the same design guidelines as Volvo design engineers. Volvo's stance is: 'you are the experts—we need you to help us.' As a result, suppliers provide a great deal of the data that is used in life-cycle assessments.

Volvo's 'Environmental Requirements for All Major Suppliers and Contractors' stipulate that a supplier must have an environmental management system in place. Suppliers of production materials and major contractors must be certified, or have a plan to become certified, either to ISO 14001 or EMAS. There must be goals and action plans for the continuous decrease of their environmental impacts. Open data sharing and dialogue is a prerequisite, as is full co-operation on environmental effects from production and products to enable the use of LCAs as strategic tools. Volvo requires full control of all chemicals and materials—there can be no materials on the 'black' or 'grey' lists, unless accounted for with phase-out plans. Planning, choice of packing materials and optimised handling of waste materials are also areas considered. Finally, suppliers must design for recyclability and use recycled materials.

Volvo uses a **'black list' and 'grey list' of controlled chemicals**, both internally and with suppliers. For example, the black list of prohibited substances includes (among others) CFC compounds, asbestos, brominated flame-retardants, halons, PCBs, chlorinated hydrocarbons, lead chromate, cadmium and mercury. The grey list covers those chemicals whose use should be limited: for example, solvents such as benzene and chloroform; metals including arsenic and lead; cadmium in batteries; and zinc chromate.

Volvo clearly communicates to suppliers and contractors its goals for leadership in Environmental Care. The company's holistic life-cycle perspective and strategies are summarised. Expectations (as described above) are also clearly communicated. Suppliers are expected to assume responsibility in turn for their own suppliers. A 'Self-Assessment on Environment' is provided, as a checklist, to be returned to Volvo.

f. Product declaration and measurement

'Cars generate pollution, noise, and waste.' Thus begins Volvo's 'Environmental Product Declaration' for the S80 introduced in May 1998. With this document, Volvo's S80 became the first car in the world with an Environmental Product Declaration certified by a third party and based on life-cycle assessment. Volvo's goal is to provide an easy-to-understand summary of product environmental attributes for customers.

The Volvo 'Environmental Product Declaration' rates progress in four areas using the 'environmental priority strategies in product design' tool described earlier:

▷ Environmental management (supplier companies, Volvo operations, dealerships)

▷ Manufacturing (solvent emissions, material use, energy use per manufactured car)

▷ Operation (exhaust emissions, evaporation of hydrocarbons, carbon dioxide emissions)

▷ Recycling (labelling of plastics, dismantling, use of recycled plastics)

The Volvo S80 2.9's environmental performance is rated and displayed in a spider chart, with explanations of the rating in each category (see Fig. 2).

3. The route: leadership, planning and implementation

a. Planning for sustainable development

Volvo's vision and strategy are supported by plans incorporating many critical factors for successful implementation: leadership priority, organisational alignment, detailed diagnosis of the current situation, transparency of data, scenario development, careful analysis and planning, clarity regarding the relevance to mainstream business, clear goals and objectives, and adequate investment of resources. Not every element was part of a comprehensive, detailed plan, yet Volvo's plans and actions reflect a strong intentional focus—Volvo is a company working progressively at integrating a core value for more sustainable transport into its business strategies and operations.

Leadership priority and organisational alignment

Volvo's management of its strategic reorientation experience put the company in the envious situation of having aligned shareholders, the board of directors, a new president and CEO (Leif Johansson, previously CEO and President of Electrolux, a leading company in integrating sustainability into strategic management and operations), senior management and employees in a singular vision and plan for positioning Volvo as an environmental leader in its industry. Managers commented frequently that 'the top' is very devoted to achieving environmental goals, and that this is a key to their success.

In addition, alignment has been consciously built, through education, communication, advancement of the life-cycle management paradigm, and the careful placement of people with environmental expertise on new product development teams. Their mandate? To bring environmental considerations to light. Most of the

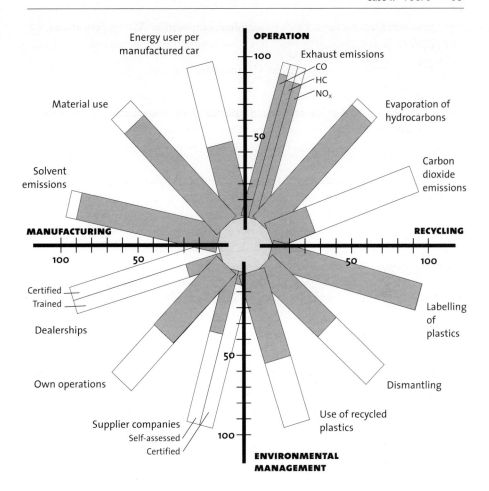

* The shaded areas on the pillars provide a measure of the environmental performance of the Volvo S80 2.9, manufactured at the Volvo Torslanda plant in Sweden and sold on the European market.

Figure 2: **Environmental performance of the Volvo S80 2.9**

managers for environment have extensive, high-level product and operations management and engineering experience, to which they have added knowledge about environment.

Each Volvo company is challenged to become the world leader in the combination of safety, quality and environment, as an essential requirement of the brand Volvo. This strong leadership and organisational alignment regarding the importance and relevance of environmental issues to its business has contributed to past accomplishments, but also means Volvo is strongly positioned for breakthrough progress in the future.

Diagnosis and analysis

As part of its planning process, Volvo conducted in-depth diagnosis and analysis. In addition to the extensive data collection described earlier, Volvo has responded to the challenge of finding a path to sustainable mobility by developing: a clear understanding of the present situation (where it stands); user and societal needs that drive development; actions based on cost–benefit analyses; the contribution of all transport modes and actors; arguments for legislation where needed; harmonised regulation and fiscal policies in Europe and the US; and infrastructure development (roads, railways, waterways, telematics). For example, Volvo developed 'global emissions scenarios' calculating estimated global emissions over a 30-year period, based on differing levels of improvement in fuel-efficiency and different traffic growth rates. The company then prepared comparisons of the differing environmental loading of its various products when operating on petrol versus biogas, taking into consideration production and waste management.

A culture of openness and transparency

Volvo is working to create a culture of openness and transparency of data, both internally and within its supply chain. In both personal dialogue and external publications, Volvo managers openly acknowledge the realities of transport as intrinsically environmentally destructive. A holistic, life-cycle perspective is the predominant framework for data collection and analysis. Suppliers are required to provide Volvo with data on environmental effects of their production and products to enable life-cycle assessments. Volvo works proactively with suppliers to build the relationship, understanding and motivation to share their data.[1]

Measurable environmental goals

Volvo has established clear, measurable environmental goals and objectives for the entire corporation and within each business area. Behind each goal is range of specific tactics and action plans. These goals include:

---

1   Volvo has not required suppliers to be certified to ISO 14001, although recently Ford has announced that it will require all suppliers to become ISO 14001-certified. This will presumably also include suppliers to the Volvo car brand.

▷ Ranking as one of the leading automotive manufacturers in the environmental field by 2000

▷ Reducing fuel consumption of cars by 25% from 1995 levels by 2008 for
cars sold in the EU

▷ Establishing an environmental management system in all 40 production
units by 1998 (34 were achieved as of 31 December 1998)

▷ Conducting environmental audits in all majority-owned production units
by year-end 1998 (all but one plant was completed)

▷ Integrating life-cycle analysis as a decision-making tool in at least ten
development projects no later than 1998 (achieved)

▷ Manufacturing the most fuel-efficient construction equipment in the
world (achieved)

▷ Natural gas trucks introduced commercially (achieved)

▷ Reducing levels of production-related consumption of resources (energy
and water down 10%), emissions (solvents down 25% and nitrogen oxides
down 5%) and waste to landfill (down 10%) (relative to 1995) by 1998 (all
achieved, with the exception of waste to landfill, which could not be
monitored globally)

b. *Organising*

Laying the groundwork
The groundwork for implementation was laid through comprehensive education
and communication, a systematic process of engagement, clear expectations for
change, and a myriad of decision tools and guidelines.

Infrastructure
Volvo established that the Volvo Group Executive Council is responsible for
environmental policy, group-wide strategies and goals, and monitoring business
area activities. The Group Environmental Council supports the Executive Council
and each of the business area management teams. Each business area has its own
environmental manager, staff, local co-ordinators and specialists. Headquarters
provides policy and goals, tools such as the life-cycle analyses, and supports the
transfer of knowledge from one area of the company to others.

The life-cycle specialists and training specialist groups described earlier were
also developed and made available to the operating units.

c. *Implementation*

As with any competitive organisation, Volvo has focused on developing a visionary and incisive strategy, and then mobilising the organisational competence and commitment to successfully launch its execution. Although the path is not always linear, Volvo exemplifies a fairly classic strategic management process of 'turning the improvement cycle' from vision and strategy formulation, through planning and goal-setting and co-ordination of initiatives, to implementation and review. What is exceptional is the rigour and thoroughness with which this is done, and that Volvo is sincerely making steps toward the development of equipment and transportation systems and services that promote 'sustainable mobility'.

Volvo seems to be making the required investments, fully embracing the immense learning and engineering requirements, and building the strategic partnerships and alliances that sustainability implies if the organisation is going to turn plans and goals into results.

Investment of resources

The Volvo Group has made substantial investments—driven from the perspective of sustainable development—in research and development, technology development, new product and service development, customer marketing and education, and learning and competency building.

For example, Volvo has systematically shifted its investment of resources to reflect the changing strategic positioning of environment internally. In the early 1990s, over 50% of VCC's total investment costs were attributable to environment-related programmes. This type of investment is expected to account for less than 30% of the total by the end of the decade as the emphasis shifts from post-treatment and purification measures to process modifications of a preventative nature, and the introduction of materials that will alleviate the environmental impact of products and production processes.

The trend in environment-related development costs goes in the opposite direction. During the first half of the 1990s, between 20 and 30% of VCC's product development costs were related to environmental improvement measures. Since 1994, however, the trend has turned upward and the proportion has risen to between 50 and 60%. The significant efforts being made by the company to reduce fuel consumption and minimise emissions account for this increase.

Partnerships and alliances

Volvo has developed collaborative partnerships and alliances with customers, city and state governments (e.g. the cities of Gothenburg, Curitiba and Shanghai), national agencies, and industry partners and competitors (e.g. research on recycling).

For example, Volvo and the Gothenburg Board of Trade and Industry Development have initiated an extensive collaboration designed to put both the company and the city at the forefront of development of efficient vehicles and transport systems. By 1997, half of the bus fleet was running on natural gas.

Volvo, the City of Gothenburg, and Swedish National Road Administration run trials on intelligent traffic information systems to examine the interaction of information technology, alternative fuels and different types of transport system and vehicle with regard to lowering environmental impacts and improving efficiency. These tests are also supported by the Department of Urban Transport at Chalmers University of Technology, and ASG, a haulage company also leading in efforts to create sustainable transport (see Chapter 7). The goal is to design the most efficient and least socially and environmentally invasive system for goods distribution in the city centre.

Volvo led the development of EPS, the Environmental Priority Strategies, a consortium of companies (including ABB, SKS and Electrolux) working together to create a computer-based comprehensive analysis of the total life-cycle impact of products. It is also leading an international effort to develop an LCA standard within the ISO 14000 series.

Practical change management strategies

In the words of Volvo managers:

▷ **Lead, lead, lead.** 'Designers are reluctant to change and critical; they need to be convinced or they won't do it.' In response to the question, 'How did you get them to change?': 'The President of AB Volvo is very convinced; it has its influence in everything he says. There is full support from the top. Also, there is a changed climate. People are facing environmental issues in and out of the company . . . everyone is more or less convinced that we must do something. It helps to have top management convinced.'

▷ **Integrate at both the strategic level and into daily work.** 'It is a problem to add extra work to people who are already so overloaded, so environment must be a property to regulate just as the others. Don't add extra activity. Include in everything you do. You must have currency for environment.'

▷ **Systematise the changes.** 'My ambition is that, in ten years, my position (environmental manager) won't be needed. Just as quality worked independently years ago and is now in the backbone and built into the systems, environment must be the responsibility of every designer, a normal part of their work. Environment in ten years won't be talked about as a special task.'

▷ **Prevention is key.** 'It is obvious when you go into production today that there is not the perspective of 20 years ago of adding filters—now we build new production plants and build processes that won't need anything to clean up.'

▷ **Provide education.** ' "Dialogue on the Environment" gave everyone the same ground level, same terminology, possibility for communication, and awareness.'

▷ **Follow education with action.** 'In some areas where we delivered "Dialogue on the Environment" [we didn't follow up with the recommended implementation of an environmental management system within six months] and there is nothing, it ends with a big question mark.'

▷ **Work through the line management.** 'We now have an organisation that really works—environmental responsibility is in every department.'

▷ **Provide simple, easy-to-use checklists and tools.** 'It is better to have a tool that is only 80%, but is used, than one that is 100%, but is not used.'

▷ **Encourage dialogue and discussion.** 'The ethical debate is interesting. For example, you can have high-impact greenhouse gases causing climate change that have disastrous outputs in parts of the world, but not our part of the world. Other impacts might be felt here. We have to validate different impacts for us as a people, but also as world citizens. There is no single answer.'

d. Review and monitoring

Volvo certainly recognises the adage, 'What gets measured gets done,' and has developed a systematic process for assessing progress against goals. Environmental objectives and results are monitored and reported within a traditional strategic planning process. In addition, an annual *Environmental Report* is developed and widely communicated. Environmental audits of operations are conducted regularly in Volvo plants, as part of the wider environmental management system. The objective, of course, is to stimulate continuous improvement.

Volvo has developed a number of key metrics. One example is the 'Environmental load unit' (ELU) metric, for calculating environmental impact throughout the life-cycle of components based on the manner in which the following five areas are affected:

▷ Health (according to World Health Organisation Standards)

▷ Biological diversity

▷ Biological production (foods, forest, etc.)

▷ Natural resources (land use, as well as metals, oil, coal, etc., valued according to their availability or scarcity)

▷ Aesthetic values

The 'Product Declaration' also provides a very visible mechanism for assessing current performance and progress by displaying in one chart product performance relating to environmental management, manufacturing, operation and recycling.

Volvo developed an 'Environmental Calculation Programme' to evaluate the impact of various modes of transport, as part of its effort to quantify the impact of internal transport operations (deliveries to plants and dealers). It was able to calculate that, in 1998, the emissions of carbon dioxide from the SEK 5.5 billion (US$647 million) of purchased transport services for its own operations totalled an estimated 410,000 tonnes. Nitrogen oxide emissions at 10,800 tonnes and sulphur oxide emissions at 5,700 tonnes exceeded the quantities emitted by Volvo's production plants! Volvo plans to reduce these transport-related atmospheric emissions by 5% in the next five years.

Volvo also tracks improvements in 'Employee Satisfaction with Environmental Performance' over time.

4. Conclusion

Volvo has many exemplary management processes and achievements, valuable to those also on the path toward developing sustainable industry in a sustainable society. Volvo's greatest contribution, though, may stem from its recognition of the power to be tapped at the intersection of environmental values and brand image. Volvo managers pointed out that:

> Customers will not buy only technological products: you must bring soul and joy . . . the product must feel 'good'; people want soul in a car.

> People are already willing to pay more for knowing how products are made.

> It's the values in the company that people really buy, not the product.

Designing and producing more sustainable products and services promises to provide this element of 'soul and values', building enormous brand equity in the process. As Volvo executives pointed out, sustainable development can be thought of as a logical extension of Volvo's long-standing commitment to safety—'taking care of life'.

References

Volvo publications

http://www.volvo.com
Documents may be downloaded from: *http://www.volvo.com/environment/index.htm*
AB *Volvo Proposed Sale of Volvo Cars* (Gothenburg: AB Volvo, 1998).
Volvo Annual Report 1996 (Gothenburg: AB Volvo, 1997).
Volvo Environmental Report 1996 (Gothenburg: AB Volvo, 1997).
Volvo Annual Report 1998 (Gothenburg: AB Volvo, 1999).
Volvo Environmental Report 1998 (Gothenburg: AB Volvo, 1999).
EcoMobility (Volvo Truck Corporation Newsletter).
Volvo Buses and Alternative Fuels: Natural Gas and BioGas
Trade and Industry Development Agency, *On the Road to a Better Environment* (Public Affairs
    612-0002).
Volvo Corporate Presentation (Gothenburg: AB Volvo).
Volvo Environmental Concept Bus (Gothenburg: AB Volvo).
Volvo Environmental Requirements for Suppliers (Gothenburg: AB Volvo).
Volvo Environmental Truck (Gothenburg: AB Volvo).
Volvo Magazine (Gothenburg: AB Volvo).
Volvo Product Declaration (Gothenburg: AB Volvo).
Volvo Requirements for Suppliers and Contractors (Gothenburg: AB Volvo).
Volvo S70V70 Bio-Fuel (Gothenburg: AB Volvo).
Volvo's Black and Grey Lists for Chemicals (Gothenburg: AB Volvo).

Other

'Integrated Transport Planning in Curitiba, Brazil', in M.L. Birk and P.C. Zegras (1993) *Moving
    toward Integrated Transport Planning: Energy, Environment and Mobility in Four Asian
    Cities* (Washington, DC: International Institute for Energy Conservation).
ECRIS (Environmental Car Recycling in Scandinavia) *Recycling Cars the Ecocycle Way* (A
    Swedish research project undertaken jointly by AB Gotthard Nilsson, JB Bildemontering
    AB, Stena Bilfragmentering AB and Volvo Car Corporation).
WBCSD (World Business Council for Sustainable Development) (1997) *Environmental Perfor-
    mance and Shareholder Value* (Geneva: WBCSD).

Organisational contacts

Jan Blennius, Vice-President, Corporate Strategy
Torsten Dahlberg, Managing Director, Volvo Mobility Systems
Bo Egerdal, Vice-President, Industry and Trade Policy
Ulla-Britt Fräjdin Hellqvist, Director, Competence Center, Environment
Lena Gevert, Director, Environmental Affairs
Inge Horkeby, MSc, Director, Corporate Environmental Auditing
Agneta Wendel, Environmental Manager, Product Development Process, Volvo Car
    Corporation

SUNCOR
Taking stakeholder relations to a new level

1. *The lie of the land*

a. *Corporate overview*

Suncor Energy's history throughout the 1990s is one of significant change and transformation. In the early part of the decade, Suncor Energy—a small integrated oil and gas company based in Alberta, Canada—faced an uncertain future, experiencing economic pressures as it struggled to meet the demands of a more competitive energy marketplace. Employee morale was low and the company was subject to control orders and citations for violating environmental regulations. Its environmental performance was considered to be weak. At one point, the provincial government in Alberta, Canada, delivered an ultimatum: improve your environmental performance or forfeit future Oil Sands growth opportunities (one of Suncor's main operations).

Today Suncor is regarded as an industry leader. The company is transforming itself from a traditional integrated oil and gas company to a sustainable energy company. Suncor has modernised its operations, dramatically improved its financial performance (shareholder value has increased more than 600% since 1992) and the company is now recognised by the government as a leader in environmental management and stakeholder relations. Suncor has taken a progressive approach to challenging issues such as developing new reserves and defining the role of an energy company in the face of global climate change.

Today, employee morale is high and the pride of the workforce in the company has increased dramatically. As one long-time company employee stated, 'the attitude of people outside the company in the late 1980s was "Why would anyone work for Suncor?" '. Now employees who leave the company are often greeted with the statement, 'I can't believe you would leave Suncor'. In under a decade, the company has moved from the brink of closure to a position where its current target of doubling shareholder value every five years seems attainable.

Suncor's stated goal is to become a 'sustainable energy company'. This means that it aspires to supply energy in a responsible way that meets the environmental, economic and social needs and expectations of its stakeholders.

This case study details the progress the company has made, and the role of environmental and sustainable development considerations, in this impressive transformation.

Corporate structure

Suncor employs over 2,600 people. Its assets are C$4.1 billion (US$2.8 billion), with market capitalisation of approximately C$6.4 billion (US$4.37 billion). Suncor is an integrated energy company with three autonomous, decentralised business units:

▷ **The Oil Sands** operation in Fort McMurray, Alberta, mines oil sand, upgrades bitumen and markets refinery feedstock and premium transportation fuels.

▷ **Exploration and production** operation explores for, acquires, produces and markets crude oil, natural gas liquids, natural gas and sulphur in western Canada.

▷ **Sunoco Inc.** refines, distributes and markets petroleum products in central Canada, with a refinery in Sarnia, Ontario, two state-of-the-art distribution terminals and a network of Sunoco-branded and company-affiliated service stations. Sunoco has also entered the newly deregulated Ontario energy market, offering natural gas and heating, ventilation and air-conditioning services to residential customers.

In addition to these business units, Suncor is a major partner in the Stuart Oil Shale Project, a C$235 million (US$161 million) demonstration oil shale plant currently being commissioned in Queensland, Australia. The project will test the viability of Canadian technology to extract oil from Australia's vast oil shale deposits.

Corporate staff at the company's headquarters in Calgary, Alberta, guide the company's decentralised operations. Their primary role is to integrate the strategies of the three main businesses and to support the implementation of those

1. Solar energy enters the atmosphere: some is reflected.
   ▷ Climate is **driven** by the flow of **energy from sun.**

2. Energy is absorbed by the earth and is re-radiated back to space at longer wavelengths.
   ▷ Earth must send some of this **energy back out to space** to regulate climate.

3. Greenhouse gases absorb this energy and re-radiate much of it back to the surface, much like an insulating blanket.

Figure 1: **The greenhouse effect**

Source: Canadian Climate Change Secretariat

strategies. Corporate responsibilities also include alternative energy projects, downstream integration, mineable oil, and corporate environment, health and safety (EH&S) management systems and performance.

b. *Business context*

The need for energy to drive the world economy is accelerating rapidly. The world population is expected to increase from the present 6 billion to around 9 billion by 2050 (UNEP 1999). With the increase in population, there will be an increased demand for abundant, reliable and affordable supplies of energy to maintain and improve quality of life.

Although the energy sector is diverse and made up of a myriad of supply options, conventional sources such as coal, oil and natural gas are dominant. The International Energy Agency estimates that, in the absence of new policies to promote energy efficiency, world energy demand could grow by as much as 65% over the next 30 years. Fossil fuels are expected to meet 95% of this energy demand (International Energy Agency 1998). This optimistic future for conventional sources of energy is offset by the ecological and economic implications of global climate change. The combustion of fossil fuels is increasing atmospheric concentrations of greenhouse gases and the weight of scientific evidence indicates that these gases are producing an enhanced greenhouse effect that is altering the global climate (Fig. 1). To address this challenge, major industrialised countries have signed the Kyoto Protocol which commits signatory countries to significant reductions in greenhouse gas emissions from a 1990 baseline. It is expected that these commitments will substantially alter the future growth and pattern of world energy demand.

National governments and international agencies are now deep into the process of identifying policies and programmes to meet their Kyoto reduction commitments. For the energy sector, this will probably result in a combination of regulatory programmes, market-based instruments and voluntary programmes to achieve emissions reductions. It will also result in policies and programmes that favour less carbon-intensive supply options. Consequently, there is a renewed and growing interest in alternative energy technologies, such as fuel cells, solar and wind, cleaner fuels, such as biofuels and enhanced natural gas, and cleaner electric power generation options, such as hydro and gas versus coal.

Equally important will be policies and strategies to support energy efficiency, establish markets for emissions trading and allow national governments and individual organisations to pursue offsets such as planting forests in developing countries to compensate for emissions from sources in developed countries. National governments, international agencies such as The World Bank, and individual companies are actively exploring a variety of policies and strategies as they strive to meet their greenhouse gas emission reduction commitments. In spite of this activity, the transition to cleaner, less carbon-intensive energy supply will probably take a number of years and, in the interim, traditional supply sources will continue to play a major role in meeting global energy demand.

In response to this situation, a number of leading energy companies are pursuing a more diversified and hopefully more sustainable approach to energy development. This approach calls for parallel paths: the responsible development of fossil fuel resources to meet current needs and taking action now to support the diversification of energy sources over the longer term. Companies such as StatOil, BP-Amoco, Royal Dutch Shell and Suncor are recognising that suppliers who can provide less carbon-intensive energy, and effectively pursue other emission reduction strategies, may be in a better competitive position for the markets of the next century.

c. *Preview*

The late 1980s and early 1990s were challenging times for Suncor. Cash costs for the extraction of oil were very high; the company was barely keeping its plants on-line; and the Oil Sands operation was in danger of being closed down. The exploration and production group was in a downward spiral. It was having difficulty replacing its reserves and was cutting costs by downsizing employees.

The crisis surrounding the future viability of the Oil Sands operation caused the company to 'hit the wall'. In the early 1990s, a new leadership team was introduced. This team, led by CEO Rick George, initiated Suncor's transformation. It was clear to the new leadership team that growth was necessary for the company's survival. This was particularly true of Oil Sands, where the options facing management were to extract what reserves were left and close down or take the longer-term view and invest. The decision was taken to invest and grow, based on the belief that closing Oil Sands would have left a lot of shareholder value uncaptured. In addition, the economies of scale of new Oil Sands development were needed to improve the company's long-term financial picture.

However, at this time, Suncor's Oil Sands emissions, particularly of SO_2, were very high, and growth would not have been possible without significant environmental improvement. This point was being made clear by government regulators and community stakeholders who were demanding improvements from Suncor. Rather than viewing environmental issues as an annoyance and a cost, Suncor shifted to a more proactive position. The company started to integrate environmental considerations into core decision-making processes and to give more equal weighting to environmental, economic and social issues.

Suncor began to look at environmental issues from a broader perspective and, at the corporate level and in long-range planning exercises, the issue of sustainability began to enter into key discussions. Gradually, a sustainability perspective worked its way into key Suncor policy documents.

The new management team brought fresh approaches and ideas to the company. Suncor changed its technological approach to Oil Sands development and, as a result, decreased operating costs by C$5 (US$3.5) per barrel over three years. Management renewed the company's emphasis on a core set of business directions. In each business unit, this involved an examination of key value drivers, the development of measurement systems, and alignment of performance and financial incentives. For example, within Oil Sands, the key value drivers were called the 'big six', comprising safety, environmental care, productivity (cash cost and production volume), product value, customer relations and shareholder return. A new 'core purpose' statement, supported by a written set of values and beliefs, was developed by senior management to reflect these business directions. The core purpose was an important document and it was carefully designed to gain support from across the company and to reflect a clear leadership position.

During this turnaround period (1992–95), there was a sea change in the way Suncor did business. The company developed a belief that being an environmental leader offered a competitive advantage. Suncor adapted and expanded traditional approaches to loss management to include environmental responsibility. Gradually, it began to shift from a compliance perspective to a commitment to meet and strive to exceed environmental regulations. While, in the past, non-compliance was viewed with little concern or indifference, today, when mistakes occur at Suncor, they are examined in detail. This examination ensures that the mistakes are quickly corrected and reported to affected stakeholders and that the lessons learned can be applied elsewhere.

Also at this time, Suncor began to fully integrate a continuous improvement approach into its decision-making practices. Previously, decision-making was top-down and good ideas had to fight to rise to the top. In the 1990s, the authority and the power to implement ideas moved down in the organisation. This change in decision-making was very motivational and it contributed to increased employee morale.

Another important turning point was a change in Suncor's attitude toward stakeholders. The company began to see the impact and benefit of stakeholder relationships and it began to pay closer attention to stakeholder consultation. This resulted in real value for the company in areas such as improved community relations, accelerated approval processes and reductions in operational costs. In the Oil Sands operation, financial incentives for employee performance based on the 'big six' business directions were established. Under this dynamic programme, incentives were adjusted to reinforce and encourage performance that supported the company's changing priorities.

During this period, the emphasis at Suncor was on survival, reducing costs, achieving excellence in execution, and maximising current assets. In 1996, with the initial phase of the turnaround essentially complete, the company entered a new stage in its history: a growth phase. This phase, which is still ongoing, involves an expansion of Suncor's existing businesses through investment in the retail network, expansion of conventional exploration and development programmes, and ambitious growth plans for the Oil Sands operation, expansion of which is well under way, with regulatory approval received in March 1999 for the C$2 billion (US$1.37 billion) 'Project Millennium'. The company is also pursuing opportunities in the international arena, starting with the Stuart Oil Shale Project in Australia.

Box 1: Suncor's climate change position

▷ Suncor Energy recognises the current scientific consensus that the balance of evidence suggests there is a discernible human influence on the earth's climate.

▷ Suncor believes there is a need to take precautionary action now, not because we're certain climate change is happening, but because we must not ignore the possibility it may occur.

▷ Climate change is a complex, global issue and Suncor believes all segments of the global community should be working together to take prudent and reasonable actions that reduce greenhouse gases in the atmosphere.

▷ Suncor believes better solutions are created when stakeholders work together. Developing the right policies is a complex process, but it believes that, by working together, we will find creative ways to reduce the impact on the environment without harming economic development.

▷ Suncor is committed to taking actions to address the issue of climate change. Its success will be measured by the degree to which it meets the environmental, economic and social needs and expectations of its stakeholders.

Suncor is moving against the grain with these projects, as it is one of the only companies pursing new development at a time when oil prices are very low. It believes that these projects will not only be economically viable, they will also be developed in an environmentally responsible manner. For example, for the Stuart project the company has established a goal of attaining 'a level of net greenhouse gas emissions equal to or less than those associated with the production of conventional oil products'.[1]

This growth phase is leading to new environmental challenges, particularly in relation to global climate change. With a growth in oil production, the company's greenhouse gas emissions are expected to increase. To counter this impact, the company is pursuing a comprehensive and aggressive action plan to limit its greenhouse gas emissions to 1990 levels. The action plan includes the management of Suncor's own emissions, investment in alternative and renewable energy, and the pursuit of offsets and other flexible mechanisms likely to be formally established under the terms of the Kyoto Protocol. For example, Suncor has achieved an annual reduction of 960,000 tonnes of CO_2 from its Oil Sands operation and it expects to stabilise greenhouse gas emissions from this facility at 1990 levels by 2000. To this end, Suncor has developed a team to study alternative energy sources such as biomass, wind and solar, and it has funded a wind electricity-generation project in Alberta.

Suncor's action plan is based on the company's parallel approach to climate change: developing hydrocarbon resources responsibly to meet current needs while taking action now to support the diversification of energy sources over the longer term. The action plan and the company's approach to stakeholder consultation are an important part of the company's ongoing journey to become a sustainable energy company. The company is confident that it is putting in place the strategy and tools needed to continue this transformation. The following sections detail some of the specific actions and approaches that have enabled Suncor to pursue its ambitious plans for the future.

2. Trailblazing: principles, people and actions

a. Business value through improved stakeholder relations

In the mid-1990s, Suncor formed a team to deal specifically with stakeholder relations. The results of this effort changed the company's philosophy from indifference, ignorance and, in some cases, fear of stakeholder processes, to a firm belief in the value of stakeholders and their different perspectives. This turnaround

---

1   Suncor website: *http://www.suncor.com/ 01 about/ 01 frames.html*

An oil sands operation is somewhat like a large open-cast mine. Once the oil has been extracted, the land must be reclaimed to pre-development capability. In the case of Suncor's northern Canadian operations, this is a boreal forest landscape. In traditional practice, this meant filling in the land and typically bringing in heavy equipment to compact and smooth out the area. Aboriginal stakeholders observed that Suncor engineers conducting the reclamation process did everything in straight lines. The ground was smooth and flat and the edges of the reclamation area were linear.

Aboriginal stakeholders pointed out that nature rarely produces straight lines and they suggested that the area be left looking more natural. This simple suggestion lead to a more natural regrowth of the area and it saved the company money as Suncor did not have to bring as much heavy equipment to straighten the area out.

Box 2: Value in stakeholder relations

was not easy for a company that had traditionally viewed stakeholders as adversaries. A key component in the new approach to stakeholder consultation was company-wide training in principle-based leadership, which emphasised Steven Covey's 'Seven Habits of Highly Effective People' (Covey 1989).

One of the core principles of Covey's approach is that, to be effective communicators and individuals, people must learn to view situations from the perspective of others prior to making judgements or decisions. In Covey's terms: 'seek to understand and then be understood'. In the case of Suncor, this principle-based approach led to a number of realisations and subsequent actions. The company began to actively seek stakeholder input and, more importantly, developed a willingness to act on this input. Suncor realised that it had to build a new level of trust with stakeholders in order to gain community support for new projects and growth plans. It helped that the business implications of poor stakeholder relations were also clear: other project developers were sometimes going through more costly and adversarial hearing processes.

Suncor management applied resources to stakeholder relations, and the company began a very open dialogue with key stakeholders as exemplified by the 'Oil Sands Environmental Coalition' which included local aboriginal groups. The result of this dialogue was a consultation process that enhanced Suncor's relationship with the local community and helped incorporate stakeholder ideas and concerns into its planning. Through the consultation process, Suncor began to reap the benefit of another core principle of Covey's approach: 'win–win solutions'.

The inherent multidisciplinary view that arose from consultations with aboriginal elders, local communities and environmental groups afforded the company a new perspective, with stakeholders bringing forward questions that may never have otherwise been asked. According to Mark Shaw, Director of Sustainable

Suncor Oil Sands opened its SO_2 reduction plant in September 1996, which reduced SO_2 emissions by 90%.

The plant uses an innovative process developed by Chiyoda Corporation of Japan. It mixes limestone, mined from deposits beneath the oil sands, with water to create a slurry. SO_2 from the emissions is bubbled through the slurry and reacts to create calcium sulphate, commonly known as gypsum.

The gypsum produced is used to help reclaim tailings ponds, in a project called 'Consolidated Tailings Technology'. In this project, fine tailings from existing ponds are combined with thickened tailings from extraction and gypsum. This mixture does not separate in tailings ponds, but stays consolidated, and squeezes water out of the mixture. It is expected to turn Suncor's tailings ponds into a solid land surface able to support a productive layer of soil in 10–20 years, rather than hundreds of years.

Box 3: Suncor's innovative product development

Source: Suncor website, *www.suncor.com*

Development at Oil Sands, many of these questions led to cost savings, innovations and better solutions. In addition, because answering these questions often required input from different parts of the company, the stakeholder process led Suncor to take a more integrated approach to problem-solving.

Shaw credits the stakeholder input and concerns over SO_2 emissions as being instrumental in the development of a new SO_2 reduction plant and a new process to improve land reclamation of tailings (Box 3). The consolidation of tailings into solid land surface drastically reduces long-term reclamation time and the associated risk and liability associated with managing tailings ponds.

Suncor's consultation process is simple in concept but sometimes challenging to implement. The first step is to identify all potential stakeholders, group them as primary or secondary in importance and determine their positions or areas of concern. The next step is to work with them to develop different consultation arrangements dependent on their needs. The level of participation is determined by factors such as resource availability, cultural issues, language barriers, historical interactions and existing relationships.

Suncor, in conjunction with the stakeholders, developed a set of principles to guide the consultation process (Box 4). These principles act as the 'rules of the game' and enable all parties to evaluate whether an individual stakeholder is in compliance. They provide a means of evaluating and assessing differences and keeping the relationship moving forward.

Working with its stakeholders, Suncor seeks to develop a common understanding of the desired outcome of the consultation process. In each consultation process, it strives to ensure that **the best business decisions are made after full, fair consideration of ideas of all key stakeholders.** The focus of the consulta-

▷ **Integrity of regulatory process preserved.** The regulatory process fulfils a legitimate function that must be met at the end of the process and thus the integrity of this process must not be compromised by the drive to become more efficient.

▷ **Open and transparent.** All information is made available to stakeholders in a format that is transparent and customised to their needs. All stakeholders receive the information within the same time-frame.

▷ **Information shared freely and early.** To facilitate early stakeholder feedback, information would be shared during the developmental stage of the project. This information would usually be distributed in draft form in order to maximise input.

▷ **Stakeholders must be able to participate effectively**. Stakeholders must have adequate resources to review information and provide valuable input. They must also be allotted time to digest this information and understand the company's proposal.

▷ **Sensitivity to all needs of participants.** The consultation process must respect the needs of all participants and their other relationships.

Box 4: Example of Suncor's principles of consultation

tion process is to build long-term, trusting relationships that will maintain and enhance Suncor's public 'licence to operate' with both governmental and non-governmental groups. Suncor recognises that disagreements between the company and its stakeholders will occur. While Suncor does not commit to agree with all stakeholders, it seeks to avoid disagreements that are based on misunderstandings.

The most dramatic example of the business benefits of Suncor's stakeholder relations activity was the approval process for the start-up of the C\$320 million (US\$219 million) Steepbank Mine at Oil Sands. The company prepared an environmental impact assessment to determine how its growth plans would impact on air, water and land, as well as the social and economic life of the region. Throughout the process, the company worked with stakeholders to achieve a balance between the growth of Oil Sands and the environment. The result of this consultation effort was approval of the mine without the need for a public hearing. Stakeholders actually wrote to the regulatory authorities in support of the project. The regulatory authorities concluded that Suncor had appropriately dealt with all the relevant stakeholder concerns and issues during the consultation process. The speed of governmental approvals resulting from effective consultation put the project ahead by two years, helped to reduce construction costs and allowed Suncor to increase production and implement environmental improvements more quickly. Suncor applied the same approach to Project Millennium, and again accelerated the approvals process for growth plans. The business value of the stakeholder process is clear when it is considered that each day that the approval process is shortened translates into tens of thousands of barrels of oil being shipped.

b. *Early action on climate change*

On the opening day of the Kyoto Summit on Climate Change, Rick George made a presentation to the Vancouver Board of Trade. In this speech, he acknowledged the scientific consensus on climate change: the balance of evidence suggests that human activity is causing a discernible effect on the world's climate. He also affirmed Suncor's belief that emissions of greenhouse gases can be significantly reduced without sacrificing the economy.

For an energy company that derives most of its production from fossil fuels, this position caused quite a stir. While most of the players in the oil industry were pursuing a defensive course of action that called for more research and warned of the economic consequences of 'premature' action, Suncor stepped away from the pack and took a very different path. Three months after this speech, Suncor demonstrated its commitment to action on climate change by participating in one of the first emissions trades in North America, purchasing 100,000 tonnes of greenhouse gas emission reductions from Niagara Mohawk Power Corporation in the US, with an option to buy up to an additional 10 million tonnes of reductions over a ten-year period.

These two events were consistent with Suncor's action-oriented approach and its stated objective of meeting or exceeding stakeholder expectations. Prior to the Kyoto conference, the company recognised that, as an environmental leader, it needed to make a public statement on climate change. High-level debate took place internally. For Suncor, it was important that the discussions on climate change included the full 'toolbox' of so-called flexible mechanisms included in the Kyoto Protocol. These mechanisms, when approved, will allow companies to achieve reductions through emissions trading and offsets. Suncor recognises that there is a large potential business risk in policies that constrain carbon. The company's

***Box 5:* Actions on climate change**

In 1998, Suncor took the following actions to address global climate change:

▷ Improved the energy efficiency of its own operations

▷ Funded the generation of wind power in Alberta

▷ Financed climate change awareness programmes in schools

▷ Participated in a forest conservation programme in Belize

▷ Entered into one of the world's first cross-border emissions reduction trades

▷ Participated in a major trial reforestation project in Australia

▷ Supported research of new climate change solutions involving leading scientists from institutions across Canada

climate change plan, therefore, involves a multifaceted approach to greenhouse gas reductions that includes efficiency improvements, alternative energy development, emissions trading and offsets. It also recognises that policy-makers will only take a broader perspective to climate change solutions (including market and voluntary mechanisms) if they see results from non-regulatory approaches. By participating in an early voluntary trade, Suncor provided a working case study of a flexible mechanism in action. This case study has increased the company's understanding of potential emission reduction trading systems and contributed to national and international discussion of emissions reduction trading.

Suncor understands that it is not just what you do but when you do it. The timing of the speech by Rick George was designed to attract attention and to influence a debate that had only just begun in Kyoto. By taking a bold, strategic, proactive position, Suncor gained a seat at the table in important climate change discussions in Canada. Governments, stakeholders and other industry players began to seek out its opinions on emissions trading and other implementation issues. The company now has the profile to effectively demonstrate the benefits of a multi-faceted climate change plan and to help shift the policy debate toward its more balanced, less regulatory approach to carbon management.

c. Long-range planning: supporting the sustainability vision

In 1998, as part of its continuing evolution into a sustainable energy company, Suncor developed a management framework to achieve progress toward environmental quality, economic prosperity and social wellbeing. The framework is based on six strategic priorities:

1. **Operational excellence**. This involves developing best-in-class environment, health and safety (EHS) management systems, achieving performance results, and tracking progress through key performance measures. Suncor is benchmarking itself against international standards such as ISO 14001 and against companies within and outside the oil and gas sector. For example, in August 1999 Suncor's Sarnia refinery became the first refinery in Canada to achieve ISO 14001 certification.

2. **Integrating environmental, social and financial considerations into core business decision-making.** To achieve this priority, Suncor will continue to develop and utilise key tools and concepts such as eco-efficiency, life-cycle value assessment, EHS performance measures and targets, as well as environmental and social impact assessments.

3. **Products and services for the future.** Suncor has made a commitment to be a leading provider of energy solutions. To achieve this priority, the company is looking at ways to:

a. continuously improve current products through projects such as fuel reformulation

b. increase production and sales of more eco-efficient fuels such as natural gas

c. incorporate renewable energy into the product mix

d. expand product and service offerings to include other energy solutions on the demand management side

4. **Issue management.** This involves the continued development of a proactive process based on early identification of trends, opportunities and threats; participation and leadership in key business and governmental forums on sustainability such as the World Business Council for Sustainable Development (WBCSD); and the application of the precautionary principle.[2] Key issues include climate change, land use management, fuel reformulation, flaring and SO_2 emissions.

5. **Corporate social responsibility.** Suncor has developed a leadership position in stakeholder relations, based on:

a. mutually beneficial relationships with communities and stakeholders

b. strategic alliances with leading organisations involved in sustainability issues

c. ensuring knowledge transfer to international aspects of the business

d. working with business partners, suppliers and contractors to employ strategies and practices that enhance sustainability

e. support to the public in making informed decisions

f. open and regular reporting on goals, targets and performance

Partnership efforts include activities with the US Environmental Defense Fund, the Alberta-based Pembina Institute for Appropriate Development, and the WBCSD.

6. **Organisational capabilities and commitments**. Suncor actively fosters a high degree of understanding, commitment and action on sustainability issues from its employees. It also regularly tracks and assesses its progress toward sustainable development. This has led to new training opportunities for employees and the integration of sustainable development issues in succession planning.

2 The precautionary principle at Suncor is that, where there are threats of serious or irreversible damage, lack of full scientific certainty will not be used as a reason for postponing cost-effective measures to prevent environmental degradation (Suncor, *Long-Range Planning Guidelines*).

The company's framework for sustainability resulted from a dialogue between the senior management team and the EHS team. Together, they recognised that a more structured approach was required to enable Suncor to implement its core purpose and to achieve progress toward the ambitious goal of becoming a sustainable energy company. Gordon Lambert, Suncor's Corporate Director of EHS, describes three main challenges to the ongoing implementation of the framework.

▷ The first challenge—organisational engagement—is common to most companies. Sustainability issues are core to the company's future but, until they are more fully integrated into the decision-making processes, they must compete with the priorities of the day. Training and communication will be key to meeting this challenge.

▷ A second challenge is the potential for a reduction in the price of oil and its potential effect on Suncor's profitability. The future may bring higher oil prices but this is not a given. Suncor's growth has allowed it to achieve economies of scale that will insulate it from prolonged periods of low prices.

▷ The third main challenge is internal competency and capacity within the company. As is the case in most organisations, the company began looking at sustainability issues using a core team of experts. Today, the responsibility for sustainability is expanding throughout the organisation. For example, the Senior Vice-President of Human Resources and Communications has taken on the issue, and sustainable development is now being integrated into areas such as recruitment and orientation. Recently, Suncor's senior management team gathered for a three-day strategy session devoted exclusively to sustainability. According to Lambert, there is a 'pretty good conversation going on' about sustainability within the company.

This conversation extends to the board of directors and shareholders, both of whom have been supportive. Sustainability is a focus of speeches by senior managers and a core part of Suncor's dialogue with stakeholders.

d. Tools for change

As Suncor began to focus more on sustainability, it recognised the need to improve the eco-efficiency of its operations and to develop performance measures to track progress. There were also increasing demands both externally and internally for information on environmental performance. This need led to an examination of a variety of tools and approaches. Working in conjunction with the Pembina Institute for Appropriate Development, Suncor is now building life-cycle considerations into the business decision-making process.

Life-cycle value assessment (LCVA) uses a systematic methodology to identify, quantify and analyse the environmental, financial (and, if desired, social) implications of each of the activities involved in producing and consuming a product or service. It can unearth opportunities to improve the technical design, upgrade operating procedures, or substitute processes and materials in order to reduce costs and reduce environmental pollutants and other impacts. LCVA's systematic analysis extends beyond direct company activities to include all life-cycle stages of a process or product. This 'cradle-to-grave' analysis ensures that decision-makers are aware of the total system impacts of a decision, and do not unknowingly shift costs or environmental burdens onto others at 'upstream' or 'downstream' stages of the life-cycle.

The LCVA methodology works through six main steps:

▷ **Goal definition**: definition of decisions and key questions, comparison and analysis of products or production systems on the basis of equivalent provision of service to the consumer

▷ **Scoping:** clear mapping of the life-cycle flow of activities involved in production, use and disposal and organising these activities into 'unit processes'.

▷ **Inventory assessment:** collection and validation of data to quantify the inputs and outputs within the life-cycle stages selected for analysis, in order to answer the key questions of the goal definition stage.

▷ **Impact assessment:** results are assessed in terms of environmental and financial impacts and significance.

▷ **Design improvement:** a series of steps taken in tandem with the four main analysis stages, to ensure that a systematic and serious effort is made to find opportunities to reduce the financial and environmental impacts of various technologies, process activities and material supply choices across the full life-cycle.

▷ **Report:** results are synthesised and summarised; conclusions and recommendations are made and compiled.

Box 6: Life-cycle value assessment (LCVA)

Source: Pembina Institute for Appropriate Development

The company initially worked with Pembina to evaluate life-cycle value assessment (LCVA) on a pilot basis. Although these pilots achieved mixed results, it was clear that a life-cycle approach provided value to the company in spite of additional up-front project planning costs. Currently, Suncor is using LCVA as a tool (Box 6) to analyse the environmental and socioeconomic aspects of development projects, the implementation of green purchasing policies and other business activities. Some specific examples include:

▷ The use of LCVA to verify marketing claims related to ethanol-enhanced fuels sold through the Sunoco distribution network, such as reduced hydrocarbons and lower greenhouse gas emissions. An LCVA evaluation of end-of-life options of a major process tower led Oil Sands to send the tower to a recycling facility instead of disposing of it in a landfill site.

The effective communication of Suncor's actions in areas such as climate change has led to the following results:

▷ Recognition by the financial sector: the company stock is owned by a number of ethical funds.

▷ Good media image: positive coverage by the business and environment press.

▷ Better relationship with regulators: Suncor is often asked by government to participate in high-level discussions on environmental issues such as climate change. In many cases, it are asked for advice in these discussions.

▷ New opportunities: as a leader, Suncor is now being approached with ideas, particularly with respect to emissions trading.

▷ In 1998 Suncor's action plan on climate change was rated fourth over all in Canada— and best in the oil industry.

Box 7: **Enhancing brand image**

▷   The use of LCVA to evaluate several pipelines and access road routing options for a new development project.

LCVA analyses include capital and operating costs as well as environmental impacts, such as greenhouse gas emissions. Suncor has adapted LCVA on a project-specific basis and now uses a range of methodological approaches. Depending on the size of the project, the method chosen may range from the use of an LCVA checklist to a full LCVA study. According to Eric Axford, Director of Strategy and Planning, LCVA has led to better-designed projects and a variety of business benefits.

Suncor has made a commitment to integrate life-cycle thinking and LCVA into all major decisions within a three-year time-frame and has established a committee to oversee the implementation of this objective. Implementation will involve more pilots, the identification of internal and external expertise, and the development of training programmes and databases. Auditing procedures are also being established within the finance group. By setting up the proper infrastructure for LCVA, Suncor hopes to ensure that this tool becomes an integral component of company-wide decision-making and an important step toward its overall sustainability strategy.

e. *Bold actions effectively communicated*

Suncor CEO Rick George often says that business success requires taking the right actions and then communicating these actions to the marketplace. Suncor has taken these two simple principles to heart. The company has a carefully focused

Suncor Energy is a unique and sustainable energy company dedicated to vigorous growth in worldwide markets by meeting the changing expectations of our current and future stakeholders.

We will actively dialogue and create congruence with our colleagues, investors, customers, partners and communities. We will involve them in our opportunities, processes and issues with the goal of creating long-lasting and mutually beneficial relationships. Our values and beliefs will be demonstrated in all our decisions and actions.

To accomplish our core purpose, we will individually and collectively:

▷ Identify and seize significant growth opportunities in strategically selected markets

▷ Transform and grow our existing businesses and continuously improve our processes, products and services

▷ Earn exceptional customer loyalty by providing quality products and services, and building relationships that are value-creating and sustainable

▷ Invest in opportunities to develop and apply our unique and diverse talents in ways that build the business and achieve our personal growth, reward and satisfaction

▷ Achieve leadership in health, safety and environmental performance within our businesses, our communities and the eco-systems in which we operate.

Our success is measured by the degree to which we deliver on our commitments and exceed the expectations of stakeholders while doubling our market value every five years.

Box 8: Suncor's 'core purpose'

plan to communicate its responses to various issues, including climate change, and to demonstrate its commitment to sustainable development through action.

Effective corporate communications involves reaching the right audience at the right time. At Suncor, communications issues are integrated directly into the policy development process to position the company as a leader. To achieve this goal, communications personnel are engaged at the front end of specific projects. For example, the communications group assisted in the development of the company policy on LCVA and handled internal employee communication on this issue. The communication group was also directly involved in the development of Suncor's action plan on climate change.

The company has pursued a very open and transparent communications strategy on environment and sustainable development issues. According to Ron Shewchuk, Corporate Manager of External Communications, this approach has benefited the company by enhancing brand image and contributing to business and greenhouse gas reduction opportunities. For example, the effective communication of Suncor's climate change position and actions, such as the emissions trade with Niagara Mohawk Power Corporation, has resulted in the company being approached by other organisations with new emissions trading projects. The

The ideal workplace is challenging, stimulating and fair; a place where each employee has the opportunity to grow and accomplish; a place where commitment is freely given and the desire to outperform competitors is strong. At Suncor, we are determined to create and maintain this ideal. Our success depends on it.

We will:

▷ Treat each other and our customers fairly and with respect.

▷ Be highly ethical and professional.

▷ Encourage the kind of open, honest communication that fosters a climate of trust.

▷ Value the judgement of employees by giving them the latitude to make decisions, take calculated risks, learn from mistakes and put ideas to work.

▷ Respect individual and cultural differences.

▷ Tolerate no discrimination, harassment or disrespect.

▷ Recognise and reward the accomplishments of our employees, and provide timely and honest appraisal of their work.

▷ Provide training and development opportunities, and encourage employees to take charge of their own learning.

▷ Be progressive in our health, safety and environmental practices.

▷ Earn customer loyalty with superior products and services.

▷ Care for and work to improve the communities in which we operate.

▷ Maintain mutually beneficial relationships with our unions and employee associations.

▷ Ensure that we do not compromise our values and beliefs in our relationships with customers, suppliers and other stakeholders.

▷ Work to exemplify our vision, core purpose, values and beliefs in all our actions, relationships and plans.

Box 9: **Suncor's values and beliefs**

trade also enhanced Suncor's brand image as it was greeted by laudatory press statements from Al Gore, Christine Stewart, the Canadian Minister of Environment, and Ralph Goodale, the Minister of Natural Resources, as well as leading non-governmental organisations.

Suncor also recognises that an act of communication is also an act of consultation with stakeholders. As a result, the communications group is strongly linked with the company's EHS department. Suncor understands that engaging stakeholders is not a secondary consideration, but is integral to the company's evolution as a sustainable energy enterprise.

f. Principle-based leadership

Suncor's managers talk about principle-based leadership, and this approach is reflected in the company's statement of values and beliefs, its interactions with stakeholders and its actions on climate change. Through company-wide leadership training, the development of the core purpose statement and other initiatives, Suncor has gained a strong, coherent sense of corporate identity. These efforts have shaped how Suncor interacts with stakeholders, how employees view the company, and the confidence the company has in its people, its business strategy and its long-term vision.

The Covey doctrines, along with the core purpose and the values and beliefs statement, have all helped create a very special culture within Suncor. It has evolved into a confident, principled and professional organisation that is not afraid to choose its own course. It has done so in important areas such as climate change and stakeholder relations and, significantly, it has made this transformation at a time when oil prices are extremely low. Led by a CEO and management team that have backed up words with concrete actions, Suncor has established itself as sector leader with a solid brand image.

Within Suncor, sustainability has progressed to the point where the issues are gradually becoming ingrained in the company's culture and business practices. As an energy company, Suncor faces significant challenges and uncertainties with respect to global climate change but is preparing to meet them by putting in place the processes, tools and management framework it needs to survive in a carbon-constrained future.

3. Conclusions

Suncor is an established leader in a sector that faces a number of challenges in addressing sustainability. Suncor's principle-based approach has helped the management team and shareholders to see the value in sustainable development and has contributed to the company's ability to take a progressive stance in environmental areas such as climate change and the development of alternative and renewable energy.

The company is an active member of the WBCSD and is using this experience to learn from other leading companies and to benchmark its performance against global standards of excellence. While achieving some early progress toward sustainable development, Suncor recognises that it still faces a number of significant challenges and must proactively continue its implementation plans if it wants to maintain strong progress.

As a smaller player in the energy sector, Suncor is in a position to react more quickly and aggressively to changes in the marketplace. The company is facing criticism for developing more oil reserves, but this is balanced by its progressive climate change action plan. In responding to issues such as climate change, Suncor continues to demonstrate a strategic, principled approach to environmental management. These efforts were recently recognised when Suncor was named top energy company in the Dow Jones Sustainability Group Index. This tracks the performance of 200 leading sustainability-driven companies in 68 industry groups in 22 countries. Criteria for inclusion include: innovative technology development; corporate governance; shareholder relations; industrial leadership; and social responsibility.[3]

Finally, the company remains committed to defining parallel paths of energy development: developing hydrocarbon resources responsibly to meet current needs while supporting the long-term diversification of energy sources. In this way, Suncor plans to build capacity to operate in a carbon-constrained world and ensure its long-term competitive future.

References

Suncor publications

http://www.suncor.com
Long-Range Planning Guidelines (Suncor, 1998).

Other

Covey, S. (1989) *The Seven Habits of Highly Effective People* (New York: Simon & Schuster).
International Energy Agency (1998) *World Energy Outlook* (Paris: International Energy Agency).
UNEP (United Nations Environment Programme) (1999) *Global Environment Outlook 2000* (Nairobi: UNEP).

Organisational contacts

Eric Axford, Director of Strategy and Planning
Mark Shaw, Director of Sustainable Development, Oil Sands
Ron Shewchuk, Corporate Manager of External Communications
Gordon Lambert, Corporate Director of Environment, Health and Safety

3   Dow Jones Sustainability Group Index: *http://www.sustainability-index.com*

AssiDomän

*Foresters integrating dual goals
of economy and environment*

AssiDomän is one of Europe's largest forest products companies, and the largest private landowner in the world. Production is concentrated on packaging paper, packaging, and sawn timber. Gross revenue for 1998 was SEK 23,993 million (US$2.8 billion). Over the last nine years, AssiDomän has pioneered a full-scale commitment to ecological forestry. Their corporate-wide policy has focused on closed-loop, sustainable operations. Through their market and ecological successes, AssiDomän has been driving the entire European forestry industry into sustainable forest management.

As a corporation, AssiDomän is committed to two goals of equal importance: (1) enduring profitability; and (2) viable ecosystems with the same or higher biodiversity (see Box 1). From this commitment, strategies are formally designed to meet both goals simultaneously. Annual action plans show direct paths to both goals. Managers and work crews are evaluated on the basis of their scores in both dimensions. And, throughout the organisation, there is a tangible sense of enthusiasm and confidence as they move forward.

At the corporate level, the two goals are broken down into specific quantitative sub-goals for economic return and for ecosystem health, biodiversity and aesthetic and recreational environmental targets. Then, as described by an AssiDomän manager, 'balancing production and ecological values requires us to do co-ordinated economic and ecological planning'. This has resulted in seven major implementation programmes designed to achieve both goals simultaneously:

For some organisations, the goal of becoming sustainable is equal to the goal of financial return for shareholders. AssiDomän sees the goals of sustainability and financial return as complementary and equal. It has positive environmental restoration goals, and is measuring positive impacts.

	BALANCING PRODUCTION AND ECOLOGICAL VALUES	
	Economy–profit	*Ecology–other values*
	⟷	
GOAL	▷ High and steady economic yield	▷ Viable ecosystem ▷ Preservation and development of biodiversity ▷ Recreation
MEANS	▷ Site-adapted forestry with functional conservation (regeneration planning) ▷ Ecological landscape planning ▷ Modified harvesting/silviculture ▷ Soil and water conservation ▷ Road and machine investments ▷ Education—ergonomics ▷ Customised timber deliveries—reserve of area planned for regeneration	

Balancing production and ecological values requires co-ordinated economic and ecological planning

Box 1: AssiDomän fully balances economic and ecological goals

1. Site-adapted ecological forestry with functional conservation

2. Ecological landscape planning

3. Ecologically modified harvesting and silviculture

4. Soil and water conservation

5. Road and machine investments

6. Education

7. Customised timber deliveries and timber reserve areas

Behind each of these implementation programmes are detailed actions that align daily work with the achievement of the dual goals. For example, the cutting crews

To evaluate how adopted goals relating to sustainable production and conservation of biodiversity have been met, the forestry group has, since 1993, used an 'Ecological Balance Sheet'. AssiDomän's Ecological Balance Sheet assigns a 1–5 score for key forest, land and water management factors. Five specially trained auditors check and evaluate more than 200 randomly chosen felling sites throughout Sweden, assessing site adaptation, soil conservation and water profile. Aggregated, these become the corporate-level measures of AssiDomän's biodiversity and conservation management goals. At the operational level, a finer granularity of measures includes: snags, seed trees, dead trees per hectare; threatened species; cut areas; percentage preserved; nature conservation areas; harvest-to-production ratio; and biodiversity. Each management area—typically 6–7 hectares—is mapped into sub-units, based on soil type and moisture, vegetation and fauna diversity and other characteristics. Each sub-unit then has its own management plan: 'final felling', which takes out all mature trees, various kinds of selective cuts, small-area managed fires, leaving whole stands intact (on average 12% of the area of management units in southern Sweden) to protect soils, species and ecological vitality. This is an example of mass customisation applied to natural resource management.

Overall, AssiDomän limits cutting to 75% of the timber growth rate, yet it is able to steadily increase harvest—projecting a 1%-per-year increase over the next 20 years—because timber growth rates are actually increasing under this management plan. In addition, AssiDomän tracks energy and raw material use, emissions (SO_2, CO_2), and waste by-products.

Box 2: AssiDomän's 'Ecological Balance Sheet'

receive two weeks per year of education in ecological forestry. In conjunction, the Human Resource System has been changed to a more team-based design. Crews are now responsible for the entire process of cut planning through harvesting; thereafter, the teams' sites are given follow-up ecological evaluations (formerly, 'teams' of individual loggers were simply told to clear-cut the entire area). The teams analyse each site, use their new knowledge to customise the cutting plan to meet ecological needs (e.g. adjusting cutting plans to moisture levels of biotopes, matching cutting plans with wildlife requirements, and working and cutting differently in riparian areas) and then harvest the site according to the plan. (AssiDomän took five years to characterise and input to a database every biotope in the forest to measure each one's impact on biodiversity.) Afterwards, forest ecologists assess the plan and the cut, and grade each team's work on an 'Ecological Balance Sheet', with scores from 0 to 5 in three major categories (See Box 2).

AssiDomän's Ecological Balance Sheet 'Grade-Point Average' scores are displayed in Box 3. Sites logged in the 1980s scored at or below '2' on all dimensions. With the commitment to ecological forestry begun in 1990, sites began receiving average scores of 3.1 in 1991, and rose every year for five years. However, 'the

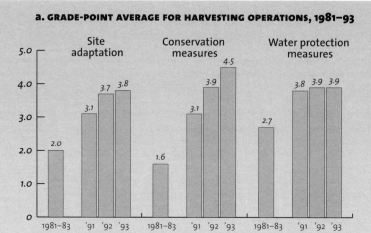

a. GRADE-POINT AVERAGE FOR HARVESTING OPERATIONS, 1981–93

b. ECOLOGICAL BALANCE SHEET, 1993–98

Internal follow-up in the form of an ecological balance sheet has been carried out since 1993 so that the progress of forest-related objectives can be monitored.

The grades for site adaptation and nature conservation in regeneration felling show that the high level, reached in the middle of the 1990s through extensive further training, has not been maintained. The number of evaluated categories, as well as the requirements to obtain the highest grade, have increased in pace with new research findings and further development of the criteria for FSC certification. A renewed advanced training campaign is planned to coincide with the introduction of the new handbook on regeneration planning in spring 1999. The follow-up of site adaptation shows that, on 83% of the regeneration felled area, the best possible combination of felling method, tree species and regeneration method was chosen. This represents a decline of five percentage points compared with 1997. It is mostly the use of natural regeneration on land unsuitable for the purpose that is responsible for this less favourable result.

The thinnings in the 1998 balance sheet show no great changes in grades compared with last year. The removal of hardwood trees in the thinnings has further decreased which means that the hardwood fraction is increasing after thinning for the first time. Pre-commercial thinning is included in the ecological balance sheet starting in 1998. In the long term, this will be of decisive importance for achieving AssiDomän's production and environmental objectives.

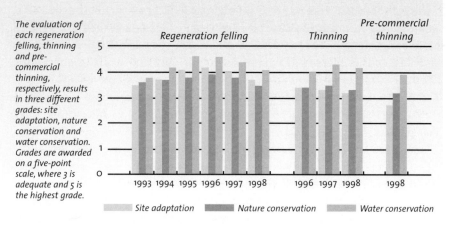

The evaluation of each regeneration felling, thinning and pre-commercial thinning, respectively, results in three different grades: site adaptation, nature conservation and water conservation. Grades are awarded on a five-point scale, where 3 is adequate and 5 is the highest grade.

Box 3: AssiDomän 'Ecological Balance Sheet' scores

number of evaluated categories, as well as the requirements to obtain the highest grade, have increased in pace with new research findings and further development of the criteria for Forest Stewardship Council (FSC) certification' (*Environmental Report* 1998). The company's proportion of FSC-labelled forestry went from 50% in 1997 to an impressive 100% in 1998. (FSC certification endorses the fact that AssiDomän's forestry operations are conducted in a sustainable manner from an economic, ecological and social perspective.) A renewed advanced training campaign coincided with the introduction of the company's new handbook on regeneration planning in 1999.

Environmental economics: financial performance

But what about financial performance? Surely, costs are increased by training loggers two weeks a year—and having them spend time planning customised ecological cutting programmes, selectively cutting rather than clear-cutting, and evaluating ecological quality. The answer to this is both 'yes' and 'no'. The chart in Box 4 illustrates AssiDomän's short-term and long-term cost payback comparison for a 38-hectare area.

As AssiDomän began measuring its costs, it found that ecological harvesting does cost more the first year for any given site, often three times as much. But over just a five-year period, the additional costs for the clear-cut area (e.g. for draining, scarifying, harrowing, road work and replanting) far outweigh the costs for the ecologically managed site.

By the start of the third year, the two sites reach break-even point, and, after five years, the ecological sites end up being, on average, 56% cheaper to manage than the clear-cut sites. And that is only the cost side. On the revenue side, the ecological sites grow better wood—stronger fibre, and more of it. AssiDomän gains both more board-feet and higher prices, so the revenue is significantly higher.

And then there's the gleam in their eyes. We questioned one AssiDomän manager hard about costs and profit margins. How could they justify this ecological forestry on a simple cost basis? 'You know,' he replied, with that gleam, 'if you have a motivated organisation, things are cheaper.'

AssiDomän provides a strong example of the long-term economic benefits of managing for environmental goals: its analysis of the costs of undertaking site-adapted forestry versus industrial forestry revealed that, during the first year, its goal of preserving biodiversity entailed cost, but, over as little as a five-year period, site-adapted ecological forestry actually generated a 56% cost saving. AssiDomän reported achieving these cost efficiencies, even given the considerable investment made in the two-weeks-per-year operator training for applied forest ecology.

COMPARATIVE COSTS FOR A 38-HECTARE CUT IN CENTRAL SWEDEN

Year	Measure	Area	Large-scale forestry Cost	Site-adapted forestry Cost	Comparison
1985	Cleared	38.0	22,800	12,800	−10,000
1986	Extra cost, felling	38.0	–	72,000	+72,000
1986	Drained	38.0	38,000	13,000	−25,000
1987	Patch-scarified	38.0	41,800	23,800	−18,000
1988	Planted	38.0	159,600	67,600	−92,000
1989	Surveyed	38.0	1,900	1,900	–
1989	Harrowed	38.0	41,800	–	−41,800
1989	Replanted	26.7	112,000	–	−112,000
1990	Replanted	4.7	19,800	–	−19,800
	Total		437,700	191,100	−246,600 (56%)

Shelterwood versus clear-cutting

Box 4: **AssiDomän comparative costs for large-scale forestry versus site-adapted forestry**

Strategic rationale

In summary, AssiDomän invests in these dual goals with the clear expectation that they will strengthen the company's profitability in the long term through increased efficiency gains and savings, strengthened brands, retention of key customers, strategic partnerships, goodwill and competence. These values are the components of intellectual capital built on a new, long-term vision of success in the forestry industry.

References

http://www.asdo.se
Documents may be ordered from: *http://www.asdo.se/english/respons/order.htm*
AssiDomän Annual Report 1998 (Stockholm: AssiDomän AB, 1999).
AssiDomän Environmental Report 1998 (Stockholm: AssiDomän AB, 1999).

Organisational contacts

Nippe Hylander, Senior Vice-President, Development and Environment
Nina Haglund, Senior Advisor, Packaging Development
Jonas Jacobsson, Director, Forest Management
Katarina Lindel, Development and Environment
Professor Jan-Erik Lundmark, Senior Ecologist
Lars Ströberg, Co-ordinator of Environmental Affairs, Development and Environment

PATAGONIA

First ascents: finding the way toward quality of life and work

1. *The lie of the land*

a. *Corporate overview*

Patagonia's brand awareness and reputation are distinctly out of proportion to its size. Nestled in a quiet street just yards from the ocean in Ventura, California, Patagonia has for over two and a half decades been renowned for supplying high-quality outdoor clothing and equipment to discriminating enthusiasts.

A stepchild of Chouinard Equipment, the leading US supplier of speciality climbing equipment in the early 1970s, Patagonia remains privately held. It is a subsidiary of Lost Arrow Corporation, established in 1984 as the holding company for Patagonia, Patagonia Mail Order, Chouinard Equipment (now Black Diamond) and Great Pacific Iron Works. Patagonia sales in 1998 were US$165 million, achieved with 900 employees.

Patagonia manages the research and development, design, manufacturing, merchandising and sales (retail, catalogue and web-based) of adult and children's outdoor clothing, hardgoods such as packs and travel bags, and, more recently (following founder Yvon Chouinard's long-standing philosophy that, if you can't find a good one, make it) surf boards!

The heart of Patagonia's success lies in relentless technical innovation that produces a continuous stream of products good enough to meet the tough and continually rising expectations of the most avid experts in a multitude of high-intensity sports: mountaineering, rock and ice climbing, surfing, skiing, snowboarding, kayaking, biking, sailing and fishing.

The soul of Patagonia's success lies in a deep, abiding commitment, at both an organisational and personal level, to preserving the diversity, ecological integrity and beauty of the natural environment that is Patagonia's ultimate source of wealth and *raison d'être*.

b. *Preview*

The first clue that Patagonia might not be a typical corporation is found on the message board as you walk into corporate headquarters in Ventura, California. Just below the visitor welcome message is a permanent space for the daily 'Surf Report', which, on the first day I visited, registered 'Pumping Swell 6'–10'; High Tide: 9:39 am'. Promoting surfing by providing flexitime to allow employees to take advantage of when the surf is up is just the tip of the iceberg (or the crest of the wave, as it may be!) at Patagonia.

Besides creating a culture that encourages employees to pursue the sports about which they are passionate, Patagonia is quietly creating a revolutionary model for business in the next millennium. With its statement of purpose, with breakthroughs in converting recycled soda bottles into plush fleece fabric, with a commitment to using only organic cotton, with a new children's clothing line carved out of scraps, and with its struggles with a new strategic direction, Patagonia is a pioneer on the journey toward more environmentally and socially sustainable industrial practices.

Patagonia is literally and figuratively integrating environmental and social responsibility into the fabric of its business. Several of its key actions and accomplishments are summarised in Box 1.

What really makes Patagonia stand out? The accomplishments listed in Box 1 are impressive, and the stories behind how they evolved are captivating and informative to other companies proceeding along this path. Yet many companies today can list a number environmental and social achievements (although decidedly less radical and encompassing). Impressive as they are, these milestones represent only the top notes of Patagonia's score. It would be a grave mistake to view Patagonia's story only from a cognitive, rational perspective—and to fail to hear the theme underlying these notes. What is truly remarkable about Patagonia, and much more difficult to define in words, is the heart and soul that has been the essence of the company since its inception, and is now broadly embraced by management, employees, suppliers, retail distributors and, increasingly, customers.

The sections below strive to convey both these elements of Patagonia's journey, process and destination, describing their philosophy and strategic actions in the following areas:

▷ Over 25 years of dedicated, hands-on and financial support to grass-roots environmental causes. The company operates a self-imposed 'Earth tax', which provides either 1% of sales revenue or 10% of pre-tax profits (whichever is greater) to environmental activism. Over $10 million has been donated since 1973.

▷ The first outdoor clothing designer and distributor to base a product line on fleece made out of recycled soda bottles (registered and branded as PCR [post-consumer recycled] 'Synchilla'), diverting plastic bottles from landfills and saving oil and toxic air emissions (1993)

▷ One of the first companies in the country to offer on-site corporate childcare; recognition in a *Forbes* article as one of the top 25 companies to work for; and over ten years of honours as one of the 100 best companies to work for by *Working Mother* magazine (see e.g. *Working Mother* 1999). It also appears in *Fortune* magazine's '100 Best Companies to Work For' (*Fortune* 1999).

▷ A revolutionary internship programme that pays employees to work up to two months for the non-profit environmental group of their choice

▷ Environmental considerations are built into the Reno Customer Service Center and into the renovation of the 'Firehouse' building at the headquarters site (e.g. recycled steel and concrete, reclaimed materials, mirrors capturing and redirecting sunlight).

▷ A corporate decision in 1994 to convert to entirely organic cotton in all product lines by the spring 1996 season

▷ A landmark supplier conference to ensure the entire supply chain was aligned in its efforts to mitigate environmental impacts (modelled after a supplier quality conference Patagonia held several years earlier, this time introducing environment as part of quality)

▷ 'Q=E' (i.e. quality and environmental protection should be one and the same): manifested in a customer education campaign, internal dialogue, and a design challenge

▷ Start-up of a new business, 'Beneficial Ts', producing blank organic cotton t-shirts (1997)

▷ Creation of the 'Seedling' infant clothing line, which patches together scraps from adult clothing fabrics—what Patagonia calls 'pre-cycling' material—which used to end up on the cutting-room floor.

▷ The first Californian company to commit to using 100% wind energy for in-state facilities

▷ Eliminating PVCs from travel bags in the spring 2000 line

Box 1: Patagonia's integration of environmental and social responsibility with business

a. Recipe for transformation: personal, heroic, magical

b. The bare essentials: ultimate purpose and core values

c. Strategic rationale: 'It's the right thing to do.'

d. Then again, we might be onto something here

e. Weaving a sustainable tapestry

Before considering the details of Patagonia's story, it is useful to examine the general business context and the market drivers toward environmentalism in the industry.

c. Business context

The market for quality outdoor clothing and equipment is heavily saturated and highly competitive. Key competitors make very-high-quality products, so it is increasingly hard to differentiate based on technical performance. Many of Patagonia's publicly owned competitors, under pressure to meet 20%–25%-per-year growth targets in an industry with overcapacity, are moving to alternative distribution channels such as large department stores. This represents a significant threat to the speciality retailers that have been the mainstay of Patagonia's business model. Although competitors claim to offer only lower-quality products (in terms of technical grade) via these channels, there is evidence that outdoor equipment retailers may be going the way of the independent booksellers. For example, in France, a major market for outdoor clothing and equipment, two major chains have bought out almost all independent stores—leaving only about 20 independent stores in the country! Furthermore, the entire retail industry is being reshaped, as are many industries, with the consumer gaining the capability of going directly to the manufacturer through the Internet. Although Patagonia has remained committed to the dealers with whom it has had long-term relationships, both Patagonia and the retailers are feeling increasing pressure.

d. What are the drivers for environmental sustainability?

Customers choose Patagonia products because of their technical excellence, performance and quality. Environmental sensitivity as a customer requirement comes in well behind these foundational expectations. In fact, for many customers, environment may not even make the list. Market research at Patagonia reveals that, today, only about 20% of customers report caring about the environmental impact of what they purchase.

So what is the incentive for going so far beyond simply complying with regulatory requirements? Where does the motivation come from? At Patagonia, concern about the environmental impact of products and processes is largely internally driven. Its has well-established roots:

66 We believe quality is not something you can do piecemeal. Either you believe in quality, or you don't. Either it surfaces everywhere and you commit to it everywhere, or you don't. There is no gray area here. I don't think it's possible to make a great quality product without having a great quality work environment.

It's all linked: Quality product, quality customer service, quality workplace, quality of life for your employees, even quality of life for all living things on this planet. If you miss any one piece, there is a good chance you'll miss it all. **99**

Yvon Chouinard, Patagonia Founder

Box 2: Patagonia's world-class approach to quality

▷ Founder Yvon Chouinard's leadership in developing innovative gear for 'clean climbing' that didn't deface the mountain—dramatically shifting the market toward removable chocks away from pitons (despite the fact that his company led the worldwide market for pitons in the early 1970s)

▷ A long-established corporate philosophy to 'do no harm'

▷ Managers and employees alike being passionate about nature and spending a great deal of time outdoors. 'What you love, you protect', one manager commented.

▷ A history of supporting grass-roots environmental causes, together with a formal system for engaging employees in activism

Patagonia is clearly leading the market. Although there is a growing confidence in the strategic rationale for sustainability, both environmental and social initiatives in Patagonia stem largely from a strong internal conviction about 'doing the right thing'.

2. *Trailblazing*

a. *Recipe for transformation: personal, heroic, magical*

What is the recipe for transforming an organisation? Based on years 'in the trenches' working for social and political change, Kevin Sweeney, Patagonia's Director of Communications, advocates that, to transform an organisation, you must: (1) make it personal; (2) take heroic action; and (3) sprinkle in a little magic.

Kevin and other leaders at Patagonia are working to integrate all three of these apparent intangibles both internally and externally. Together, as implemented in Patagonia, these ingredients are creating a powerful formula for change.

Make it personal

In most industries, the daily grind of strategic planning, technology development, product design, marketing, manufacturing excellence, and sales and service allow managers and employees to remain far removed from the environmental and social impacts caused by their products. Exacerbating this, most environmental interventions to date have focused primarily on 'end-of-pipe' actions to ameliorate the negative effects of production processes. Only in the past decade has conscious-ness been raised to understand that a business must be concerned with, and assume responsibility for, the entire life-cycle of the products or services it is providing, from raw materials extraction to end-of-life disposal. Patagonia is a leading exam-ple of a company that has examined the life-cycle impacts of key products and used this analysis to prioritise aggressive action. That is the rational part. Added to this are several factors that have elevated environment to a personal level, and turned this technically sophisticated life-cycle impact analysis into a powerful lever for transformation. Patagonia's conversion to organic cotton illustrates this well.

In 1990, Patagonia managers' thinking underwent a significant shift. They began to look at the environmental impacts of the primary materials that composed their products. Up until this point, like many organisations, they thought of environ-mental performance primarily in terms of regulatory compliance and internal office paper recycling. More proactive than most, Patagonia also had a long-standing programme to support grass-roots environmental groups, and had led the market in producing products for 'clean climbing' to minimise environmental degradation of climbing routes. With the latter, they contributed substantially to the transformation of climbing culture and practice worldwide.

In the early 1990s, with an increasing realisation that its business was contribut-ing to environmental problems, Patagonia embarked on an effort to understand the life-cycle impacts of the four major fibres used in its products: polyester, nylon, cotton and wool. What it found was surprising, and led to a decision that would take the company's production co-ordinators, employees, customers and suppliers in a dramatically different direction.

Although they anticipated issues with synthetic fibres, surely, they thought, cotton is pure and natural? Not so, as it is currently treated. Contrary to expecta-tions that natural fibres would prove to be the most environmentally benign, the life-cycle analysis revealed that conventionally grown cotton had negative impacts through every stage of life-cycle from the fields to the washing machine. On getting these results, Patagonia immediately embarked on an effort to better inform itself, its employees, and even its customers, about its unintended but undeniable collusion in environmental degradation. (Synthetic fibres and wool, as expected, had negative impacts as well, but cotton was chosen as the area in which Patagonia could make the most substantial reduction in the environmental impact of its products.)

Patagonia's next actions provide a vivid example of 'making it personal'. Typically, manufacturers in the apparel industry are several steps removed from the production of raw material from which their suppliers make fabric and accessories. Patagonia broke ranks with this tradition in 1992, taking a group of representatives on a tour of cotton farms in the San Joaquin Valley with farmer and organic agriculture activist Will Allen. What they saw was a dramatic contrast between the conventionally grown and organically grown cotton fields.

Conventional practices for growing and harvesting cotton—undertaken in the vast majority of the valley's one million-plus cotton acres—farm cotton as a monocrop supported by an onslaught of chemicals that toxify the soil, air and groundwater—making cotton one of the most damaging fibres Patagonia uses to make clothing. The soil, chemically sterilised, becomes merely structural support for holding the cotton plant upright. Seeds are fumigated to prevent fungi. Synthetic nutrients, herbicides and pesticides are applied to feed the plants, kill competitive weeds and exterminate insects. Chemicals are used to regulate the rate of growth, maximise the number of bolls, and ensure uniform opening. Prior to picking, defoliants are applied to kill the plants and remove the leaves, in order to facilitate harvesting. The chemicals also reach unintended targets: drifting from cropdusting planes onto nearby water supplies and farmhouses; seeping from discarded concentrate cans into stream beds; washing with flood irrigation into drinking-water sources; spreading as run-off into irrigation ditches; and exposing workers in gins and spinning mills, resulting in extensive and pervasive health problems. Additionally, resistant strains of insects thrive and reproduce despite the chemicals, spurring research to find ever-stronger chemicals, while beneficial insects are wiped out along with the harmful. Ecosystem damage from monoculture farming and chemicals impact plant, bird and wildlife populations. Equally threatening is the fact that cottonseed (containing herbicides, pesticides, synthetic fertilisers and defoliants), treated as a by-product, ends up pressed into oil for use in snack foods and transported for use as animal feed. Furthermore, conventional cotton farming is part of the larger agri-business industry, which has been linked to 20,000 deaths annually from unintentional chemical poisoning, reports of concentrated incidence of cancer clustered around agricultural communities, diminished biodiversity, and topsoil loss at a rate of 8.1 tonnes per acre per year (see e.g. Briggs and Carson Council 1992; Tyler Miller 1996; Jeyaratnam 1990).

Organic cotton production involves very different practices. As Patagonia puts it, 'Life, and cotton growing, is possible without synthetic chemicals.' In stark contrast to the bare-dirt ditch-banks of the conventionally farmed fields, organic irrigation ditches are green and alive. Building on both traditional and newly developed knowledge about sustainable farming and land stewardship, organic farmers condition the soil with compost, organic matter, crop rotation and natural fertilisers; they discourage weeds by using cover crops; and they deal with pests by developing healthy plants, encouraging beneficial insects, planting trap crops, and occasionally using natural pesticides. Artificial growth regulators are not used. There are no defoliants to strip and kill the plants; instead, picking is undertaken by hand, or by machine-picking with the leaves on, and the process is supported by withholding water or by capitalising on frost. Organic farming requires more labour and increased knowledge and skills. The rewards are a healthy ecosystem, reduced topsoil erosion, and withdrawal from the chemical dependence that is responsible for such far-reaching negative side-effects.

This review of cotton farming was a seminal event in the history and evolution of Patagonia. It set in motion intense internal debate about the pace with which Patagonia could and should convert to organic cotton. Will Allen brought a slide show and vivid descriptions of the tour to the spring 1994 sales meeting. The audience and other managers, shocked at the effects of conventional cotton farming, developed a conviction that knowing without acting would contradict every value the company had come to stand for. The ultimate board of directors' decision in summer of 1994 was to take the assessed risk, absorb some of the additional costs, and switch Patagonia's entire product line to organic cotton.

Over one-third of Patagonia employees have retraced that first tour of the cotton fields. They come back different people, passionate about Patagonia's potential contribution to creating a sustainable industrial system, but also about changing their personal buying practices. Sweeney comments: 'This is not a strategic decision . . . We took 350 people on tours and they come home and buy organic . . . we have changed people's lives.' What could be more personal?

Patagonia has extended the effort to 'make it personal' well beyond its employees. The story comparing conventional and organic cotton has been told in catalogues, brochures, web pages and meetings to customers, shareholders and the general public. The most powerful impact, though, has been effected through a corporate and personal appeal, bolstered by a riveting video, with others in their value stream.

In 1996, Patagonia held a three-day supplier conference that still holds an emotional charge three years later for those who were there. The conference included everyone who had anything to do with the creation and sale of Patagonia products. Four months before the conference, participants had been asked to send in a photograph of their children. The introductory message from Patagonia was clear: 'It is not Exxon—it is us. The problem is ours. It is not OK to assign blame for environmental degradation elsewhere—the production, distribution, and use of Patagonia products is causing damage.' Participants were then swept along on a video tour of the cotton fields presenting stark facts and striking visual images comparing conventional and organic cotton-growing processes. At the close of the video, with the music of Louis Armstrong playing in the background, Patagonia

▷ Cotton accounts for approximately 25% of the world's insecticide use.

▷ 8%–10% of world pesticides (fungicides, herbicides, insecticides and defoliants) are applied on cotton fields: 40 million lb of pesticides are applied to cotton fields worldwide every year—13 million lb per year on California's cotton crops alone.

▷ Conventional cotton crops in six California counties alone are dusted every year with 57 million lb of chemicals, including both pesticides and fertilisers.

▷ Pesticides used on cotton are among the most hazardous.

▷ Children are particularly vulnerable to pesticide-related health problems.

▷ Farm workers exposed to excess toxins are at risk from poisoning and health problems.

▷ Further problems are: over-spray from aerial delivery; run-off into irrigation ditches; leaching through soil to contaminate groundwater; soil erosion; loss of biodiversity; ecosystem damage.

Box 3: **Environmental impacts of conventionally grown cotton**

said: 'Let us show you what you folks love.' With a montage of young faces making tangible the importance of our legacy to the future, in the words of Kevin Sweeney, Patagonia's Director of Communications, 'It was impossible not to cry.'

Patagonia thus explained their rationale for switching to entirely organic cotton, and invited their suppliers and distributors to join them in developing the technical and managerial knowledge that this would require. The reaction of supplier Rob Koeppel, a textile laminator, summed up many participants' personal alignment with Patagonia's decisions and strategy: 'I came as a representative of business; I left a citizen of the earth.'

The tour, by providing a first-hand, personal experience of the impact of its product design and production process decisions and specifications, created the conviction that Patagonia had 'no choice, knowing what they now knew' but to convert to using only organically grown cotton. It also created the commitment in the entire organisation and value stream that would be required to overcome the challenges that this shift would entail.

Patagonia went on to develop marketing and communications materials to inform their customers and consumers—and anyone else who would listen—about the negative environmental and health impacts of conventionally grown cotton (summarised in Box 3), and requested others join them in creating a market for organic cotton. Farmers need a stable market in order to convert to organic, and handling costs would decrease substantially with increased volume. Patagonia was instrumental in getting Levi's, Nike and Adidas to commit to ordering three bales of organic cotton for every 100 they use.

Now, using sustainable farming practices that actually restore ecosystems, organic cotton is the least damaging fibre used in Patagonia's clothing.

Take heroic action

Patagonia has on numerous occasions chosen the heroic route, rather than the easy one. Each time, it weighed the costs and increased difficulties inherent in siding with its core values, then determined to find a viable way to meet *both* business and social responsibility goals.

In the case of the conversion to organic cotton, for example, Patagonia accepted the challenge of solving a myriad of economic, technical and managerial problems. The more conservative strategy might have been to avoid the issue altogether, or to slowly introduce more organic cotton products as fabric variety increased. Instead, Patagonia chose the heroic route of totally eliminating cottons grown with synthetic chemicals. This meant absorbing an economic hit due to higher costs for growing and handling organic raw materials,[1] and relying on business acumen and relationships with mills, distributors and customers to solve technical problems and maintain consumer perceptions that Patagonia was in no way sacrificing quality.

Other examples of Patagonia's heroism pepper its corporate history. As mentioned above, 20 years earlier founder Yvon Chouinard decided to opt out of the extremely successful, high-quality piton climbing equipment market and convert to clean climbing equipment with lower environmental impacts. The company leads the outdoor clothing industry in using fleece fabric made out of recycled soda bottles in order to reduce the impact of extracting and refining crude oil used in commercial synthetic fleece—a shift that simultaneously provided consumers with a high-quality new product while saving tens of thousands of barrels of oil and diverting over 100 million bottles from landfills in just six years. Patagonia dared to visibly support grass-roots activism; it openly disclosed the real environmental impact of its products; and, more recently, led by CEO Dave Olsen, it committed to renewable energy use for Californian facilities and decided to phase out PVCs from hardgoods. Looking into the eyes of courageous employees, it is clear that many people would rather work for a heroic company such as Patagonia.

In each of the above cases, however, answers and outcomes were not apparent to the people as they first made the strategic decisions. Although the company is privately held, concerns about potential impact on the financial viability of the business were nonetheless acute, and in fact may have been heightened by a sense

---

1   Increases in production costs for organic cotton varied between 15% and 40%. Although some of the additional costs for labour and separation of organic from conventional cotton within the production process are counterbalanced by reduced costs of chemicals, organic cotton currently remains more expensive. Patagonia absorbed some of the additional costs itself, and also asked customers to share costs but limited price rises to a maximum of 20%.

of deep obligation to the employees who had devoted a portion of their lives to Patagonia.

Sprinkle in a little magic

How do you create organisation-wide caring about the environmental and social impact of the products you make? Patagonia has a rather unique answer. Most of it has to do with establishing a very personal relationship with the outdoors. Loving a sport or outdoor activity is not only encouraged, but one of the key hiring criteria. Spending time in nature with Yvon Chouinard, whether fly fishing, surfing or climbing, is high on many managers' lists of most memorable experiences. Perhaps most significant, though, are the efforts Patagonia has made since its inception to 'give back' to the community. Since 1985 Patagonia has donated 10% of pre-tax profits (or 1% of sales revenues, whichever is greater) to grass-roots environmental programmes, as part of their corporate tithing programme. Where 'giving back' turns to magic is in the Patagonia internship programme, where individual employees, or groups of employees, are supported in taking up to two months' paid leave to work for a non-profit organisation of their choice. Almost 20% of the workforce has participated in front-line action from Tibet to Alaska, camping out in redwoods to prevent logging of old-growth forests, monitoring emissions in tidal flows in Puget Sound by kayak, or helping protect an endangered habitat. The important point here is that this is not a one-way relationship: the connection with these groups began to change the company. Employees built a whole new skill base, and came back passionate about the environment. They returned re-energised, and shared their slide shows, convictions and learning with the rest of the company. This combination of nature, tithing and internships has led to an explosion of activists in Patagonia. More importantly, from a business perspective, it has led to a mobilised community committed to transforming almost every aspect of Patagonia's products and processes. As one manager stated, 'For me, it is easy to follow the path of greening from love of mountain places to choice of dyes.'

The source of magic at Patagonia seems to be a unique combination of personal, very tactile, connection with nature and a dedication to contributing to solving the earth's environmental problems; this has become the lifeblood of the organisation. All this is combined with the quality and excellence required to serve a clientele who care primarily about purchasing extremely high-quality technical performance gear.

b. *The bare essentials: ultimate purpose and core values*

> Patagonia exists as a business to inspire and implement solutions to the environmental crisis (Patagonia, *Louder than Words*, 1999).

Purpose

Patagonia exists as a business to inspire and implement solutions to the environmental crisis.

Core values

Quality:	pursuit of ever-greater quality in everything we do
Integrity:	relationships built on integrity and respect
Environmentalism:	serve as a catalyst for personal and corporate action
Not bound by convention:	our success—and much of the fun—lies in developing innovative ways of doing things.

Box 4: **Patagonia's purpose and core values**

Source: Patagonia, *Louder than Words*, 1999

Patagonia's purpose and core values speak for themselves (see Box 4). As with a few other select, leading-edge companies, it is articulating and enacting a purpose that is much greater than making a profit, or even providing high-quality goods and services to customers. This definition of its ultimate reason for being has galvanised the entire organisation, provided a rationale for continued growth that fits with its values, and defined a heroic, visionary objective. The core values— 'quality', 'integrity', 'environmentalism', and 'not being bound by convention'— form the guideposts for strategic and operational decisions.

Strikingly, this purpose and values statement is not a wish-list of aspirations for some future state. Rather, it is the result of a collaborative process by which Patagonia management and employees articulated and came to a shared under-standing of their current operating purpose and values. This purpose statement builds on, and extends to a more active, positive stance: Patagonia's long-standing objective to 'do no harm'.

CEO Dave Olsen commented about their purpose:

> We want to use what we know about managing a successful business to lead others in finding solutions to the environmental crisis. We have a couple of million customers we can tell our stories to, whether it is about organic cotton, or renewable energy. We have built an audience. We do feel great urgency that as a society we can't continue on the high consumptive path we're on. We need leadership to find a different way of being.

Standard business objectives are not left out of this equation. Olsen goes on to say, 'In order to be inspirational, we must be successful.'

Yvon Chouinard and Mike Brown, in a 1997 *Journal of Industrial Ecology* article, reflected on Patagonia's choice of environmental principles: 'We were interested not only in reducing our impacts—pollution prevention was a given—but also in keeping a focus on creating an economy that might someday allow us to restore the ecological health of the world.' Today, Patagonia is moving full speed ahead toward achieving these goals.

c. Strategic rationale: 'It's the right thing to do.'

We discussed earlier that Patagonia's innovations in environmental and social responsibility have not been led by legislative requirements, market pressures, or even a far-sighted strategic plan. Rather, the guiding principle has been a sense of 'doing what's right' at each branch in the road. Patagonia's penchant for 'doing the right thing' permeates every level of the organisation, from the CEO to production managers, team leaders, quality managers, operations leaders, new business managers, environment managers, human resource managers, and even finance. For example, with a 'build it and they will come' attitude, Patagonia is beginning now to design for disassembly and closing the loop, even though the infrastructure for dealing with products at end-of-life is not there. Their philosophy is that making products for reclamation will drive the need and prove the viability. As with organic cotton, in many areas Patagonia is leading the market—making the changes; collaborating with suppliers; then educating and enrolling customers in the rationale.

Dave Olsen related that Patagonia has many examples of doing things because they were the right thing to do, and of being fortunate, because they turned out to be commercially successful.

> Organic cotton was a big risk: we were prepared to take substantial losses for several years. In full sight of the risks, we decided to go ahead. We knew it was possible—that we had adequate supply, that organic cotton could be ginned, spun, etc.—but not that it would be commercially successful. It turned out not to be a commercial penalty.

Retrospective analysis would suggest that Patagonia did not leave this positive outcome to chance. Instead, it appears it is making strategic choices based on values about what is right, but putting all the energy of an integrated, aligned organisation around reducing any downside risks and laying the groundwork for positive outcomes now and in the future. Patagonia's work to reduce the incremental costs of its decision to use only renewable energy in Californian facilities (described in Box 5) illustrate this characteristic.

There is increasing evidence in the marketplace that proactively integrating environmental considerations into core business strategies, product design and production processes through the entire life-cycle will have synergistic effects in

Patagonia's motivation for converting to solar and wind power is once again that 'it is the right thing to do'. Although using renewable energy will carry an incremental cost, the company has taken a number of steps to neutralise the additional costs. By investing in energy conservation—such as new lighting, insulation, new more efficient motors to drive the conveyors at the Reno distribution centre—Patagonia has achieved a roughly 20% reduction on its 800,000 kWh/yr consumption. Although it will pay a premium for using 100% renewable energy, its net costs will be less. Thus, with planning and organisation, Patagonia is able to do the right thing environmentally, at no extra cost.

Patagonia is actively working to sell the concept of renewable energy to its suppliers by helping them discover that the economics really do work, that they can make investments in energy reduction and cleaner waste-water that provide tangible financial gains.

Of course, it might have been possible to attain the reductions without incurring the additional costs for renewable energy, but combining these provided a noble purpose that very probably contributed to the success of the conservation efforts. Additionally, converting to solar or wind power lessens the life-cycle impact of Patagonia production processes, and provides another model for employees, customers and other organisations of more sustainable business practices.

Box 5: Conversion to renewable energy— with strategies to make it cost-neutral

improving profitability and value—from cost reductions found through eco-efficiencies, to increased customer loyalty, to new product and business development. When asked if a strategic assessment of this business case for sustainability was part of Patagonia's strategic planning, Olsen replied: 'That is our hope. It is the substance of things hoped for, the evidence of things not seen.'

There are, however, signs that indicate this hope may prove justified and that the investments Patagonia has made may pay off soundly in the future.

d. Then again, we might be onto something here

On a variety of fronts, Patagonia's moves toward more sustainable products and practices have resulted in tangible strategic and operational benefits to the business, suggesting there is a solid business case for proactive improvements in environmental and social performance.

Customer loyalty and increased revenue

There is a certain percentage of customers—around 20%—who purchase Patagonia equipment because of its reputation and long-standing commitment to social and environmental responsibility. In this highly competitive market, even a few points of additional market share can be very valuable.

Differentiation in the marketplace

Environmental performance can serve to differentiate Patagonia products from those of competitors, in a market where differentiation based on technological performance is becoming increasingly difficult. As Randy Harward, Patagonia's Director of Fabric Development Quality and Environmental R&D, put it, environmental performance may even offer a way out of the 'game' Patagonia in which finds itself:

> The evolution here has been because of heart, and what is the right thing to do. It has occurred to us that it might be a good business strategy, but that is not where it started. In fact, our environmental stance causes many problems, like dealing with increased costs, or ensuring we were not compromising quality. We have done it because it is the right thing to do, from an ethical stance.
>
> Increasingly though, we are seeing benefits from an efficiency standpoint, from an innovation standpoint. It may even offer a way out of the game that we find ourselves in, where Patagonia is in a very saturated market where it is harder and harder to differentiate. We have existed on quality and technical innovation, but this is harder and harder to do. There are now hundreds of companies in a field where there were only one or two when the company started. All of these companies keep driving innovation forward—but always in smaller and smaller increments. Then they compete with each other, but, because significant technical innovations are hard, they are generally shared by suppliers, so many of competitors get them at the same time, so it is even harder to differentiate. So we are in that game—we are participating in creating a tweak war based on technical innovation. The question is how to get out [of this dilemma] and still be interesting. Living up to environmental and social values might just be the key here.

Customer trust

In one catalogue, Patagonia went on record saying 'everything we do pollutes'. It committed to making incremental steps, and invited its customers to accompany it on the journey. Managers were amazed when customers responded by saying, 'keep doing this; keep trying; thanks for being honest'. Patagonia's openness about the negative impact of its products has created a high level of trust among its customer base. This trust is likely to be transferable to other elements of customer relations and view of Patagonia as a brand. (Additionally, it is exactly this candour that provides the foundation for problem-solving that is leading to breakthrough new fabrics, modified production processes, and even new businesses, at Patagonia.)

Brand enhancement and free media coverage

Patagonia has a strong brand presence primarily based on the technical integrity and quality of its products. Yet social consciousness has always been a part of its value proposition, and it has a portion of customers who buy because of company values. Karyn Barsa, Director of Operations, noted that environmental initiatives have contributed to the health of Patagonia's brand, allowing it a price point better than others, and increasing its help to dealers.

In the past, Patagonia has been fairly modest and understated about its activities in social responsibility. Now, it intends to be more explicit to each customer group in the marketplace, reinforcing this aspect of the Patagonia brand.

There have also been unintended side benefits to Patagonia's social stance. Patagonia estimates that, because of its social activism and environmental initiatives, it receives an impressive US$5–7 million a year (3%–4% of sales) in free media coverage, which is much more powerful than advertising.

New business development

Patagonia has started new business and product lines directly related to innovations stemming from its environmental efforts. Its new business, 'Beneficial Ts', which in one year became the largest supplier of organic cotton blank t-shirts, stemmed from a work team going outside to acquire commodity contracts in an effort to increase the organic cotton market. 'Seedling'—a bright, colourful line of infant apparel made from unused material cut from the gaps in the patterns of adult clothing—originated from a problem-solving discourse with a vendor about attempting to recycle fabric that no one wanted following Patagonia's environment-focused supplier conference. It was the brainchild of Patagonia's product designer, Janna Vaattainen, who creatively pieced together this new clothing line, using patterned and solid pieces of various colours, all in one garment, in an effort to reduce the estimated 18% of fabric that typically ended up on the cutting-room floor. (The 'Seedling' line, plus continuous improvement in positioning 'markers' for greater efficiency, is slowly reducing this volume of fabric scrap at Patagonia.)

Efficiencies and waste reduction

Patagonia's internal environmental improvement efforts have reduced waste by about two-thirds through re-use and recycling, improved efficiency of lighting, heating and cooling, and reduced use of toxic substances and emissions. In the $2\frac{1}{2}$ years since Patagonia's new worldwide distribution and customer service centre in Reno opened, only three 36-40-yard dumpsters of waste have been hauled away. Energy conservation achievements already described are supplemented with architectural design innovations adding up to more than a 30% reduction in energy costs.

Broader market segments

The growing percentage of Patagonia business devoted to sportswear belies an underlying current of internal conflict which is only recently becoming resolved—because of Patagonia's new clarity on its fundamental purpose. Moving into the general sportswear consumer market represented a strategic dilemma that shook the company—founded on providing high-quality, technically superior products to devoted athletes and outdoor enthusiasts—to its core values.

The rationale for entering the sportswear market is clear: an increasing number of people are wearing sportswear clothing, the margins are better, volumes are higher, and demand is more uniform, avoiding the off seasons that exist in most highly technical sports activities. The problem with this direction—according to Patagonia management and employees—is that these products have lower technical specifications and represent a move away from 'expert' customers. No one wanted to sell out on the original mission of the company—to provide high-quality technical equipment and clothing—purely for increased profits.

Ironically, the redefinition of Patagonia's purpose and commitment to organic cotton has provided a rationale for making sportsgear and brought about a resolution to the conflict that everyone could get behind, as all cotton used in sportswear production is organic. One moral purpose has been replaced by another!

Employee commitment and loyalty

Patagonia has truly won the hearts and minds of employees, most of whom are passionately committed to ensuring Patagonia's business success and achieving its purpose. The following striking comments demonstrate a level of dedication seldom found in industry:

> The employee base feels this is where our destiny lies.

> For any organisation where you get a person so totally committed to a whole approach, they can't imagine being anywhere else! It becomes your life when you work for a values-driven organisation. We don't compete on salaries, or benefits. People are here because it integrates into their life.

> Our strength is the quality of our people—people have the passion.

Attracting and retaining employees

Patagonia's breakthrough human resource practices and environmental responsibility agenda have resulted in high employee commitment that turns into bottom-line results. Employee retention is high compared to industry averages in both retail (turnover is only 20%–30% a year versus a typical 100%) and administration (administrative turnover is running at ~5%, sometimes 3%). Here are some comments from management:

> We have low turnover here—we are connected to a greater purpose than making a profit.

> We have zero turnover among employees who have children in our on-site childcare.

> We have issues of retention that other companies wish they had.

Recruitment, selection, and development experiences of organisational members are all aligned to achieve the corporate purpose and values. Terri Wolfe, Patagonia's Human Resources Director, emphasised that the employment culture is not only intentionally linked to, but is entirely contingent on, Patagonia's business mission. Her philosophy is that, although they look for technical skills, these can be trained or learned, whereas personal commitment to a cause and being passionate about things must be selected for.

Deeper knowledge and new competences

The most significant internal impact of Patagonia's environmental initiatives was unexpected. As Patagonia worked to better understand the life-cycle impacts of its products, as it met the challenge of converting to organic cotton, as it researched for substitute materials and dyes, it has gained invaluable benefits in increased knowledge, competences, and confidence about managing the entire production process. Despite the fact that it had established pivotal relationships with suppliers and customers and designed a production process that was one of the finest in the outdoor and apparel industries, it still found tremendous scope for learning from being forced to develop a more external focus, to work outside of its industry, and to create new alliances for change with vendors, suppliers and customers.

In converting to organic cotton, for example, production managers found they couldn't simply go to a textile mill and say, 'Please send me organic cotton with the same quality features.' So Patagonia had to take responsibility through the entire process—fibre production, ginning, fabric design, spinning and weaving, distribution and transportation, etc. Managers stated that the company is now more confident in taking hold of the entire process chain, and with specific elements such as the handling of fabric lamination internally, allowing 'middlemen' to be cut out of the process.

CEO Dave Olsen highlights more generally the value to marketing of learning to tell their environmental story effectively:

> There is a great opportunity to raise awareness and concern with all people. The challenge is for us to become better marketers. We have to make it simple and straightforward, even though it is not a simple story. Really, this particular challenge will help us become a much more successful business. If we can tell the environmental story in ways that get people to change their behaviour, it will really help us in other areas of business. We are too much in the details, too close to it—tend to say too much, haven't spent enough time with customers to know what sells. The better we get at that, the better we'll be at marketing other issues.

Stimulus for excitement and innovation

'There is an evolving sense within the company that, if Patagonia can design and make products correctly from an environmental perspective, not only will it be the right way to do it, but it will make the company more exciting and innovative at the same time,' according to Randy Harward. Patagonia staff members, even their suppliers, are embracing the challenges that becoming more sustainable implies.

At a pragmatic level for Patagonia, these innovation challenges include: discovering or developing high-quality substitutes for product components to eliminate toxic materials; 'closing the loop' by designing products for construction from recyclable materials, disassembly and re-use or eventual recycling; minimising material and energy inputs; restructuring global production processes to reduce transportation; reinventing design patterns to fit colour palettes limited to the least-toxic dyes; and finding effective ways of communicating with each customer segment.

From a supplier's perspective, Patagonia is most often seen as a prized customer with whom there has been a long-term relationship focused on continuous improvement to achieve stringent quality levels. Patagonia's commitment to reducing environmental impact has meant drastically shifting requirements. Many suppliers were not able to adjust, although some of these are now developing new technology and capabilities and coming back.

Patagonia veteran Director of Contract Management, Roger McDivitt, tells of one notable example illustrating a very positive response within Patagonia's supply chain to the shift toward organic cotton. Johnny Yeung from Thai Alliance Textiles, a mill in Bangkok that spins yarn for a Patagonia shirt supplier, on being told of the new requirement, adapted his organisation to provide organic cotton at great expense and trouble. His rationale? According to McDivitt,

> Personally, he became attuned to the ethical issues of organic cotton. But, from a strategic business perspective, Yeung was interested in keeping his organisation from stagnating. To counter the sense that 'what we do for a living is what we do', he saw the shift to organic cotton as a chance to force his organisation to respond to something new. Thus he used this as a business opportunity to remain flexible. Right now, spinning organic cotton is a niche business, but Yeung has determined that, if he can figure out how to do it well, it is a competitive advantage to him. Since it is a difficult process, he can distinguish his business from the guy down the street. He was looking for something that isn't easily copied—organic cotton certainly is that. He also did it out of consideration to us.

Yeung has gone on to find innovative ways of spinning organic cotton with polyester, an important capability for Patagonia's product line. (Patagonia is looking into the life-cycle recycling implications of multiple-materials fabrics.)

Strategic positioning for the future

Patagonia is focused on the future, not just the rear-view mirror. It is positioning itself for what managers project will eventually be increased demand from customers, critical requirements of the marketplace, and a key source of excitement and innovation internally and externally.

'Do you *know* what's in that shirt you're wearing?' Patagonia managers jokingly laughed at the fact that each of them had fallen prey to this 'conversation stopper' at a party. Their point, though, is that, although for the most part consumers have no idea what is in the garments and other products they purchase or the social conditions under which they are made, there is increasing awareness on the part of customers and consumers, and increasing transparency of organisational activities and impacts. Patagonia intends to continue to lead the customer in coming to these understandings. Harward comments:

> It really is scary, what is in products . . . I believe that this value awareness will become more mainstream. I don't know when, but it will become apparent to consumers at some time. We have a strategy of trying to match a growing awareness of environmental impacts. Culturally, we hide a lot of those costs; at some point the real costs of environmental impacts is going to reach consumers, and those [companies] that have figured out this strategy will be in a much better position.
>
> It may be that incorporating environmental criteria causes us to approach solving customer problems in a unique way—and we stand out in the marketplace. Customers respond to what we are calling the 'elegant solution'. When you can put all that together, [what you offer] is the newest cool product—it really does perform and, by the way, it is environmentally sound. This is a combined value that is generated and can't be pulled apart. That's very appealing to us.

Geoff Cline, Patagonia's In-House Counsel, adds:

> Our marketing message is not that this is important because it is good for you, or even the right thing to do—but instead that these products have a lot of excitement, innovation, sex appeal and dynamism.
>
> With the right marketing approach to go with this business approach, we will win the hearts and minds of people, because, if you have the choice between the two products, why would you buy the one to hurt your kids' future? It is intuitively impossible—but it has to be exciting.

Enhanced value proposition

As part of its strategic planning, Patagonia management is re-examining the value proposition both for existing products and for the new products and services that it might offer.

It would be lax to describe the environmental aspects of Patagonia products without mentioning a characteristic that has been built in for years: durability and longevity of product. Of course, the longer the life-span of a product, the fewer needed by the consumer—hence the lower potential negative environmental impacts related to the production of the commodity in general. Patagonia designs for endurance and longevity. A company newsletter article jokingly tells the story of 'Joe's ten-year-old long underwear' which constantly fails to receive a very deserved retirement from the lifetime of adventure and abuse through which Joe has been putting it. Children's clothing is so strongly over-built that it is easily passed down multiple times. Performance guarantees are part of the Patagonia promise.

Patagonia shows a sophisticated understanding of providing increased value to the customer. In talking about the social conditions in factories where garments are made and the environmental impact of products, managers clearly realise that the product history and product future are part of the value proposition. As they shape, understand and meet the needs of customers regarding these social and environmental impacts, they are banking on the fact that values have value. Patagonia is also exploring ways of providing services as well as products, for example, renting rather than selling highly specialised technical products, or leveraging the Patagonia image and sense of 'club' membership without selling goods.

e. *Warp and weft: weaving a sustainable tapestry*

It is one thing to commit to creating more sustainable industrial practices and to inspiring and implementing solutions to the environmental crisis—another to bring it to reality. As might be expected, Patagonia has done many things well, but has also encountered strategic and operational challenges. Below is a discussion of its approach to implementation.

Platforms, playgrounds, and protesting

What most differentiates Patagonia's efforts from those of many others is that it is moving beyond isolated environmental and social improvements dominated by the mainstream thrust of production-as-usual to a coherent strategic platform integrating all aspects of design, production, supply management, marketing and human resource management.

On multiple fronts, Patagonia is experiencing the synergistic benefits of a unified 'platform' approach, and it is poised to increasingly reap these benefits. It has achieved: increased commitment and retention of employees attuned to working in a values-driven organisation; clarity of branding and customer understanding from a unique message; suppliers committed and confident enough to invest in radical shifts; and human resource practices that align on-site childcare and activist training with strategy—to name but a few examples.

Redefining design, production and operations management

Patagonia's strategic integration of environmental criteria has had reverberating ripple effects in every aspect of its business.

Product design changes were mandatory if environmental impacts were to be reduced. Life-cycle analyses revealed negative environmental impacts in every stage of Patagonia's products' life-cycles—but high-impact areas most under Patagonia's control are materials choice and colouring. Patagonia's products are known for their deep, vibrant colour, and one of Patagonia's key selling features distinguishing them from competitors has been unusual fabrics. Given this, designers were at first disconcerted by having limitations imposed by constraining

Patagonia has created for designers, suppliers and customers a concise overview of the environmental impacts of modern fabric-dyeing techniques as a guide for decision-making. In it, it developed for each major fabric type (nylon, polyester, cotton and wool) an 'Impact Matrix' table summarising the relative impacts of various dye types and dyeing methods on water usage, energy consumption, toxins (primarily metals, chlorine, azo dyes and sulphides) and biodiversity.

WOOL

Method	Water	Energy	Toxins	Biodiversity	Comments
Acid-metallicised	High	Med	High	Med	
Acid reactive	High	Med	Med	Med	
Acid milling	High	Med	Med	Med	
Acid levelling	High	Med	Med	Med	
After chrome	High	Med	Very high*	High	* Due to metals
Natural	High	Med	Med	Low	

Product assessment

NYLON

Method	Water	Energy	Toxins	Biodiversity	Comments
Disperse	Low–med	Med	Low–med	Med	
Acid	Low–med	Med	Low–med	Med	
Direct	Low–med	Med	Low–med	Med	

Product assessment

POLYESTER

Method	Water	Energy	Toxins	Biodiversity	Comments
Disperse	Low–med	High	Very high*	High	* Due to carriers
Basic	Low–med	Med	Low–med	Med	

Product assessment

COTTON

Method	Water	Energy	Toxins	Biodiversity	Comments
Reactive	Low–med	Low–med	High*	Med	* Due to salt
Vat	Low–med	Med	Med	Med	
Direct	Low–med	Med	Med	High*	* Due to oxidation
Sulphur	Low–med	Med	High	High*	* Due to oxidation

Product assessment

Box 6: **Patagonia's 'Impact Matrix' for dyes**

materials and colour palettes. With time, however, they did develop attractive and viable solutions to retaining product quality with lower environmental impact (see Box 6 for a sample of Patagonia's assessment of the environmental impacts of dyes). Once they recovered from the initial shock, designers rose to the challenge, and even identified additional benefits from these constraints, such as efficiencies gained from simplification.

Patagonia's hardgoods division also illustrates the integration of environment into product design. Beyond its immediate focus of eliminating toxic materials (for example, in the spring 2000 travel bag line, a replacement product has been introduced with higher quality and technical functionality, yet at the same price to the customer and produced without PVC), Patagonia is exploring design for disassembly, re-usable materials, and dematerialisation. The vision is design for 'closing the loop', where materials are easily separated into either a technical materials cycle of re-use–recycle or a natural cycle that is compostable. Although there is not currently an infrastructure in place for dealing with end-of-life of travel bag and footwear products, managers believe that it will come, and are designing the products for reclamation. The philosophy put forward by hardgoods team leader, Gary Eckwortzel, is that 'If we don't take the first step, others won't take the second.' Once again, he articulated that Patagonia's motivation is that it is the right thing to do, and that, although customers won't buy solely because a product is environmentally right, if they don't have to compromise quality between two identical products, they will choose the environmental option.

Contracts management ensures all product elements are available to the factory, on time, to meet the 'recipe' of each style slated for production. Contract managers have integrated environmental and social considerations as part of the style definition of Patagonia products, and work carefully to select and develop suppliers capable of meeting Patagonia's quality, social working conditions, and environmental standards.

From a pure vision of sustainable commerce simultaneously achieving business, social and environmental needs, this area is probably one of Patagonia's greatest challenges. In an industry where cost is critical to competitiveness, as McDivitt puts it: 'There is a gentle breeze blowing to find a cheaper place. This gives incentive to be transient, to only develop a supplier until I can find a cheaper place.' Unfortunately, these dynamics have been exacerbated even further by the efforts to reduce environmental impacts: increased materials costs (of organic cotton or non-toxic materials) often means labour costs are squeezed, which can amplify the negative social costs and disruption to community if meeting environmental criteria requires moving to a new supplier. Although Patagonia may be one of the industry leaders in providing prevailing industry wages and 'acceptable working conditions', the bottom line is that the entire industry is participating in a value-sharing structure that leaves little at the bottom end for those providing raw materials, cutting and sewing.

Production changes in fabric layout and use have greatly improved materials efficiency. Patagonia used to put small, medium and large patterns each on their own marker. Now, before any fabric is cut, teams supported by computer-aided design and manufacturing software carefully set markers to optimise fabric efficiency, integrating all three adult sizes, plus the infant 'Seedling' line patterns, to optimise materials use.

The markers are the easy part of the 'Seedling' product line. It was the production operations to create this line that required phenomenal commitment and flexibility. From the cutter, the Seedling pieces are gathered, shipped to Reno, separated and sorted to match arms, legs, etc., and then, the next season, sewn into mix-and-match outfits for infants. (The Seedling line currently piggybacks on the adult season.) The challenge doesn't end there, however. Ironically, Patagonia's continued strides in improving markers may eventually threaten their new Seedling business!

Packaging waste has also been minimised, resulting in many successes (as is evidenced by the minuscule amount of waste hauled from production and distribution facilities), but also some failures. For example, what were thought to be improvements replacing plastic bag packaging on capilene underwear with rubber bands holding on a 'face plate' tag have turned out to have numerous logistical hassles for barcoding, merchandise handling and product display.

Involving the entire value stream has been a key part of Patagonia's success. Patagonia's conference to engage its suppliers and distributors in including environment as part of their quality definition, and its work to bring energy conservation techniques to suppliers have been described above. This is part of the ongoing work to align its entire value stream in integrating environmental excellence into product design and production management. Patagonia describes its stance with suppliers not as prescriptive, but as 'co-venturing'. As indicated earlier, this closer involvement with the entire value stream has created new competences and capabilities at Patagonia. In addition, it has put the company in a position of trying to initiate dialogue with chemical and pesticide companies (which also make fabric dyes). Sweeney's advice from his days in civil action is to 'invite the enemy into your camp, . . . to push the envelope, but not close the door'. He also noted that getting to know organic farmers forced them to make the connections between environmental and social issues, in ways they had not previously considered.

Environmental principles and goals, listed in Patagonia's 1995–96 *Environmental Assessment Report*, guide design and decision-making in all areas. The principles are:

- Maximizing the efficiency of systems: using less and changing systems to improve use of time and resources
- Closing the loop: using recycled materials and maximizing recyclability of materials and products

1. Include environmental costs in accounting and production systems.
2. Eliminate all solid waste sent to landfills from domestic facilities and reduce waste from international facilities.
3. Establish stewardship requirements for all products.
4. Increase customers' awareness of product impacts and benefits.
5. Educate suppliers to meet environmental standards.
6. Increase the efficiency of our use of resources.
7. Reduce the impacts of facility construction and operation.
8. Expand the use of sustainable paper products while reducing the use of paper.
9. Reduce our use of energy and increase our use of sustainable forms of energy.

Box 7: Patagonia's five-year environmental goals

- Protecting public and worker health: avoiding toxic materials and hazardous processes
- Using renewable resources wisely: using sustainably grown or harvested products and materials appropriately
- Conserving nonrenewable resources: specifying particular conditions of use and increasing efficiency of use
- Educating ourselves and our customers: increasing understanding of our environmental impacts and what we can do about them

Each department is expected to achieve the goals summarised in Box 6.

Secret formula for brand loyalty: brand qualities are verbs, not adjectives.

We are a high-visibility company, totally out of proportion to our size.

Selling for Patagonia is like being ISO-certified.

Banks compete to finance us—Patagonia is viewed as a trophy credit.

We are also a trophy customer for suppliers.

This company stands by its friends; this is a big part of our brand.

Patagonia's brand has evolved not from clever marketing, but instead as a reflection of their bold, far-reaching corporate actions over 25 years. Producing only the highest-quality goods; actively supporting retailers; taking an activist stand on redwoods; guaranteeing its products for life; giving back with both money and time; daring 'not to be bound by convention'—all these demonstrate the action orientation that has defined what Patagonia means in the marketplace. As it moves into the future, Patagonia is just as proactively taking the initiatives that will define it as a leader in integrating the concepts of environment and innovation.

Transition to a values-driven culture

Several years ago, Patagonia's leadership recognised the need to make a transition away from the day-to-day operational leadership of the original founders and management group. To accomplish this, they determined that they must develop a 'values-driven' culture, where all people take responsibility for their individual actions, aligned around a commonly shared purpose and set of values. Thus began their values discussion, where three times a year the entire employee community breaks up into groups to discuss each of the key values, how Patagonia is living by them, how not, and what could be done to be more values-focused.

CEO Dave Olsen has attributed a great deal of importance to the development of the cultural elements of the shift that he sees as fundamental to the transformation Patagonia is making. In addition to the values discussions, the organisation has provided education and leadership focused on building within the entire workforce these key attributes: curiosity, risk taking, mutual support and flexibility. His rationale:

> . . . to introduce a grand vision of sustainability too far ahead of culture that can get us there is a big strategic mistake. I have been focused on creating the culture that all employees can embrace. Unless we do this, we won't be effective, because there is too much learning required in all areas. The problem is not technical, it is socio-technical.

Sustainability as a values discipline

Patagonia's self-appointed (but organisationally empowered) cross-functional team responsible for finding the bridge from principles to action is working to define Patagonia's long-term strategic plan and to integrate environmental principles with business practices. They are enthused with the idea of looking at environmental performance, maybe even sustainability, as a value discipline—the core organising principle of the company. They suggest extending the concept put forward by Treacy and Wiersema (1996), who propose a strategy for reinventing competitiveness that focuses on one of three value disciplines—customer intimacy, product leadership or operational excellence—to a fourth value discipline that actually has values! The goal would be to 'organise the business around a sustainability paradigm (or whatever the right word is for building a product that is designed around principles of no waste, that is useful, consumed, then re-used, and disposed of in a way that is friendly and feeding at the end of life)', according to Randy Harward. Thus this new value discipline would bring together the values of innovation and customer intimacy and product leadership (other types of value) in a new way of doing business that changes the competitive landscape and reshapes customers' value expectations.

3. *Conclusion*

Patagonia's vision is to create a concrete message of hope: to model for society a new way of designing and producing value that is restorative, rather than damaging, to the environment.

Perhaps because they know more about what the real requirements are, what it really means, managers at Patagonia are cautious about using the word 'sustainable' to refer to their business operations. Yet Patagonia clearly stands out as a leading example of a company proactively, with passion and high integrity, making the transformation to a more sustainable business model. These same managers reveal a level of dedication and commitment unheard of in most business ventures: 'We honestly want to give our lives' purpose to this company; this is an opportunity to do that—you don't get that very often.'

Patagonia has made much progress, but still has a long way to go. In Kevin Sweeney's words:

> In any entity where ideology is involved, there is a disparity between ideology and reality. A potential pitfall is that this gap will always be the subject of intense conversations. This can be constructive or destructive. A positive vision is much more constructive. What is important is the ability to create a vision—what the country could be like, what a company could be like. It is a rare skill, but, when it is done, it is magic.

Patagonia is creating that vision.

References

Patagonia publications

http://www.patagonia.com

Organic Cotton Story (company brochure; Ventura, CA: Patagonia Inc., 1996).
Defining Quality (company brochure; Ventura, CA: Patagonia Inc., 1998).
Louder than Words (company brochure; Ventura, CA: Patagonia Inc., 1999).
Environmental Grants Program, May 1, 1997 to April 30, 1998 (Ventura, CA: Patagonia Inc., 1998).
Environmental Assessment Report 1995–1996 (Ventura, CA: Patagonia Inc., 1998).
Environmental Assessment Report 1996–1997 (Ventura, CA: Patagonia Inc., 1999).

Other

Briggs, S.A., and the Rachel Carson Council (1992) *Basic Guides to Pesticides: Their Characteristics and Hazards* (Washington, DC: Taylor & Foster).
Chouinard, Y., and M. Brown (1997) 'Going Organic: Converting Patagonia's Cotton Product Line', *Journal of Industrial Ecology* 1.1.

Fortune (1999) '100 Best Companies to Work For', *Fortune* 139.1 (11 January 1999).

Jeyaratnam, J. (1990) 'Acute Pesticide Poisoning: A Major Global Health Problem', *World Health Statistical Quarterly* 43: 139-43.

Sweeney, K. (1997) 'Keynote Address', *Eco-Conference*, The Anderson School of Business and UCLA Institute of the Environment, 11 April 1997.

Treacy, M., and F. Wiersema (1996) *The Discipline of Market Leaders: Choose your customers, narrow your focus, dominate your market* (New York: Addison Wesley Longman).

Tyler Miller, G., Jr (1996) *Living in the Environment* (Belmont, CA: Wadsworth, 9th edn).

Working Mother (1999) '100 Best Companies for Working Mothers', *Working Mother*, October 1999.

Organisational contacts

David Olsen, CEO
Lu Setnicka, Director of Public Affairs
Randy Harward, Director of Fabric Development, Quality and Environmental R&D
Kevin Sweeney, Director of Communications
Gary Eckwortzel, Team Leader, Hardgoods
Neil Edwards, Director of Finance
Mike Brown, Environmental Assessment
Eric Wilmanns, Environmental Assessment
Julie Ringler, Production
Geoff Cline, In-House Counsel
Adrienne Moser, Team Leader, Kids'
Roger McDivitt, Director of Contract Management
Karyn Barsa, Director of Operations
Terri Wolfe, Director of Human Resources
Bruce Barbour, Team Leader, Watersports

INTERFACE FLOORING SYSTEMS

Driving industrial standards higher

1. *Company profile*

With operations in North America, Europe, Australia and Asia, Interface Flooring Systems (IFS) is a leading global supplier in the commercial interiors market. Its product lines include floor coverings, fabrics, speciality chemicals and interior architectural products. The company is the world's largest manufacturer of modular carpet tiles and it is also a leader when it comes to the implementation of industrial sustainability. Led by a unique and visionary Chairman and CEO, Ray Anderson, the company has embarked on quest to 'build the world's first sustainable—and eventually restorative—enterprise'. To help it achieve this vision, the company has set out a series of sustainable objectives that give new meaning to the concept of stretch targets (see Box 1).

Interface is a leading example because the company has benefited greatly from its sustainability initiatives both financially (its 'QUEST Zero Waste' initiative saved US$90 million between 1995 and October 1999) and in less tangible ways such as employee morale (IFS was named one of the '100 Best Companies to Work For' by *Fortune* magazine in both 1998 and 1999). In 1998 Interface recorded net sales of US$1.281 billion, the highest level in the company's history. This represented a total net sales increase of 12.8% over 1997. In addition, cost of sales as a percentage of

1. We must eliminate waste.
2. We must emit nothing harmful into the biosphere.
3. We must use renewable energy sources.
4. We must create closed-loop products and processes that are inherently self-renewing.
5. We must develop alternatives to the physical movement of people and material and use resource-efficient means of transport.
6. We must take thousands of small steps by creating a culture that integrates the principles of sustainability into what we do every day.
7. We must pioneer sustainable commerce.

***Box 1:* Interface's sustainability objectives**

net sales decreased to 66.2% in 1998 compared to 66.6% in 1997. The company attributes this decrease in part 'to decreased manufacturing costs in the company's floor covering and interior fabrics operations through the company's QUEST waste reduction initiative' (*Interface Annual Report 1998*).

There are many aspects to Interface's sustainability work that could be profiled. To offer deeper insight into how Interface is implementing its ambitious plans, this short vignette examines its work on toxic substance management, using its operation in Belleville, Ontario, Canada, as an example. The Belleville plant has been the company leader in a number of IFS environmental programmes, including the elimination and management of listed toxic substances.

2. *Drivers*

There are many environmental and business drivers that have led IFS to systematically address the issue of listed toxic substances in its products, operations and supply chain.

▷ **Business risk.** Plastics are a major raw material for carpeting systems and IFS is very aware of issues related to potentially toxic substances (e.g. flame-retardants, smoke suppressants and stabilisers) that may end up in their product. This poses a business risk and IFS needs to understand what substances are in their product.

▷ **Solid waste.** Landfill is the primary fate of most carpet today and this issue represents a potential risk to the future use of carpet. Leaching of toxic substances such as brominated flame-retardants and antinomy into municipal landfill poses risks with respect to future liability.

▷ **Employee satisfaction.** IFS openly communicates within the company on issues related to toxic substances. Health and exposure issues are discussed, and, as substances are eliminated, this is communicated to employees. By actively managing the issue of toxic substances and communicating issues directly to employees, IFS has been able to address issues before they are even raised as employee concerns. This approach has increased morale.

▷ **Brand image.** By reducing its use of toxic substances IFS has been able to create a clean fresh environment in its facilities. Visitors to the Belleville site often comment on this clean environment. This enhances IFS image and customer visits are encouraged to demonstrate this aspect of its operations.

▷ **Product stewardship.** IFS is actively demonstrating its product steward-ship through participation in labelling and certification programmes. Examples include Canada's eco-logo programme 'Environmental Choice™', and work IFS has done with the Canadian Lung Association. By pushing for strong criteria in these programmes, IFS is raising the environmental standards across its sector.

▷ **Raw materials.** Toxic substances are sometimes expensive. As the regu-latory burden on these substances increases, the costs of using these compounds will further increase. By eliminating these substances, IFS can reduce costs and reduce the demand for toxic substances in society. IFS is actively encouraging suppliers to find safer, cleaner alternatives to toxic substances in their processes as well.

▷ **Technology development.** The push to design toxic substances out of their products has led to innovations with respect to new products and new technology. This has increased the profile and effectiveness of environmental issues as a driver for business innovation.

When examined in combination, these drivers provide powerful incentives to reduce or eliminate toxic substances from the company's operations and supply chain.

3. *Strategy*

Taking the drivers outlined above into account, IFS has developed a clear strategic approach for its environmental work on toxic substances.

▷ **Drive industrial standards higher.** IFS is working in partnership with government, labelling programmes and other stakeholders to develop standards in areas such as indoor air quality.

Interface actively works with suppliers to ensure that toxic substances are eliminated. IFS explains its long-term objectives to suppliers and talks about the positive aspects of eliminating toxic substances both from a business and an environmental perspective.

In these discussions it finds that, although this approach can be difficult—for example, in communicating with various environmental, technical and sales staff—the end result is better relationships with their suppliers.

In one case, IFS identified a compound in a supplier's material that led to the identification of a leak in the supplier's operations.

Box 2: Supplier relationships

▷ **Communications of environmental work to customer.** By providing products that are free of toxic substances, IFS is adding value for the customer. This is actively communicated to the customer through labelling and certification programmes, the sales staff, conference presentations and the company's website.

▷ **Emphasise the health connection.** Indoor air quality is an increasingly important issue in modern society and IFS takes strict measures to ensure that its products are free of toxic substances.

▷ **Become an industry leader.** IFS has a list of targeted substances for elimination from its products and it closely examines its operations to achieve this goal. First, all raw materials are treated using a gas chromatograph/mass spectrometer for airborne emissions of organic compounds. Then, compounds created from these raw materials are tested in the same manner. Finally, the product is also tested.

IFS has found that its approach has led to better relationships with government. It emphasises that, by reducing toxic substances, it is lessening the burden on ecosystems and water treatment systems. This message is well received by government and other stakeholders.

4. *Implementation and results*

IFS has a toxics team working on the elimination of selected toxic substances throughout the company. Through strategies such as product redesign and materials reformulation, Interface is attempting to eliminate toxic elements from all of its products and manufacturing facilities (*Interface Sustainability Report*, 1998). Interface Canada was successful in eliminating targeted compounds by taking the following steps:

For each targeted compound, a flowchart is prepared that outlines its use. There are essentially two common classes of compounds the company uses: (1) compounds that are *arrestors* (e.g. smoke- and flame-retardants); and (2) compounds that *contribute* a property (e.g. stabilisers). For arrestors, the possibility of increasing non-toxic substitute arrestors is investigated. For example, increasing the use of fillers or reducing the amount of polymer can reduce smoke generated from polymers. In each case, trials are undertaken to check that: (1) quality is not compromised; (2) there are no cost impacts (often costs go down); and (3) other non-related performance impacts such as electrostatic properties and conductivity are not affected. At this point, some informal life-cycle assessment screening may also be performed.

If the targeted substance is a contributor, similar strategies can be pursued. The possibility of increasing non-toxic contributors is investigated. If this is not possible, substitutes are investigated and life-cycle and cost issues are examined. A key strategy is to try to redesign the product while using the same technology. If this is not possible, research and development is conducted.

Using existing regulatory lists, IFS has developed a company-wide target list of substances for elimination. It includes compounds such as zinc borate, DBDPO,[1] antimony oxide, molybdenum trioxide, lead, cadmium, barium, dispersing agents containing formaldehyde and silica products. All of the targeted compounds were eliminated one after another at the Belleville operation. In addition, traditional solvent-based adhesives were replaced by water-based products.

All this activity is reinforced by financial incentives. Employee bonuses are linked to environmental improvement through eco-points related to progress in key areas such as the reduction of greenhouse gases, the use of sustainable energy and the elimination or reduction of non-renewable materials.

5. *Cost and financial performance*

Toxic substances can sometimes be very expensive on a pound-per-pound basis while their use is often limited. Eliminating these substances often reduces costs. IFS has also found that the elimination of toxic substances can increase the performance and quality of its products.

---

1   Decabromodiphenyloxide (DBDPO) is one of the most commonly used flame retardants.

Product that does not meet quality standards and is unsaleable has been reduced from 5.25% four years ago to less than 0.4% today. This reduction cannot be entirely attributed to reductions in toxic substances, but this was a factor in reducing off-quality product. Certain flame-retardants can interfere with fusion or tensile strength of products which is reflected in performance. By eliminating these toxic compounds, performance has improved.

IFS has also found that customers want to be associated with an environmental leader. Some customers will always be motivated almost entirely by cost, but increasingly other factors such as environment are becoming important. IFS has had great success in meeting its market share targets. Production in 1997 increased by 58% over 1996, and 1998 production increased a further 38%. This represents a roughly 100% increase over a two-year period in product going out of the gate.

Because IFS has integrated its environmental and technical work throughout the company, it has been able to achieve results with relatively low investment. According to Rahumathulla Marikkar, manager of Interface's Belleville operation, this integration of environmental considerations throughout the company means that the solutions are in the hands of the technical experts who know the operations and the products best.

References

Interface publications

http://www.interfaceinc.com

Interface Annual Report 1998 (Atlanta, GA: Interface Inc., 1999).

Interface Sustainability Report (Atlanta, GA: Interface Inc., 1998).

Other

Fortune (1998) '100 Best Companies to Work For', Fortune 137.1 (1998).

Fortune (1999) '100 Best Companies to Work For', Fortune 139.1 (1999).

Organisational contacts

Rahumathulla Marikkar, Manager, Technical and Environmental, Belleville Plant

SONY

Operationalising the slogan 'Entertaining the world: caring for the environment' *

1. *The lie of the land*

a. *Corporate overview*

The Sony brand is one of the strongest in the world. From the invention of Japan's first tape recorder and transistor radio by Sony's late founder Masaru Ibuka, to the latest hit products in electronics, games, music and film, Sony has consistently been a powerhouse of innovation and new product development. Now, mostly behind the scenes, the company is applying this ingenuity and creativity to making all Sony products and production processes more sustainable.

Sony is one of the world's foremost companies in the development, design, manufacture and sale of consumer and industrial electronic equipment and devices. Additionally, Sony leads in the development, production, marketing and distribution of entertainment—music, games software and consoles, motion pictures, and video technologies and products. A leader in technological innovation, Sony has made rapid progress in the new digital age. Sony's sales for the fiscal year ended 31 March 1999 were ¥6,795 billion (US$56.621 billion) with 177,000 employees worldwide.

---

* This slogan was created in summer 1994 as an environmental communication concept for Sony in Europe. It has been widely used in company publications ever since.

In addition to electronics, constituting 64.1% of total sales for fiscal year 1998, Sony has recorded the following results in the entertainment and other segments: games (11.2%), music (10.6%), film (7.9%), insurance (5%) and others (1.2%). Sony's electronics products include: video (22.3%), audio (24.6%), television sets (16.1%), information and communications (21%), and electronic components and others (16%).

With its global production operations, Sony develops and manufactures products and provides customer services worldwide. Sales in fiscal year 1998 by geographic area, as a percentage of consolidated sales, were: Japan (28.1%), United States (31.8%), Europe (24.5%), and other areas (15.6%).

The force of Sony's technological know-how is now being applied to operational-ising its slogan 'Entertaining the world: caring for the environment' (see footnote on previous page). Sony represents a powerful example of what can be achieved when a world-class organisation fully integrates environmental considerations into products and processes.

b. The business context

Sony's field, the electronics and entertainment business environment, is charac-terised by intensely competitive markets, continual new product introductions, fast-paced technology developments, and rapidly shifting consumer preferences. In addition to electronics and games, music and film, and insurance and financing markets, Sony has initiated activities in digital broadcasting and Internet-related business. Although many of these industries are extremely dynamic and challeng-ing, Sony maintains a strong competitive position in all of the major product lines in which it is engaged.

c. Preview

Sony is used to being number one, so in the early 1990s when a widely read consumer report-type journal rated Sony Europe's television set well below competitors on environmental performance, it focused attention on improvement. Such reports significantly affect purchasing decisions in Europe, and, as one manager put it, 'If we fail with the environmental features, we can never reach the "best buy" qualification.' This event sparked Sony's 'Eco TV' project. J. Günther, a Sony design engineer, passionately led the effort to redesign Sony's colour TVs to lessen environmental effects. Now, with the Eco TV in its second generation, Sony has succeeded in developing an 'environmentally conscious' TV for the European market: it eliminates hazardous materials and dramatically eases disassembly for recycling.

More specifically, Günther reports that this second-generation TV has reduced environmental impact (it is halogen-free, with no antimony trioxide, no PVC, has reduced plastics by 52%, and uses less total material), increased recyclability to 99%, reduced costs of the cabinet by 30% and the speaker box by more than 50%, and can be dismantled quickly with only two tools (it has only nine screws). Assembly time was also reduced, due to minimisation of parts. This TV Design won a Grand Prize in 1994, and a Management Prize in 1996 in Sony's internal worldwide environmental award contest. Packaging has also been addressed: the TV is packed in Beeboard®, a cardboard made of low-density paper.

Contrary to traditional views that environmental performance costs money, the Eco TV not only dramatically reduces negative environmental impacts, but simultaneously has lower materials costs, is cheaper to produce, and offers increased retained value at end-of-life through recycling.

This project is important not only for itself, but because it is illustrative of Sony's proactive, integrative stance toward 'harmonising' environment and advanced developments in technology. Sony has systematically moved beyond limited solutions, travelling instead along the path toward integrating sustainable development principles and practices into the mainstream of its products, services, relationships, and even business models. Sony's exemplary work in the following areas are described in this chapter:

▷ Long-standing commitment and comprehensive approach

▷ Worldwide infrastructure for driving, co-ordinating and disseminating learning

▷ Priorities and clear targets for improvements in product design and production

▷ Systems for environmentally sound product development

▷ Environmental management systems and production management

▷ Technology development aimed at environmental performance and recycling

▷ Education, communication and promotion programmes

▷ Leadership within industry and government

An overview of Sony's accomplishments in what they call 'incorporating a sound respect for nature in all of its business activities' is presented in Box 1.

Sony's efforts toward more sustainable products and production processes are be part and parcel of organisational management, supported by the genuine concern of many committed managers. Below, we look at the business drivers more closely, then examine Sony's advanced approach, systems and implementation processes.

▷ Sony's Greenplus 2000 programme goal requires that all Sony products incorporate environmental issues as part of the product development process by 2000. To support the Greenplus 2000 goals, Sony has established environmental product assessments at each phase of the new product development process.

▷ Sony is advanced in ISO 14001 and EMAS certification, with 94 of 105 (90%) of manufacturing sites worldwide ISO 14001-certified as of 5 July 1999 (100% of manufacturing sites in Japan and Europe are ISO 14001-certified).

▷ Sony has a goal of reducing negative environmental impact by emphasising energy conservation and prevention of global warming, product recycling and resource conservation, industrial waste reduction and reduction and management of chemical substances, Sony is incorporating consideration for the environment into product design, production processes, facilities design and operation, and procurement management. Examples of product and process innovations include:

  – Sony designed and produced its Eco TV—significantly reducing environmental impact, increasing recyclability and reducing costs

  – Audiotapes are no longer manufactured using chromium oxide as a surface polishing material

  – A number of models of home video recorder sold in Europe incorporate a power-saving mode

  – A compact radio on the Japanese and US market uses hand-wound power generation

  – R&D efforts focused on reducing environmental impact of products and production processes include lead-free solder, re-use of waste polystyrene and ABS plastics (used in cassette cases), and recycling of CD-R optical disks

  – Changes in production facilities reduce energy consumption for heating and cooling.

▷ Sony has introduced a computer monitor take-back programme in Germany, and is actively developing recycling technology in Europe and Japan.

▷ Internal environmental education and promotion activities reach every employee, and the head office in Japan conducts a variety of courses aimed at specific audiences.

▷ Sony initiated the 'CARE' project, an industry-wide effort to develop environmental R&D and recycling knowledge. The company now assumes a central role as one of the steering board members.

▷ New technologies are being developed in Sony's 'Center for Environmental Technologies'—and are even being commercialised to applications outside of Sony.

Box 1: Environmental activities in Sony today

d. *The key drivers*

Sony, and the electronics industry more broadly, is experiencing a number of forces moving it toward more sustainable industrial practices: pressures toward recycling, market demand in the form of consumer pressure, eco-labelling and media attention; legislative requirements regarding materials handling, emissions and product take-back; increasing costs for resource use and disposal; and competitive pressures. These external factors, in combination with the genuine concern of management and employees about the issue of environmental protection, have been driving forces in Sony's commitment to environmental ideals and practices.

As in many industries, market segments vary in the intensity and focus of environmental concerns. In general, within Sony's business areas, Europe appears to be driven mostly by consumer demand, competitive pressure, legislation requiring product take-back and recycling, elimination of hazardous materials, and limits on waste to landfills. Japan is increasingly concerned with recycling, energy conservation and hazardous emissions, whereas North America is more driven by government regulation on factory production processes. General consensus about who should be responsible for the costs of dealing with products at end-of-life also vary by region, with the European Union asserting that industry is responsible,[1] whereas common feeling in Japan places responsibility with the consumer. Sony General Manager in Corporate Environmental Affairs, Y. Sasagawa, commented that perceptions of Japanese customers are changing dramatically toward environmental conservation, spurred by daily news, TV reports, and announcements regarding environmental issues.

2. *Trailblazing: exemplary systems and practices*

a. *Long-standing commitment and comprehensive approach*

The Eco TV project is not a stand-alone project for Sony; rather, it is one initiative embedded within a long-standing, comprehensive framework to promote environmentally friendlier products and production.

Sony has a long history of systematic endeavours to advance environmental performance. As early as 1976, Sony established what it called an 'Environmental Conference'—an internal group responsible for driving environmental performance improvements—focusing initially on the reduction of hazardous waste,

---

1   In January 1999, recovery of all large home appliances became mandatory in the Netherlands, the first EU member state to legally require a comprehensive product recovery programme.

safety and hygiene. The group was chaired by Sony's President, with high-level management support. Sony began environmental audits in 1985, chartered a special committee to study ways of eliminating the use of CFCs in 1989, signed the Business Charter for Sustainable Development in 1991, and by 1993 had terminated the use of class-1 ozone-depleting substances (ODSs) in all its manufacturing processes worldwide, well ahead of the introduction of international regulations to phase out CFCs.

Today, Sony has moved well beyond this narrow production process focus to an 'integrative' response, where environmental issues are addressed comprehensively in business strategy, business objectives, product design, production process design and management, technology development, and even intra- and inter-industry relations. Environment has been made one of Sony's central long-term management themes. Change initiatives incorporate a perspective on the environmental impacts of Sony products at each stage in the product life-cycle, from natural resource extraction through to end-of-life. Sony's approach is to reduce the overall variability of environmental performance, recognising that it is important to move beyond demonstration projects or products to improvements throughout the entire organisation. Sony has successfully achieved significant environmental improvements in all products, fully implemented environmental management systems, and endeavoured to educate every employee. Additionally, breakthroughs achieved in one geographic area are widely publicised for adoption in other areas.

To support this higher-level focus, Sony has instituted changes on many fronts simultaneously: organisational structures and planning and control systems to drive improvement and diffusion of innovations, breakthrough improvement targets for products and production processes alike, design guidelines and environmental screens within the product development process, ISO 14001 certification for all production facilities, new technology development and collaborative R&D efforts, intensive management education, and industry-wide collaboration. This comprehensive approach not only explains much of Sony's success to date, but leaves the company well positioned for the future.

b. A worldwide infrastructure for driving, co-ordinating and disseminating learning

Sony has developed an organisational infrastructure that simultaneously optimises localised initiative and global standardisation. In this way, individual business units pursue innovations customised to their individual markets and competitive and legislative environments. The resulting new products and processes are widely communicated regionally and globally through 'Environmental Conservation Committees' (ECCs) in each of four major markets (Japan, the rest of Asia, America and Europe).

Corporate-wide global strategies and guidelines are determined and co-ordinated through the Sony ECC, headquartered in Japan. This corporate decision-making body on business and product strategy acts as the global hub for diffusion of innovation, alignment and linkages. It drafts policy, directs planning, and co-ordinates company-wide task force subcommittee meetings, environmental awards, etc. The committee is led by a corporate vice-president responsible solely for corporate-wide Sony environmental issues. Chief environment officers from each of the businesses are appointed to the Sony ECC. Each member has assumed responsibility for corporate-wide implementation of a particular theme (e.g. environmental education, recycling, green purchasing, logistics, environmental R&D, the 'Greenplus' programme (see below), environmental PR, environmental advertising, environmental audits, and regional issues). The four regional ECCs hold annual environmental conferences and multiple interim meetings which serve as a forum for dialogue, global information exchange, progress review, planning and recognition. At the corporate level, there are also several ongoing task forces focused on specific issues (e.g. life-cycle assessment, product assessment, environmental management, etc.).

Through this local–global structure, Sony operationalises its strongly held view about implementation: market-sensitive innovation, systemisation, then the freedom to customise. The way it achieves this 'systemised customisation' is to focus a great deal on providing strategy, a basic template, development and training, knowledge transfer and consulting to establish the system, then give operating units freedom to customise to their specific situations and needs. Then, following implementation, co-ordination through global committees assures that innovations in one region are disseminated to other areas.

What this process reflects is conscious attention to the creation and diffusion of innovation and a structure to continually push the entire organisation toward new, higher performance standards. The structure and process themselves are identical to those developed by other leading Japanese companies for managing implementation of Total Quality Control. Sony is elevating this to a new level in what it calls its 'unified dispersed' management model, especially designed to fit its business context of global, widely diverse business operations and network-centric interactions.

c. Priorities and clear targets for improvements in product design and production

In order to minimise the environmental impact during the entire life-cycle of Sony products, indicators were developed to allow managers to monitor impact and improvement. For example: waste volume versus sales is used to show resource conservation from waste reduction and recycling; unit energy consumption and reduction in power consumption of products are used as indicators of energy conservation to prevent global warming; product dismantling time and recycling rates show progress in product recycling and resource conservation; and the number of ISO 14001-certified sites indicates the adoption of environmental management systems.

Several years ago, each regional Sony ECC established individual 'Environmental Action Plans' to be accomplished by March 2001, reflecting the unique conditions in each marketplace. These were modelled after the Japan ECC's 'Green Management 2000' plan. Targets of the Japanese plan for the reduction of environmental impact of business processes (reported in Sony's 1999 *Environmental Report*) include:

1. ISO certification of all manufacturing bases by the end of March 1998 and all non-manufacturing bases by March 2001

2. Prevention of global warming through a 25% reduction at all Sony business locations in the ratio of petroleum-equivalent energy consumption to net sales by 2000 compared with 1990 levels

3. Zero disposal through at least 50% reduction in the ratio of waste volume to net sales compared to 1991, and total elimination of landfill use by 2010

4. Reduction of environmental pollutants through complete elimination of certain substances, 50% reduction of others by 2000, and close monitoring of many chemicals (specifically defined)

5. Reduction in paper resources by 2000: 10% reduction in computer and copy paper from 1995; 100% recycling of paper; and 100% recycled content in paper usage

6. Increased capability to respond to natural emergencies

7. Green purchasing that includes environment as a high-priority criterion in every purchase decision (materials, parts, facilities, office equipment)

8. Green perspective in new plant location and overseas expansion

9. Use of 'green' cars.

Plans for the reduction of environmental impact of products include:

1. Product recycling and re-use through 50% improvement in recycling ration of parts and materials from 1992; 50% reduction in dismantling time by 2000 from 1990 levels; and 50% reduction in the use of styrene foam from 1990 levels

2. Prevention of global warming by reducing the power consumption of all major product types by 30%–50% from 1990

3. 'Greenplus 2000', requiring that every product must show significant improvement in at least one of these areas by 2000: materials with

environmental impact, energy efficiency, resource conservation (reduction in resources used, product life-cycle, percentage of re-usable materials), recycling (ability to be recycled, labelling of plastic materials, time needed for disassembly), environmental packaging, and benefits to new product planning (see also below)

These clear, measurable goals form the basis for planning, data collection, reporting, progress reviews, and business unit operational improvements. Simple graphs provide clear visual displays of progress against targets.

In November 1998, Sony created a corporate-wide 'Green Management 2002' programme outlining goals for reducing environmental impacts of business processes and products to be achieved by 2002. This medium-term Environmental Action Plan extends the breadth of activities covered to include sales, training, accounting, etc., and sets unified global goals wherever possible. What is noteworthy about Sony's Green Management 2002 goals is that they show, in most areas, a clear commitment to breakthrough levels of improvements; and a strong progression from local to global, from selected models to all models, and from pilot projects to company-wide adoption (see Fig. 1).

d. *Systems for environmentally sound product development*

Sony has created the organisational culture and structure to foster innovation in product design. First, it closely monitors customer requirements and 'in-use' needs. Then the Sony teams are given the freedom and resources to innovate.

Not only does Sony recognise that the greatest leverage for environmental improvement is in the design phase, but it has systematised processes for ensuring that environmental impact criteria are considered in the early stages of product design and manufacturing. Fully informed of the life-cycle impacts of Sony products, the company provides product planning and design guidelines, comprehensive product assessments, design tools to measure environmental impact, manufacturing guidelines, and standardised environmental data sheets (summarised below).

These actions reflect Sony management's in-depth knowledge of what it takes to systematise a process change. In the new product development area in particular, the enthusiasm and energy of individual managers (who want to ensure that the progress they make is institutionalised) drive this approach.

'Greenplus 2000' guidelines

In 1994, Sony launched the company-wide 'Greenplus 2000' project, with the goal that all products achieve significant improvement in at least one of the following areas: environmental impact of materials, energy efficiency, resource conservation, recycling, environmental packaging, and benefit to new-product planning. These

COMMITMENT TO BREAKTHROUGH LEVELS OF IMPROVEMENT

Design of products for reduced power consumption   *Dismantling time*

Power   Standby power   Possible
consumption   consumption   recycling rate

Emissions reduction in production processes   *Waste materials reduction (Japan)*

Use of recycled paper

**PROGRESSION FROM LOCAL TO GLOBAL, SELECTED MODELS
TO ALL MODELS, PILOTS TO COMPANY-WIDE**

Lead-free solder   *PVC reduction*

Halogen reduction

Elimination of halogen flame retardants

Figure 1: Examples of targets in Sony's Environmental
Action Plan, 'Green Management 2002'

Sony examines environmental soundness as one of the key quality criteria that must be designed, controlled and improved in all products. Every product in development must undergo comprehensive product assessments (PAs) which include ascertaining a product's overall impact on the environment during its entire life-cycle, including use and what happens to a product after its disposal. These considerations are incorporated into design.

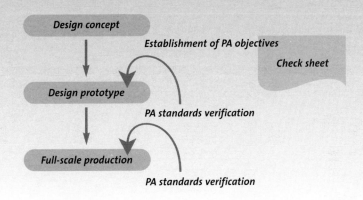

Box 2: Sony's product assessment process

guidelines were distributed worldwide, with explanations of global and national regulations, and successful product examples.

Product assessment process

Sony's product assessment (PA) process, mandated for all products, ensures that the design of new products considers environmental impacts during the entire life-cycle of the product, from materials procurement through production, use, disassembly and end-of-life (see Box 2). In addition to evaluating products in the prototype and full-scale production phase regarding their environmental soundness, the product assessment tool is used to verify the design interventions intended to diminish environmental impact.

This rigorous process for understanding design implications and making corrections early in the concept and prototype phase is another carry-over from advanced Total Quality Management. The principles can be generally applied to any enterprise. Although it is early in the product development process, the vast majority of the costs (and often the environmental impacts) are determined or committed during the design phase. Design is, therefore, the point of greatest

Sony has developed a 'DAC–LCA' design tool to assess environmental impact: design for assembly/disassembly cost-effectiveness based on life-cycle impacts. Using this tool, designers gauge the total environmental impact of various products or components, and assess the costs of assembly and dismantling. In the future, it is planned to determine the environmental impact by assigning a standard quantification of the total amount of CO_2 generated through the life-cycle of the product.

This tool is just one example of Sony management's recognition that goals and policies are best achieved if they are supported by tools that allow fast, effective decision-making and design choices based on new thinking and criteria.

AN EXAMPLE OF DAC–LAC ASSESSMENT OF A PRECISION MOTOR

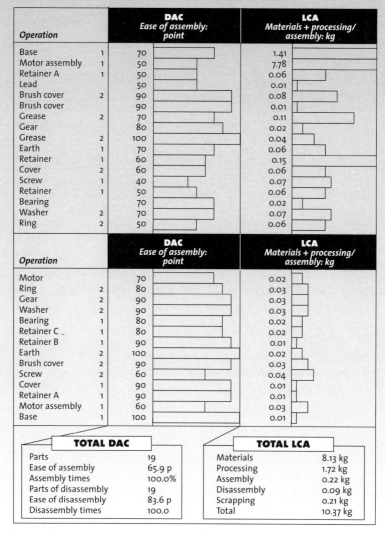

Operation		DAC Ease of assembly: point	LCA Materials + processing/ assembly: kg
Base	1	70	1.41
Motor assembly	1	50	7.78
Retainer A	1	50	0.06
Lead		50	0.01
Brush cover	2	90	0.08
Brush cover		90	0.01
Grease	2	70	0.11
Gear		80	0.02
Grease	2	100	0.04
Earth	1	70	0.06
Retainer	1	60	0.15
Cover	2	60	0.06
Screw	1	40	0.07
Retainer	1	50	0.06
Bearing		70	0.02
Washer	2	70	0.07
Ring	2	50	0.06

Operation		DAC Ease of assembly: point	LCA Materials + processing/ assembly: kg
Motor		70	0.02
Ring	2	80	0.03
Gear	2	90	0.03
Washer	2	90	0.03
Bearing	1	80	0.02
Retainer C	1	80	0.02
Retainer B	1	90	0.01
Earth	2	100	0.02
Brush cover	2	90	0.03
Screw	2	60	0.04
Cover	1	90	0.01
Retainer A	1	90	0.01
Motor assembly	1	60	0.03
Base	1	100	0.01

TOTAL DAC			TOTAL LCA	
Parts	19		Materials	8.13 kg
Ease of assembly	65.9 p		Processing	1.72 kg
Assembly times	100.0%		Assembly	0.22 kg
Parts of disassembly	19		Disassembly	0.09 kg
Ease of disassembly	83.6 p		Scrapping	0.21 kg
Disassembly times	100.0		Total	10.37 kg

Box 3: Sony's design for assembly/disassembly cost-effectiveness (DAC–LCA)

leverage for improvement. This understanding is institutionalised through the 'Product Assessment Guidelines'.

Sony has PA representatives in the design sections, materials and peripherals of each product category. They set out objectives, study new technologies and exchange information at regular meetings. A top priority has been the creation of company-wide PA guidelines, covering:

▷ The establishment of design standards to minimise the environmental impact of each product

▷ Verification that the prototype meets these standards

▷ Further verification that these standards are met in full-scale production

▷ Methods of handling the results of verification

▷ Clarification of responsibilities throughout the assessment process

Sony's PA drive is building a solid framework for managing every aspect of product design and production, such as lowering resource and energy requirements, using environmentally friendlier materials, and simplifying recycling procedures.

Clear objectives, formal regular task force meetings, design review meetings, checklists, and an ever-increasing body of knowledge about design to reduce environmental impact support the successful design of products and production processes that minimise negative environmental impact.

Design for assembly/disassembly cost-effectiveness and life-cycle assessment (DAC–LCA)

Sony has developed a powerful tool for rating a product's ease of assembly (driving cost reductions) and disassembly (easing and lowering costs of recycling). The DAC (see Box 3) is used in early stage design of all Sony products, including TVs, PCs, audio equipment, and VCRs. Use of DAC is promoted through an education curriculum for DAC and regular meetings to announce improvements.

e. Environmental management systems and production management

ISO 14001 certification

We have already outlined Sony's success with wide-scale environmental management system implementation (ISO 14001 and EMAS). Sony is very advanced in ISO and EMAS certification, with almost all of its of manufacturing sites and operating bases globally ISO 14001-certified at year-end 1998. ISO certification has extended beyond manufacturing to include all major non-manufacturing sites.

Sony also made a commitment to build the infrastructure and internal competences that would make this rapid implementation possible. As of March 1998, over 2,000 internal environmental auditors were trained and certified.

f. Technology development aimed at environmental performance and recycling

Recycling

In addition to a functional requirement to be ISO 14001-certified, the entire electronics industry is also being pushed toward recycling. As J. Günther noted: 'We can take it for granted that in the future the consumer goods industry will be obliged to recycle their products.' The Netherlands 1 January 1999 law mandating industry-wide recovery of all large home appliances exemplifies a more general European Union trend toward Extended Producer Responsibility for products at end-of-life.

Sony has been proactive in applying technology to advancing viable recycling. The company embraced the challenge of finding ways to enable economically viable recycling using product and process design, technology, management processes, information labels and education. Sony operates a disassembly facility, the DC Recycle Research Center in Japan. Sony's Environmental Center Europe entered into co-operation with a local recycler. As part of this, Sony established a disassembly line at the recycler's site. In addition to the normal disassembly of products, the line is used for experiments in new recycling technologies. Results from the line about disassembly and materials are transferred to product designers.

In Germany, Sony initiated the industry's first computer monitor take-back scheme, whereby consumers receive with each new monitor purchased a label allowing free recycling of computer displays returned to any of 800 collection sites. Sony partnered with another firm for the collection and recycling of these monitors.

Packaging innovations

Sony's environmentally conscious packaging focuses on the four 'Rs': reduction, replacement, re-use and recycling for lower environmental impact. Innovations have come from internal R&D for technology development and from partnerships with packaging suppliers to develop new materials and processes.

Innovations and partnerships developed in the pursuit of sustainability sometimes result in new business opportunities. In solving the problem of recovering its packaging material in Europe, as legislated by the EU Packaging Directive, Sony developed a technological breakthrough to enable the recycling of polystyrene (outlined in Box 4). In Japan, Sony started recycling waste styrene foam from manufacturing bases using the limonene method in December 1998. Sony is well positioned to respond to increasing EU pressures for recycling, as Japan has well-advanced requirements.

Collaboration in early state technology development

At the R&D level, Sony is helping to leverage investments already made—and share the burden of huge investment while accelerating innovation—by participating in

Sony's Center for Environmental Technologies has developed a new natural and safe technology for recycling expanded polystyrene (EPS) where EPS is reduced to $\frac{1}{25}$th of its volume. The process uses a natural, safe and non-flammable solvent called d-limonene—extracted from the peel of citrus fruits. EPS is dissolved **in the truck that picks up the styrene foam from the Sony distribution centre**. Through a distillation process, both the solvent and the polystyrene can be recovered and used many times in a closed-loop process. High-quality recycled polystyrene packaging is produced and used for Sony products. From several sites, packaging material is picked up and compressed using limonene in the truck during transfer to the recycling centre. Finally, recycling results in recovery and reproduction of high-quality recycled polystyrene and re-use of limonene.

Box 4: **Sony's technology for recycling polystyrene**

the 'CARE Vision 2000' initiative (an industry-wide consortium of voluntary collaborative research), described in Box 5.

g. *Education, communication and promotion programmes*

Sony has in place a comprehensive process for educating its 170,000 staff on environmental issues. At its head office, Manufacturing Business School courses cover environmental management workshops and environmentally responsible product development and design. There are programmes for managers on the corporate role in addressing environmental issues; general orientation programmes for new staff covering social responsibility, environmental issues and the environmental connections to Sony activities; specialist courses for environmental affairs managers such as internal environmental auditor certification and follow-up seminars; and correspondence courses introducing ISO 14001 requirements to staff members.

In Sony Europe, great attention is given to educating engineers. Video training is used to describe innovations, learning, step-by-step procedures and practical examples. Additionally, a small disassembly line (cell) was set up within the environmental function to test product design. There is good communication between the environment and design areas. Education on recycling covers the big picture of mass flows, materials and dismantling tests.

Sony sees educational programmes as the beginning of a full-scale programme of employee involvement. Many other mechanisms are also used to promote greater understanding and commitment. For example, to initially raise the environmental awareness within the employees in Europe, a touring exhibition was created several years ago, translated into five languages and highlighted general environmental topics as well as Sony's commitments and actions. The distribution of information folders, newsletters, promotional posters, along with the develop-

The programme 'CARE [Comprehensive Approach for Recycling of Electronics] Vision 2000' was launched in 1993 as a research platform to pursue joint solutions for the recycling of electronics. As an official European Umbrella (EU 1140) of the EUREKA initiative, the CARE programme brings together more than 200 participants from European electronics, computer and recycling industries. These industries, together with industrial associations, research institutions and universities, co-operate on cutting-edge research to facilitate eco-design and the recycling of electronic products.

Sony initiated CARE Vision 2000 in 1993, and now assumes the role of one of the steering board members. The day-to-day operations and management is now the responsibility of the International CARE Vision 2000 Secretariat in Vienna.

'CARE Innovation' is a major biennial congress event organised by CARE Vision 2000. The first of three such events was held in Frankfurt in 1996 in co-operation with the German Federal Ministry for the Environment, EUREKA and Expo 2000. The second event, 'CARE Innovation 98', was held in November 1998 attracting more than 300 participants to the venue in Vienna. The third, and most probably the largest, event is scheduled for 2000 at Hanover's World Exposition, 'Expo 2000'.

For more information, contact: International CARE Vision 2000 Office, c/o SAT (Austrian Society for Systems Engineering and Automation), Adlergasse 3/1, A-2700 Wiener Neustadt, Austria. Tel: + 43 2622 27367; Fax: + 43 2622 2736722; E-mail: *care_vision_2000@magnet.at*; Contacts: Mr Bernd Kopacek and Mr Bernd Habiger; Website: *http://members.magnet.at/care_vision_2000*

Box 5: The 'CARE' initiative

ment of Internet and intranet pages, are further tools for continuous awareness-raising. In addition to these internal activities, the Sony Eco Plaza at the head office in Japan has opened its doors to the public.

As well as educating management and employees, Sony has targeted consumer education—in part stimulated by the life-cycle analysis finding that the environmental impact (in terms of energy use) is much higher during the working life of the TV set than at the manufacturing stage. Environmental reports have been produced since 1994, site reports must be prepared and distributed by all manufacturing facilities by the end of March 2000, and regular exhibitions are held at the Tokyo EcoPlaza to increase consumer awareness of the environmental effects of Sony's products. Sony Europe was also an active participant in the development of *The Sustainable Business Challenge*, a project of the World Business Council for Sustainable Development (WBCSD)'s educational outreach to business students. The project developed an Internet-based primer on business and sustainable development and an on-line exam (Willums with WBCSD 1998). Sony uses the exam to screen students for acceptance into its six-month internship programme at Sony Environmental Center Europe. Sony recognises that change cannot occur if management doesn't invest in this kind of comprehensive effort which is required for creating an adequate knowledge base among workers and suppliers.

h. Sony's brand of eco-leadership

Leading companies in many sectors face tension between being a market leader and co-operating with competitors to move the entire industry forward. The top competitors manage to do both. Sony's role in CARE Vision 2000, which is recognised as the primary European environmental research platform of the electronics industry, is just one such example. In addition, Sony has a proactive approach to standardised self-declarations for products, an initiative within ECMA (European Computer Manufacturers' Association), an international standardisation organisation. Based on the compiled ECMA Technical Report 70, manufacturers can report the environmental attributes of information, communication and consumer products in a standardised and therefore comparable way. Environmentally relevant product information on energy conservation, noise, emissions (including ozone-depleting substances and VOCs), materials (PCBs, cadmium and mercury) and recyclability (number of re-usable parts, disassembly information, etc.) is provided and assessed. Sony has also led the WBCSD working group on 'Eco-Efficiency in the Electronics Industry'.

3. The route: leadership, planning and implementation

a. Leadership commitment, priorities and targets

Sony's most senior leadership demonstrate an understanding of the corporation's reliance on and obligation to the environment. Sony's Chairman of the Board and CEO, Norio Ohga, in the 1999 *Environmental Report*, states:

> This is truly a time to devote serious thought to how we can ensure that Earth remains a pleasant place to live . . . Energy is an urgent environmental issue, in large part because its production is closely linked to global warming. If we continue to rely on the limited amount of fossil fuels, I am convinced that we will no longer be able to sustain today's living standard. Now more than ever before is the time to develop energy sources that are environmentally benign, safe and clean . . . Sony is well aware of its obligation to society. We are working diligently on ways to make our products more environmentally friendly and recycle end-of-life products to conserve the Earth's precious resources.

Sony's President and Co-CEO, Nobuyuki Idei, voices intentions about Sony's role in innovation to support the environment: 'The 21st century is already being coined "the age of the environment" and I am determined to see Sony become a significant force in this era through the development of unique and distinctly "Sony-like" environmental innovations.'

Sony's leadership currently focuses on three aspects: (1) power conservation; (2) materials issues; and (3) manufacturing processes, including the number and types of materials, water consumption, and oil and energy use. In Japan, Sony has joined a number of other corporations in attempting to operationalise a zero emissions facility, where all waste is re-used or recycled. Corporate guidelines regarding reduction of environmental impact are applied in every product design. Recognising that every business manager must worry about profit and deliberate about investing to reduce hazardous material and waste, and solve other environmental problems, Sony Corporate in Japan provides both decision-making and financial support. Especially in instances where solutions to a problem might be helpful to other groups or manufacturing sites, Sony Corporate will fund design research.

b. Integration into corporate planning and control systems

A common strength of many leading Japanese companies is their management systems for planning, deploying and controlling improvement. The 'Management by Policy' system (or *Hoshin Kanri* system) (Akao 1991) is a top-down–bottom-up process for identifying and then deploying major improvement 'policies' within the company or business unit. At the point an improvement objective is officially announced, cascading levels of management and each department and team will already have negotiated and agreed on exactly the actions they are expected to take to achieve the stated goal, and the precise amount of improvement their areas and their actions will contribute. A formalised process for developing improvement plans and setting targets is undertaken that involves the whole organisation—from senior executives to shop-floor management. The 'Cross Functional Management' system creates a structure for achieving breakthrough improvement in selected core functions such as quality, cost, time-to-market and new product development, usually involving collaboration across the entire organisation. Finally, the 'Daily Management' system integrates the improvement actions into standard reliable methods for work performance, to 'hold the gains' and continuously improve.

Sony treats environmental objectives within these proven managerial systems and processes for planning and deployment of key corporate-wide business initiatives. As part of this, they establish and monitor key performance measures, and create visible displays of progress against targets.

c. Change management savvy

It is important to note that Sony's implementation process reflects a number of principles of major organisational change:

▷ Linking efforts to business strategy for improved customer satisfaction, competitive advantage or profitability

▷ Promoting flexibility and stimulating innovations that are responsive to the marketplace

▷ Setting extremely demanding 'breakthrough' goals or stretch targets that require fundamental re-examination of the product or process if they are to be met (e.g. zero emissions)

▷ Clear policy statements that are backed up by actions (e.g. using only recycled paper by 2000)

▷ Clear plans and methods for how these goals will be achieved (down to the responsibility of each department), most often established in concert with the goal establishment process

▷ Effective programmes for educating employees, suppliers and customers

▷ Mechanisms to disseminate innovation throughout global operations

▷ Widely communicated visual displays of progress in simple, easy-to-interpret graphs

▷ Direct corporate funding of innovative research projects.

Additionally, Sony has achieved a constructive balance of localisation–globalisation and of inspired individual mid-managers in a context of top corporate-level support. Sony has implemented a structure that is attempting to achieve the best of both centralised and localised management.

d. *Review and monitoring*

As was evident in the list of Sony's goals, objectives have been clearly quantified. Data is monitored regularly, performance against targets is visually displayed, and information is widely shared internally and externally.

Sony also produces an extensive *Environmental Report*, detailing philosophy, objectives and performance against targets. Their goal is to have the *Environmental Report* mirror the quality and presentation of their *Annual Report*.

e. *The environmental award programme*

Initiated in 1994, Sony Environmental Awards are presented once a year by the president of the company. Recognition is given for accomplishment in the previous fiscal years in the fields of technology, products and management related to the environment. The fifth annual competition in 1998 attracted 126 applications: 85 from Japan and 41 from overseas. Twenty-one projects were presented with awards on 2 July at Sony's Tokyo head office to commemorate World Environment Day. Grand Prize winners have been responsible for key innovations such as the development of an ecologically sound recycling method for styrene foam, an automated mass TV dismantling and cathode ray tube recycling system for the Association for Electric Home Appliances, new recycling technology that transforms polystyrene plastic into a water-soluble polymer, and the development of a new lead-free solder.

4. Conclusion

What Sony's response in all these areas represents is a concerted investment in moving forward and truly improving performance. Rather than putting time, money and energy into fighting increasingly stringent legislation and maintaining the status quo, Sony has become a leader in the evolution toward a new industrial system.

As Sony pursues this path proactively (for example by focusing on design for disassembly and recyclability), it is challenging old assumptions about the economic viability of environmental improvements, investing in new technologies, and creating new business value opportunities. In the words of Sieglinde Hahn, Manager, Sony Environmental Center Europe:

> Sometimes hidden benefits turn out if you decide to go for an issue, although in the beginning it probably didn't look like it would be economically viable. That is exactly the area where environment can open new business opportunities for companies. But of course you can only define these areas if you stop seeing environment as a burden for a company and start to approach the topic more proactively.

A strong impression gleaned from visiting Sony's Environmental Center is that of an extremely competent team of people working to do the right thing. Yes, Sony is successfully integrating environmental considerations into corporate strategy, new product design, business design, production management, customer relationships, supplier and dealer management, and product end-of-life solutions. However, besides these technical and performance accomplishments, there is a vitality to the discovery process, a joy of moving on the journey, a sense of community purpose, which is evident when talking with Sony's managers.

Sony has consciously put action before advertising, choosing to get the results rather than trying to market its environmental actions externally. The image of building wealth in harmony with the environment is a strong motivator for many Sony managers. Communicating their position and intention in a few memorable words, these leaders provided ample evidence that Sony's slogans 'Never follow others' and 'Future is the place to be' are as true for their environmental performance as they are for their technical performance.

Sony is clearly integrating sustainable development principles into product design and production operations. Hopefully, the next step will be integrating these goals into their ultimate sense of purpose. Sony advertises that 'We are here to pursue infinite possibilities. We allow the brightest minds to interact freely, so the unexpected can emerge. We invite new thinking, so even more fantastic ideas can evolve. Creativity is our essence. We take chances. We exceed expectations. We help dreamers dream.' Imagine the contribution and infinite possibilities if Sony continues to apply its creativity and innovation to actualising the dream of a truly environmentally and socially sustainable economy!

References

Sony publications

http://www.world.sony.com

Sony Annual Report 1996 (year ended 31 March 1996; Tokyo: Sony Corporation, 1996).

Sony Annual Report 1997 (year ended 31 March 1997; Tokyo: Sony Corporation, 1997).

Sony Annual Report 1998 (year ended 31 March 1998; Tokyo: Sony Corporation, 1998).

Sony Environmental Report 1997 (Tokyo: Sony Corporate Environmental Affairs, 1997).

Sony Environmental Report 1999. For the Next Generation: Sony's Commitment to Environmental Ideals (Tokyo: Sony Corporate Environmental Affairs, 1999).

The Second Sony Environmental Award Booklet (Tokyo: Sony Corporate Environment and Community Affairs, 1994).

The Third Sony Environmental Award Booklet (Tokyo: Sony Corporate Environment and Community Affairs, 1996).

Entertaining the World, Caring for the Environment (Sony brochure; Fellbach, Germany, 1994)

Sony System for EPS Recycling using Limonene (pamphlet; Tokyo: Sony Research Center, 1996).

Sony Environmental Center Europe and Corporate Communications Europe, *EcoTopics*, March 1996, June 1996, July 1996, September 1996, November 1996, December 1996, February 1997 (Fellbach, Germany: Sony Environmental Center Europe).

Sony-Wega Productions, *Made in Germany* (product brochure; Fellbach, Germany: Sony).

Günther, J., *The Second Generation of Eco Design for Sony Television Sets* (internal company handout; Fellbach, Germany: TV-Europe, Sony-Wega Productions GmbH).

Other

Akao, Y. (ed.) (1991) *Hoshin Kanri: Policy Deployment for Successful TQM* (Portland, OR: Productivity Press).

CARE (1996)'Eco-efficient Concepts for the Electronics Industry towards Sustainability', *CARE Innovation '96* Invitation Brochure (International Symposium and Brokerage event).

Fussler, Claude (1996) 'Viewing the Future through the Green TV', in C. Fussler with P. James, *Driving Eco-Innovation: A Breakthrough Discipline for Innovation and Sustainability* (London: Financial Times/Pitman): 177-84.

Willums, J.-O., with the World Business Council for Sustainable Development (WBCSD) (1998) *The Sustainable Business Challenge: A Briefing for Tomorrow's Business Leaders* (Sheffield, UK: Greenleaf Publishing/Foundation for Business and Sustainable Development).

Organisational contacts

Jürgen Günther, Senior Manager, Mechanical Engineering, Sony TV Europe
Oliver von Quast, PhD, Project Manager, Environmental Center Europe
Christian Ridder, Project Manager, Environmental Center Europe
Y. Sasagawa, Assistant General Manager in Corporate Environmental Affairs, Japan
Karl Sturm, Manager, Environmental Center Europe
Dietrich Wienke, PhD, Project Manager, Environmental Center Europe

ASG

*Trailblazing toward sustainable
logistics and transport*

Leave stereotypes at the door. Spend just a few hours with ASG executives, and any expectations that transportation is boring or unsophisticated are quickly dispelled.

Internationalisation of production and markets, advances in information technology, and trends toward outsourcing are revolutionising this highly competitive industry. Today and in the future, the prosperity and even survival of transport companies depends increasingly on global alliances, integrated logistics services, precision deliveries, and ever-improving cost performance through efficiencies. Beyond advances to meet this general industry evolution, ASG adds customer-focused solutions, an integrated, strategic approach to moving toward more sustainable logistics and transport, and a European flair for colour and design in innovative marketing materials.

The ASG Group is one of northern Europe's leading transportation and logistics companies. Operations include road, rail, sea and air-based transport and logistics activities. ASG operates warehouses and terminals, and contracts most of its transport services. Gross sales for ASG in 1998 were approximately SEK 12 billion (US$1.4 billion) with 5,700 employees, in four business areas: 'logistics', 'road transport' (formerly 'domestic' and 'parcel and European road transport'), 'air and sea', and 'specialist companies'. ASG customers include Baxter, Dell Computer, Ford, Eastman Kodak, Mazda, Nike, Johnson & Johnson and Shell.

▷ Many successful environmental initiatives and demonstration projects: for example, testing an electric vehicle (1993), an ethanol-driven vehicle (1996), and a hybrid vehicle (electricity and diesel) (1998); the establishment of a 'Green Return' programme for the efficient return of used products and packaging for recycling; co-ordinated city logistics tested, Hamburg (1994) and Gothenburg (1996); 'Green alliances' with customers.

▷ A clear strategic rationale that environmental performance leads to increased shareholder value and 'option value' (or licence to operate in the future)

▷ A positioning to move toward sustainable logistics

▷ Extremely specific operational implementation objectives for group environmental work, complete with targets, measures and monitoring

▷ The environment viewed as key element of brand

▷ Publishing the transport sector's first environmental performance report (1995) and first environmental and social report (ASG's *Values Report*, 1998)

Box 1: **Key elements of** ASG**'s environmental work**

The strategic rationale for ASG's environmental platform

ASG managers have a clear strategic rationale for aggressively tackling the company's environmental impact. It starts with the customer. ASG customers are increasingly concerned about environmental performance. In fact, ASG data from an annual survey of customers and employees indicates that the percentage of customers in Sweden who regard environmental issues as important when choosing a transport company has risen from roughly 25% in 1994 to almost 50% in 1998. In Europe in particular, the requirement for lessening the environmental impact of products is rippling through supply chains. As a company becomes concerned about its environmental profile in the marketplace, and with this the impact of its products and services from a life-cycle perspective, it will begin to examine the negative impact contributed by its suppliers, including transport. With customers such as Dow Europe, Eastman Kodak and Baxter selecting their transport suppliers based in part on environmental performance, sustainability quickly became a strategic and competitive issue for ASG. The company summarised this trend by saying that the customer value equation for what customers want to pay for has shifted from quality:cost to quality+environment:cost, with the implication that ASG must be able to differentiate its services on the basis of all three factors.

Supplementing this current market demand is an expectation that environmental considerations will drive significant changes in transport and logistics processes and technologies in the future. ASG managers projected that public environmental awareness, and therefore demand for superior environmental performance, will 'explode'. They reason that acting now will give ASG more degrees of freedom, and that waiting would mean higher costs for transition. Additionally, scenario planning, led by ASG's Scientific Board, projecting the future of transport in 2015, predicted the more efficient use of each means of transport, greater flexibility between means of transport, and the introduction of renewable fuels, primarily in urban distribution.

Besides the current and projected market demand, ASG's Scientific Board determined that 'Being ahead of the competition and the market means that surprises from legislation and market demands that threaten the company's survival can be avoided' (*1997 Environmental Performance Report*). Additionally, the board identified that there is profit potential in being ahead of competitors. They agreed that the greatest environmental gains will come from better logistics, especially as technical development stimulates the combination of transport and information technology. Thus, rather than simply complying with legislative requirements, the objectives of ASG's environmental improvement efforts have been to genuinely reduce the burden on the environment, and to improve the company's profitability. It is expected that, although environment is a relatively free resource today, it will be subject to high costs in the near future.

According to Environmental Manager, Magnus Swahn, the strategic rationale of ASG's environmental efforts has broadened from these market, customer and competitive positioning drivers to also include:

1. Increasing shareholder value—from eco-efficiencies, cost reductions, environmental savings, new environmental products, new product differentiation and reduced risks (e.g. dangerous goods accidents), thus reducing capital costs

2. Increasing what ASG calls 'option value', or the licence to operate in the future. Here, the company is considering the social and ethical value side—its brand image, and the values in the company that are preferred by customers.

Jörgen Ekberg, ASG President and CEO, states in the company's 1998 *Values Report*:

> In 1998 ASG began work formulating the Group's future brand name strategy. Ethics and morals have been included as an important part of this work . . . Our ambition is that ASG shall generate shareholder value, assume social responsibility, and show consideration for the environment.

Swahn further added that

> . . . the last five years have been about trying to increase shareholder value, but in the future, competition will increase, and the way to compete will be more and more through brand—thus we have to differentiate

our products and services. In the future, such questions as: What is ASG? What is our core mission? What values do we represent? will increase in importance. Sustainability will come to mean much more now than in the last five years.

ASG participates in an annual assessment of the image of Swedish transport companies, and is targeting improvements focused on the four image factors evaluated: (1) brand name; (2) customer service; (3) human capital; and (4) consideration for the environment. Close attention is paid to ASG performance compared to industry average: in 1998 ASG outperformed the industry average in brand, customer service and consideration for the environment, but lagged in its perception that human capital was a strength—although this ranking has improved over the last four years. However, as might be expected, ASG, and the transport industry generally, is perceived as having a negative impact on the environment. ASG has attempted to address such perceptions by focusing initiatives on improving environmental performance: the development of environmental management systems; better risk management and safety measures; tests of alternative fuel technologies; and monitoring the impacts of new distribution patterns of on-line shopping and home distribution.

Short- and long-term vision: resource efficiency to sustainable logistics

ASG's overall environmental strategy is called 'Resource-Based Management' (RBM), and is intended to promote the integration of both priced and free production resources and values. The aim in the first five-to-ten years is 'greater efficiency in use of resources and thereby greater profitability with reduced environmental impact' (*Environmental Performance Report* 1997). The longer-term aim is to switch to renewable resources and the means of production to achieve sustainable logistics.

Vision to reality

At an operational level, ASG has a sophisticated suite of environmental policies and programmes that support the integration of environmental management into their core business strategy. Examples include: an internal environmental management system (since 1994) and, more recently, ISO 14001 certification in several ASG companies; training programmes for employees and hauliers; sustainable transportation technology development (alternative fuels, electric vehicles, combined transport, emissions treatment, urban logistical systems); environmental ratings systems for hauliers; and environmental profiles of different transportation and fuel options. Since ASG does not own its own vehicles, working to educate and enthuse contractors has been critical.

An important starting place for ASG was guiding an understanding of the process by which it develops transport and logistics services, and identifying the environmental impacts associated with each process step. Managers identified ASG's significant environmental aspects, then detailed the environmental impact and environmental effect of each aspect. They then developed action plans, complete with indicators, to address each key environmental aspect. This analysis is summarised Box 2.

ASG developed explicit environmental objectives and targets in 1995, and by 1998 had met a large number of them. Progress toward these targets has been visually summarised in a chart in ASG's *Environmental Performance Reports* (see Box 3).

Another noteworthy practice in ASG was put in place to monitor and communicate its development in the area of environment. A select group of key performance indicators monitors:

▷ Net sales per tonnes of fossil CO_2

▷ Operating results in SEK per tonne of fossil CO_2

▷ Known environmental liabilities

▷ Number of environmental disputes in progress

▷ Number of environment-related incidents

▷ Fossil CO_2 per tonne-km[1]

▷ Nitrogen oxides and sulphur dioxides per tonne-km

▷ Non-methane hydrocarbons per tonne-km

▷ Percentage of customers who regard ASG as industry leader in the area of environment

▷ Percentage of staff who regard ASG as industry leader in the area of environment

▷ Number of incoming environmental complaints (*Environmental Performance Report* 1997)

In 1994, in conjunction with their 'Forward Logistics'—the planning and co-ordination of the flow of materials from the supplier of raw materials to the end-

1   ASG measures transport energy consumption and emissions in relation to the number of tonnes of energy consumed/emitted multiplied by the number of kilometres travelled.

ENVIRONMENTAL ASPECT	ENVIRONMENTAL IMPACT	ENVIRONMENTAL EFFECT	ACTION	INDICATORS
Accident with hazardous goods	Foreign substances are spread in nature.	Serious local impact on health	ASG is striving to reduce risk exposure.	Number of incidents
Transport subcontractors ▷ hauliers	Fossil fuel is mainly used, which generates carbon dioxide (CO_2). This increases carbon dioxide levels in the atmosphere.	Carbon dioxide in the atmosphere contributes to the greenhouse effect, i.e. higher temperatures on earth, resulting in climate change.	Energy needs and emissions of carbon dioxide can be reduced through more efficient logistics and means of transport that use renewable fuels.	Fossil CO_2
	Combustion of oil forms nitrogen oxides (NO_x) and sulphur dioxide (SO_x), which acidifies the ground. Nitrogen oxides also contribute to over-fertilisation.	Acidification damages plants and leaches out metals from the ground that end up in lakes and watercourses. Over-fertilisation means that lakes and watercourses become choked.	The sulphur content of the fuel determines the quantity of sulphur dioxide. Reducing sulphur is a question of cost and availability. Purification of nitrogen oxides requires new technology.	$SO_x + NO_x$
▷ shipping companies ▷ airlines ▷ railway companies	Lower atmosphere ozone is formed through the exhaust gases nitrogen oxides (NO_x) and hydrocarbons (HC) reacting to ultraviolet radiation from the sun.	Lower atmosphere ozone damages flora and fauna.	Particle filters and catalytic conversion of exhaust gases can reduce emissions of hydrocarbons.	HC (excluding methane)
	ASG uses land areas, seas and the air for its operations.	Noise and congestion are problems that lead to negative effects on health and reduced quality of life.	ASG's business concept is joint utilisation of transport resources, which reduces the number of vehicles.	No. of complaints regarding noise and congestion
Business travel	See subcontractors for transport services.	See subcontractors for transport services.	See subcontractors for transport services.	Being investigated
Energy use at permanent sites	Use of fossil energy, hydro power and nuclear power	Emissions to air, development of rivers, nuclear waste	Improving energy efficiency	Fossil CO_2
Involuntary discharge of refrigerants	The ozone layer is damaged by freons, which in ASG's operations are used in small heat exchangers	Depletion of the ozone layer leads to increased UV radiation, which damages flora and fauna	Changeover to other alternatives is taking place.	Phasing out in accordance with the law
Waste	ASG generates office waste, truck batteries, used transport packaging and worn-out tyres. Tyres contain hydrocarbons and heavy metals.	Local impact on health and growing waste dumps	ASG is striving for reduced resource consumption, recycling, and replacement of tyres with toxic hydrocarbons.	Recycling systems

Box 2: **ASG's significant environmental aspects**

Source: ASG *Values Report* 1998

ENVIRONMENTAL OBJECTIVES

ASG has achieved most of its environmental objectives during the year. The challenge that remains is to obtain uniform environmental work throughout the group.

Objective	Completion target	Outcome 1998 (0 – 100%)	Comments
Environmental and safety management			
An environmental project per business area	1997		The project shall support the entire group
Develop and introduce environmental key data	1997		For more information, see ASG's website
Training of all staff	1997		Conducted using new video-based material
Appoint safety advisor	1998		Formally established at start of 1999
Environmental management system in Nordic companies	1999		Not a requirement under ISO 14001
Develop risk management	1999		Conducted by ASG's Risk Manager
Environmental management system in all ASG companies	2000		Implementation plan to be presented in 1999
Environmental standards for all suppliers	2000		Transport suppliers and other suppliers
Environmental index for all hauliers	2000		Gradually being introduced in the group
Training of all drivers	2000		Training material is being produced in the industry.
Resource efficiency			
Full reporting of environmental data	1997		The percentage of sites reporting is increasing.
Measure energy and emissions for transport	1997		Taking place within the framework of industry co-operation
Introduce electricity-saving programme	1997		Initial investigation conducted.
Establish ASG's primary energy needs	1998		
Recycling of paper, cardboard, plastics, wood, electronics, strip lights and toner cassettes	1999		Specifies percentage of recycling system in operation
Logistics and technology			
Pilot tests of ethanol	1997		Tested since 1995, discontinued in 1999
Pilot tests of methane	1997		Results reported on ASG's website
Establish strategy for refrigerants	1997		Included in the environmental management system
Pilot tests of rapeseed methylesters	1998		Results reported on ASG's website
Tests of hybrid operation (electricity/diesel)	1999		Successful tests
Develop environmentally adapted long-distance lorry	1999		Includes exhaust gas purification, fuel gauge, etc.
Develop environmentally adapted distribution lorry	1999		Includes fuel and logistics
Market development			
An environmental alliance per business area operations	1997		Aimed at integrating the environmental work into business
Develop supporting sales materials	1997		Taking place in 1999
Develop supporting software	1997		Based on the Internet

■ *Outcome in 1997*
▨ *Outcome in 1998*

Box 3: ASG's environmental objectives and monitoring

Source: ASG *Values Report* 1998

user—ASG initiated a 'Green Return' service (see the advertisement reproduced on page 164) for customers and customers' customers, hauling used product, packaging and pallets for re-use or recycling. The company worked with contractors to optimise the efficiency of this reverse logistics business opportunity. One element of this involved compressing material for transport and selecting goods that could be loaded together, since ASG didn't want the image of a waste-hauling company. Certainly, ASG's customers were concerned with growing regulatory pressures on packaging waste, but for ASG this became a business opportunity.

Examples of other initiatives led by ASG include:

▷ The pick-up and delivery of small packages in a Mercedes-Benz vehicle with an electric-diesel hybrid engine

▷ Special handling for warehousing, repackaging and recycling Baxter's medical equipment and products

▷ Co-ordinating 'Just-in-Time' deliveries for Saab automobile production lines—within a 15-minute window of scheduled deliveries in a system of loops in Germany, Netherlands, Poland, Belgium and Switzerland, characterised as '5–1–1–1': five departures per week, one fixed loading time, one fixed unloading time, and one fixed price (*FLOW* magazine, 1998)

▷ Reducing inventory, and therefore waste (typically not calculated as an environmental cost issue)

▷ Reducing emissions (and simultaneously reducing costs) by increasing capacity utilisation in and out of facilities, flexibility in modes of transport, replacement of older transport vehicles, improving route planning, employing information technology, and educating drivers

▷ Managing the outsourced warehousing operation for Ford Europe, eliminating the need for investment in new warehouses on Ford's part (ASG was able to manage transportation that had involved multiple warehouses in each Scandinavian country with a single central warehouse for the region)

▷ Donating US$5 to the World Wide Fund for Nature (WWF)'s environmental efforts for every customer survey filled out

▷ Integrated third-party logistics, managing for customer companies' warehouse and transport, but also value-added services such as inventory management, order scheduling and fulfilment, repackaging, relabelling, and even product assembly and installation—reducing costs, but also reducing environmental impact from waste of transportation, excess inventory and packaging

Now, in 1999, ASG is at the point of moving from demonstration projects to consolidation within strategic business operations. Its proactive work with stakeholders (employees, customers, suppliers, shareholders, general public) has intensified the link between environmental performance and the ASG brand—for example:

▷ Marketing the launching of a new product or service

▷ Annual seminars for customers, government authorities and suppliers centred around themes such as ISO 14001, alternative fuels and key performance indicators

▷ Information available to hauliers via the Internet on how to become more sustainable

▷ Seminars for stakeholders with invited speakers on topics such as new engines, new fuels, new tyres, E-commerce and the environment, home delivery, and new Swedish environmental legislation

There is a clear understanding and acknowledgement that ASG, and transport in general, is not environmentally friendly—but ASG is trying to lower environmental impacts and contribute to the dialogue and technology development that will lead to sustainable logistics. Customers have reacted positively to the fact that ASG has an action plan, is making progress in this field, and is trying to minimise the environmental impact of transportation. In 1998, ASG market surveys found that 47% of transport customers rated ASG as number one transport firm in Sweden on environmental concerns.[2] The company has set a target of reaching 51% in order to surpass its only major competitor in Sweden's duopoly, Schenker-BTL. Currently, customers rank environmental considerations number ten, behind such aspects as precision/reliability and cost—but this is the parameter that is rising most quickly in importance, with almost 50% of customers in 1998 reporting that they consider environment when choosing suppliers.[3] In the transport industry, ASG data indicates that this trend is still localised in northern European countries; it is mostly found in Sweden, Finland and Germany (but not yet in Norway, the UK and Denmark).

Customers are very aware of price, so ASG aims for solutions and technologies that decrease costs and increase revenues, as well as reduce environmental impact (such as increasing loads, educating drivers, and developing smart logistics systems).

Reducing accidents with dangerous goods and increasing safety levels for employees are visible examples of the 'option value' part of the ASG equation.

2 Independent study by Image Survey International, reported in ASG's 1998 *Values Report*.
3 *Ibid.*

Managers are aware of how vulnerable profitability and shareholder value are to negative publicity from transport accidents with negative environmental or social consequences.

The provision of third-party logistics services has become the fastest-growing business in the group. Swahn reported that

> . . . the customer buys not only what we deliver today, but what we will deliver in the future . . . they are buying *systems* from suppliers, expecting suppliers like ASG to have development as well. For example, Baxter told us they liked ASG but wanted increased environmental performance, and that ASG would need to meet 65% of Baxter's state-of-the-art internal standards. ASG aimed at 80%, made it, then aimed at 100%, and met that, becoming the first third-party supplier to reach this.

The goal of ASG's seminars is to solidify its leadership position in environment and logistics. Its experience is that customers are becoming increasingly aware, requesting more and more details. To this end, ASG has created a new service: customers now have their own page on ASG's website, highlighting their own environmental profile, so that companies can see the volume of goods ASG has transported for them and the associated environmental impact. ASG has created a 'customer web' containing customers' own statistics, costs, tracking and tracing, simulation of other transportation options, and environmental impact. ASG services now include consulting with customers on ways of improving efficiency and reducing environmental impact. Swahn commented: 'We have to take part in this dematerialisation trend. We suggest to customers how to do it: for example, changing packaging to facilitate loading, or redesigning products to be transport-smart.'

In addition to these initiatives to reduce the impact of current patterns of distribution, ASG is weighing the implications of emerging distribution patterns. For example, it is attempting to envision distribution systems in the megacities of the future and incorporate these scenarios into their business strategies. The company is seriously examining the implications of the Internet for its business, and for the environment. Managers recognise that, while shipping one book may be good for ASG business, it is not good for the environment. It is pushing itself to be more creative in the generation of alternatives.

The process of change

When asked how change really happens at ASG, managers reported that strategy development unfolds in the following way: a new idea is generated, a pilot project is undertaken, then there is internal political negotiation for adoption. This last stage requires first of all that the champion and project be credible; second, that the champion knows his or her supporters and opponents; and, third, that the champion gets the informal leaders on-side (sometimes top-down, sometimes bottom-up). Managers emphasised the importance of creating and widely publicising early successes.

Despite impressive progress in many areas, ASG managers critique themselves and the organisation, saying that they are not creative enough, are too operationally stressed, are not linked to databases, are not systematically looking at outside world trends, and don't have a culture where people can think freely and fail. The company is trying to change this. Their vision of the Environment Department in the future is to develop more new concepts and to embed the practices into operations. There have already been structural changes. Because they determined that initiatives were still too much driven by the corporate environment manager, the Environment Department appointed an environment manager in each business, and an environmental co-ordinator at each site. At the group level there is a corporate environmental manager and assistant environmental manager as one of the five business-support areas assisting the president. This structure is displayed graphically in Figure 1.

ASG's education sessions, seminars and intranet are aimed at increasing commitment to and competence in environmental work. Internal awards stimulate involvement and reinforce success. ASG's intranet is also used for operational improvement.

Advancing the corporate mission

Over the last decade, ASG has been diligently building the foundation for sustainability as a core competence contributing to increased competitive advantage, shareholder value and customer value. It has developed new managerial capabilities and intellectual capital—for example:

▷ Forming alliances with customers on improvement projects to address the future business context

▷ Managing logistics for reduced environmental impact

▷ Integrating environmental considerations into lean operations management internally and with customers and suppliers

▷ Assisting customers in packaging and product design

▷ Offering new on-line services to support customers in their transport and logistics decisions

▷ Co-ordinating internal operations, customers, contractors and suppliers in life-cycle analysis

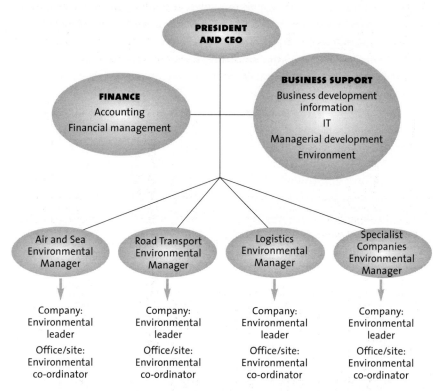

ASG's environmental organisation is integrated into the line organisation. Each company has an environmental leader, and line managers are responsible for ensuring that the environmental work is implemented.

Figure 1: **Structure of ASG's management for the environment**

Source: ASG *Values Report* 1998

▷ Providing increased value-added to customers

▷ Developing and applying new technologies for increased efficiencies

▷ Being ahead of and anticipating legislative processes for more stringent environmental requirements

▷ Developing a forward-thinking brand strategy

▷ Forming alliances to analyse and help transform city distribution, corporate culture and strategy, and global industrial practices. ASG is looking at the big picture of traffic and transportation.

ASG's stated mission is 'to develop, market, and produce efficient transport and logistics services that create competitive advantage for customers' (*Environmental Performance Report* 1997). There is little doubt that its proactive environmental measures are contributing to the accomplishment of this mission, and will increasingly do so in the future.

References

http://www.asg.se

ASG Environmental Report 1994 (Stockholm: ASG AB Corporate Environment, 1995).

ASG Annual Report 1995 (Stockholm: ASG AB Corporate Communications, 1996).

ASG Environmental Report 1995: The Environment in Facts and Figures (Stockholm: ASG AB Corporate Communications, 1996).

ASG Environmental Performance Report 1996: The Environment in Facts and Figures (Stockholm: ASG AB Group Staff Environment, 1997).

ASG Environmental Performance Report 1997 (Stockholm: ASG AB Group Staff Environment, 1998).

ASG Values Report 1998 (Stockholm: ASG AB Group Staff Environment, 1999).

Organisational contacts

Magnus Swahn, Environmental Manager
Johan Saarm, Controller

Varje år skrotas 60 000 ton elektronikutrustning i Sverige

Det handlar om mer än 300 000 TV-apparater, över 100 000 datorer och otaliga radio- och stereoapparater, videor, faxar, kopiatorer, telefoner med mera. Praktiskt taget allt hamnar i naturen, på våra soptippar. Det är ett enormt resursslöseri och ett av våra största miljöhot.

I Bräkne-Hoby i Blekinge har företaget Technoworld tagit sig an det här snabbt växande problemet. I samma lokaler där Nokia tidigare tillverkade datorer demonteras nu datorer och andra elektronikprodukter som ska återvinnas. Man har så att säga vänt på tillverkningsbandet, och av exempelvis en dator återvinns i dag så mycket som 97 procent. Alla giftiga ämnen (bly, kvicksilver, strontium, PCB m m) tas tillvara på ett betryggande sätt.

Det är en stor miljöinsats, som i sin tur kräver största möjliga miljöhänsyn i transporterna.

FRÅN HELA LANDET

ASG hämtar in uttjänt elektronik från Technoworlds kunder över praktiskt taget hela Sverige. Mellan 50 och 100 ton per månad fördelar sig ungefär lika mellan kontorselektronik och hemelektronik (från kommunernas hushållsavfall).

ASG ställer ut så kallade transportburar på 1,5 alternativt 3,0 kubikmeter, och kunderna fyller dem själva. På signal från från Technoworld hämtar vi och kör de fyllda burarna till Bräkne-Hoby. I överenskommelsen ingår att transporterna ska ske när det uppstår ledig transportkapacitet i en ordinarie transport. Inga onödiga körningar således med tomma bilar i någon riktning. Det är vad vi kallar Grön Avgång.

Det innebär att enstaka burar med gods kan bli stående på en ASG-terminal i väntan på lämpligt frakttillfälle. Det är helt i sin ordning för detta gods.

"ASG STÄLLER VERKLIGEN UPP FÖR MILJÖN"

Anders Pålsson, Technoworld:
"Idag lägger vi en stor del av våra transporter hos ASG. Styrkan med ASG är deras lastbärarsystem med transportburar som finns ute i hela organisationen, plus deras gröna avgångar. Deras inställning vittnar om hög servicegrad och känsla för miljön."

> *RETUR FÖR MILJÖN*
>
> *Retur för miljön står för den specialistkompetens ASG skapat inom området återvinning. Den grundar sig på 60 års erfarenheter av transport- och logistiklösningar. Retur för miljön bygger på en helhetssyn av de speciella krav som återvinning ställer. Det är transport- och logistiklösningar som förenar kostnadseffektivitet med hänsyn till miljön.*

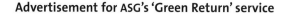

Advertisement for ASG's 'Green Return' service

SC JOHNSON

Eco-efficiency and beyond

1. *The lie of the land*

a. *Corporate overview*

SC Johnson was founded in 1886, originally as a manufacturer of parquet floors, but soon thereafter as a supplier of wax products for hardwood floor care. It is now one of world's leading manufacturers and marketers of household products for floor, furniture and air care, as well as home storage, personal care and insect control. SC Johnson produces dozens of major well-known brand names including Pledge®, Windex®, Drano®, Vanish®, Fantastik®, Edge®, Ziploc®, Saran Wrap®, Glade®, Scrubbing Bubbles®, Raid®, and OFF!®

In addition to the consumer products enterprise, the Johnson family of companies also includes Johnson Professional, with products and services for commercial, industrial and institutional building maintenance and sanitation, and SC Johnson Polymers, selling polymer intermediates to the inks and graphic arts, architectural and industrial coatings, and adhesives industries. At one time, all Johnson companies were part of a single corporate entity, but now operate as distinct, separate legal business entities.

SC Johnson, the consumer products company, is privately held, with sales estimated to be in excess of US$4 billion, up by about 100% since 1992. It has just paid for two one-billion dollar investments in cash. It would rank among the *Fortune* 150, were it a listed company and it employs 9,500 people worldwide, 3,500 of those in the US (2,500 in Wisconsin). It has business operations in 60 countries and its products are sold in nearly 100.

b. *Preview*

Perhaps more than anywhere else on our journey of trying to understand these leading practitioners in sustainable development, we heard a simple phrase repeated over and over at SC Johnson: 'Because it's the right thing to do.'

It wasn't a corporate script; everyone thought individually and carefully about their answers, frequently arrived at after extended contemplative pauses. Nonetheless, the answers to a range of diverse questions—Why did you pursue this path? Why did you do this when it was unpopular, or more costly, or not required, or too much of a burden to take on, or too hard?—were often identical: 'Well, because . . . it was/is the right thing to do.'

SC Johnson takes pride in its accomplishments to date, but shows genuine concern about the amount of work still to be done. Ask anyone in SC Johnson and they will readily acknowledge that they are not now sustainable, that they do not have a comprehensive sustainability programme, that it is very possible they may be many years away from sustainability being a core driving force in their major business strategies. However, the company has managed to achieve many things—bottom-line success, comprehensive implementation, integration with business strategies—with its eco-efficiency work, with its community responsibility efforts, with its commitment to employees, and with its new product development processes.

Elements of enlightened corporate practice that have been leading the way in corporate America for a century are now being pieced together in a grand struggle to create a sustainability effort. These include the following:

▷ An extraordinary commitment to eco-efficiency resulting in enormous cost savings and dramatic environmental impact reduction

▷ Pioneering human resources management practices that have inspired employee loyalty

▷ The company supports the 'Sustainable Racine' initiative (their main local community in Wisconsin)

▷ It donates five times the national average in corporate philanthropy.

▷ Chairman Sam Johnson was a founding member and still serves on the President's Council for Sustainable Development.

Such practices are the bedrock on which sustainability will be built and, at SC Johnson, in the midst of uncertainty and concern, there is a realistic hope that the organisation has the necessary tools to begin.

2. *Trailblazing*

a. *The start of the SC Johnson journey*

The journey rightfully begins over 100 years ago. Founded in 1886 and growing into the new century, SC Johnson was a family business grounded in the values of high product quality, careful attunement to customer needs, genuine care for employees, and a vigorous commitment to community responsibility. These principles have become the guiding light for five generations of family leadership and formed the basis for SC Johnson's growth.

The principles were initially formalised in 1927 by H.F. Johnson Jr, the son of the founder in a speech to employees. The most famous quotation from that speech still resonates throughout the company today:

> The goodwill of the people is the only enduring thing in any business. It
> is the sole substance. The rest is shadow.

The company has lived with the conviction that goodwill—from employees, customers, the general public, local neighbours and host communities, and the international community—can only be earned through integrity.

Throughout the Depression, for example, H.F. Jr, the third family leader of the company, guided the enterprise without laying off a single employee. In 1935, H.F. Jr flew into the Brazilian interior to see first-hand the ecological impact of harvesting the Carnauba palm leaves used in the company's wax products. His mission—to personally ensure that the impact was environmentally benign, that it was a renewable resource, and that it provided fair trade for local people—has served as a role model for 'doing the right thing' that continues to pervade the company to this day.

Throughout the first half of the century, the company made a strong commitment to its employees, instituting vacations with pay in 1900, profit-sharing in 1917 (long before such a notion was even conceivable by most corporations), group life insurance in 1917, and a pension programme and health insurance scheme during the 1930s. It created perhaps North America's first corporate environmental audit in the mid-1930s. It commissioned Frank Lloyd Wright to design their corporate headquarters, to create an exciting, beautiful work environment. (The headquarters, completed in 1939, is currently still the centrepiece of SC Johnson Administration, has been designated a National Historic Landmark by the US government, and is toured annually by 10,000 visitors.)

In 1935, SC Johnson initiated a corporate policy of donating 5% of pre-tax profits, and has sustained that level or higher for 50 years (contributions in the 1990s alone will far exceed US$100 million). The company expanded to international locations very early in the century, ahead of most US corporations, but has always remained committed to local management and local community development.

In the early 1950s, it installed catalytic converters at its major manufacturing operation to reduce the distressing air emissions from that facility. It also began the process of moving to water-based aerosol formulations for its consumer products, achieving enormous environmental benefits. By the 1960s, it extended this development, creating water-based polymers for printing, paints and coatings.

Of course, none of these initiatives was dictated by a clear-sighted strategic commitment to sustainable development. The term—even the concept—didn't exist at this time! Rather, SC Johnson was guided by a set of principles and a sense of character embodied by the family members and embraced by the company's employees. They were out to build and maintain a great company, a moral company, predicated on the foundation that they had to deeply understand customers, continuously innovate to serve them, commit to true collaboration with their employees and the communities in which they operated, and ensure protection of the environment for the generations to come.

b. *Principles in action*

At the dawning of the modern environmental age, then, SC Johnson already had some of the spirit of sustainable development and corporate social responsibility in operation. The question would soon arise, however, as to how it would respond to the ever more explicit, more direct pressure that would be exerted on businesses as global environmental degradation worsened, as the scale of the problem became evident, and as the requirement for more radical restructuring became clear.

The decision of current Chairman Sam Johnson in 1975 highlighted how the company would respond. On his own initiative, with no regulatory obligation, he unilaterally and voluntarily removed all CFC propellants from all SC Johnson aerosol products worldwide, based on the emerging understanding that CFCs were depleting the ozone layer. Scientific debate on ozone depletion was still continuing, but Sam Johnson and the company's leaders arrived at the decision by asking themselves, 'What is the right thing to do?' So, despite significant challenges to the manufacturing processes, despite pressure to innovate, despite uncertainties about whether they could still provide full customer satisfaction, the decision was made. Having grown up with the SC Johnson principles, virtually all employees felt committed to the decision and stood proud of the 'rightness' of the choice. Three years later, the US banned all CFC propellants, based in large part on SC Johnson's leadership.

With its environmental commitment becoming ever more explicit, SC Johnson restated and clarified its core principles in 1976, codifying them into a statement called, 'This We Believe' (see Box 1). None of the principles is particularly revolutionary, but two things are unique: the focus on serving people, and the integrity with which SC Johnson puts the beliefs into action.

'THIS WE BELIEVE'

'This We Believe' states our beliefs in relation to the five groups of people to whom we are responsible and whose trust we have to earn.

Employees
We believe that the fundamental vitality and strength of our worldwide company lies in our people.

Consumers and end-users
We believe in earning the enduring goodwill of consumers and users of our products and services.

General public
We believe in being a responsible leader within the free-market economy.

Neighbours and hosts
We believe in contributing to the well-being of the countries and communities where we conduct business.

World community
We believe in improving international understanding.

These beliefs are real and we will strive to live up to them. Our commitment to them is evident in our actions to date.

The sincerity of our beliefs encourages us to act with integrity at all times, to respect the dignity of each person as an individual human being, to assume moral and social responsibilities early as a matter of course, to make an extra effort to use our skills and resources where they are most needed, and to strive for excellence in everything we do.

Our way of safeguarding these beliefs is to remain a privately held company. Our way of reinforcing them is to make profits through growth and development, profits which allow us to do more for all the people on whom we depend.

***Box 1:* 'This We Believe'**

(SC Johnson's belief statement, first codified in 1976, based on speeches given by H.F. Johnson Jr in 1927. Revised to this version in 1987.)

The full set of principles speaks solely to its responsibility to five groups of people: employees, customers, the general public, 'neighbours and hosts', and the world community. It believes that the fundamental vitality of the company lies with its employees, whom it seeks to protect, respect and collaborate with. It seeks 'the enduring goodwill' of customers. It commits to being a 'responsible leader' in the economy, contributing to the wellbeing of its host communities, improving international understandings.

And profits? 'Profits allow us to do more for all the people on whom we depend.'

3. The route: leadership, planning and implementation

a. Leading with eco-efficiency

And thus began the modern era of environmental responsibility at SC Johnson. Unquestionably, eco-efficiency has been the main focus of implementation thus far.

Beginning in the 1980s, SC Johnson began to concentrate on improving the environmental performance of its manufacturing operations. Again, it was not a particularly explicit or integrated strategy designed to carefully position itself in customers' minds or achieve new brand equity. Instead, the subtle forces were rising concern about environmental problems, combined with increasing regulation and consumer concern. And it was clear that there were business benefits to be won from reducing waste, improving efficiency and minimising liabilities. So, over a five-year period, SC Johnson undertook a series of manufacturing improvements, waste reduction projects and manufacturing engineering initiatives that resulted in significant breakthroughs.

The main SC Johnson manufacturing plant in Europe, for example, achieved zero waste-water discharge from its manufacturing operations by developing a unique filtering and recycling system inside the plant. The major US operation, 'Waxdale' in Racine, WI, achieved a 75% reduction in waste-water discharges using a similar system. The European plant in Surrey, UK, invented a technology to capture some of the waste solvent gases and use them to create steam power for the plant. The Waxdale plant began to use methane gas from a local landfill, eventually producing 33% of its steam power from it. SC Johnson invented new methods of waste-water treatment—the Japanese manufacturing facility growing local fish species in their waste-water ponds. The company created new ways of reducing volatile organic compound (VOC) emissions, with Waxdale eliminating 99% of VOC releases in the summers and more than 60% annually. Overall, improvement project by improvement project, it dramatically reduced its solid waste—by 60% in the US and Australia, and by 80% in the UK. Manufacturing benefits were clear to the company. At the same time, SC Johnson appointed one of its key business leaders, Jane Hutterly, to the position of Vice-President for Environment. Hutterly was a respected manager who had come up through marketing, probably the most respected 'track' in the company. The appointment of someone of her stature made tre commitment to environment even clearer to all employees.

Subsequently, eco-efficiency began to take on a greater role on the product side. Hutterly started what she and others describe as the Chinese water torture method of education and communication. Along with other members of her small group, she relentlessly talked about the benefits of greater eco-efficiency throughout SC Johnson.

The team worked their way onto the agenda of every SC Johnson meeting and worldwide conference they could. They created education programmes, eco-efficiency workshops and communication initiatives. Hutterly even handed out crisp new dollar bills at the ten-day training programme at the SC Johnson Management Institute—highlighting for 'fast-track' managers in the company the money to be made from driving eco-efficiency.

She talked 'environment' for those who resonated to that. She talked 'efficiency' more than 'eco' for those who were primarily focused on business pressures. They worked on consensus-building at the senior management level and throughout middle management ranks. They avoided pushing a strong *sustainability* agenda, instead keeping the focus on eco-efficiency and its more immediate and more tangible business benefits. The group convinced executives to speak throughout the company about the eco-efficiency aspects of each of their new products. They made sure that results—business results more than environmental results—were publicised. They created employee awards (the 'WOW' awards), given to people and teams who created breakthroughs that were simultaneously gains for the business and gains for the environment. And, perhaps most critically, they created measurable five-year goals and held the company accountable to tracking performance against those goals and to reporting on it publicly.

Today, when you ask anyone in SC Johnson how they came to embrace eco-efficiency so deeply, they look at you almost quizzically, as if they aren't aware that it is resisted in other companies, as if it had never really been a choice, as if there really was no other way. 'How did we accept it so well?' they contemplate. 'Just because it is the right thing to do.' As an afterthought, they add, 'Oh, and by the way, we had a senior leader who championed it in a persistent way for five years, a way that matched our culture of involvement and consensus and respect, of action and accountability.' And then, finally, '. . . and of course, we have had a great deal of business success from it.'

And, indeed, the results have been impressive. After several years of driving manufacturing eco-efficiency improvements in the late 1980s, Hutterly led the company in the establishment of specific and measurable improvement targets against a 1990 baseline level.

By 1995, SC Johnson had reduced the use of virgin packaging by over 26%, exceeding its target of 20%. It had reduced VOC ratios in all formulas by more than 16%, again ahead of its target and on the way to a total of 25% reduction by 2000. And it nearly made its ambitious target of 50% reduction in its factory wastes and emissions (air emissions, water effluents and solid waste), reducing factory emissions by an additional 47% below its already significant reductions from the 1980s.

These accomplishments came about from a series of projects, as well as the integration of several key lessons throughout the company. Lightweighting, for example, became a priority for all packaging. Using recycled content in packaging reduced the amount of virgin packaging. Shrink-wrap was eliminated in some cases, corrugated dividers in others. Multi-packs reduced packaging and improved customer satisfaction. More than 25% of the steel used was recycled. And it continued to drive down the use of VOCs in its formulas, shifting increasingly to water-based formulas. 'WOW' projects identified innovative ways to lightweight, to use more recycled plastic, to eliminate packaging altogether, or to have the package serve as part of the product delivery or value provision. Collapsible plastic refill bottles reduced plastic usage in Canada by 90%, and by 60% in Australia and New Zealand.

The company altered new product development processes to require the integration of packaging design at the ideation stage, thereby tightly linking product development and consumer value with packaging design. They created Design-for-Eco-efficiency workshops, bringing together multi-function teams to make product ingredient and packaging decisions in tandem.

Perhaps more so than percentage reductions, the absolute numbers are striking. More than US$20 million are saved per year company-wide. Glade Plug-In air fresheners alone—through packaging innovations, reformulation, increased concentrate, refillable containers and more—reduced material usage by more than 1.3 million lb per year and saved US$3.5 million per year. More than two million lb of plastic were eliminated each year by lightweighting the caps on Pledge cans.

The Professional Division created the 'Enviro-Box', an ultra-lightweight box that uses 92% less plastic than traditional five-gallon pails previously used to transport floor-care products to institutional customers, eliminating more than three million lb of plastic each year. In Europe, lightweighting HDPE bottles reduced HDPE (one of the most commonly used plastics for liquid-holding bottles) use by nearly a million lb per year. Lightweighting the packaging on Lemon Pledge and Shout saves a million lb of material a year, and nearly a half million dollars. Reformulating carpet cleaner into concentrate and lightweighting the packaging reduced material usage 50% and increased gross profit margin by 10%.

Company-wide, the waste reduction success has meant more than 420 million lb of waste from products and processes have been eliminated over the past five years. The company has blacklisted (totally eliminated the use of) more than a dozen chemicals which were previously mainstays in their formulations.

Since 1995, SC Johnson has set new five-year targets, to bring it to 2000. It has already achieved, or is on track to achieve, all of these—despite 50%–70% production volume increases in many businesses, bringing a large new polymer plant on-line in Europe, and making two major acquisitions.

In addition to spearheading the case for eco-efficiency, SC Johnson has also created several new structures which have moved the eco-efficiency orientation more deeply into product development and brand identity. The Global Sourcing Council brings together marketing, R&D, manufacturing and procurement to work with vendors to extend eco-efficiencies at the design stages up the value chain. The SC Johnson Worldwide Business Council for the Environment is the group of senior managers convened to develop leadership commitment to the five-year environmental goals.

More publicly, the company has helped to found the World Business Council for Sustainable Development (WBCSD), with Chairman Sam Johnson serving as a catalytic member of the group. Further, the Chairman was also one of the original members of the President's Council on Sustainable Development in the US. These highly visible public roles have inspired the whole organisation with pride and with the conviction that their work inside makes a difference.

b. New product development

SC Johnson illustrates the level of improvement that is possible with a steady yet vigorous commitment to eco-efficiency. As it looks back on nearly 15 years of eco-efficiency work, however, the company feels that much of the 'low-hanging fruit' has now been harvested. Therefore, although it is confident that breakthrough thinking will continue to create significant eco-efficiency improvements, it is also beginning to look more broadly beyond eco-efficiency toward achieving a fuller definition of sustainable development.

In this vein, it has begun to rethink the nature of how it provides value, of what its products are, of how best to satisfy customers. Now, for example, instead of investigating how to reduce noxious chemicals in a formula, it is contemplating how to meet the need with no chemicals at all. It has, for instance, developed a flea killer using no insecticide—a plug-in green-light attractant 'house', which fleas enter to find sticky paper.

More fundamentally, managers are beginning to rethink the very nature of how they fulfil customer needs. For example, SC Johnson has recently convened an external advisory panel of researchers and pharmacologists to examine the nature of allergies, and how the company's existing products and formulas could be improved. As the company conducted intensive customer-focused analyses of the nature of allergies (with researchers spending time in people's homes), what became clear was that, rather than chemical products, improvements to the design of vacuum cleaner bags and bedding pillow cases (which attract dust mites) would be more beneficial to sufferers than any chemical reformulations. Such products are not core competences of SC Johnson, but a decision has been made to proceed with product development, even though such products will probably make their current formulations obsolete.

Extending its view of sustainable development, it has joined with a national environmental group to create a comprehensive database of all chemicals in all its product formulas, as well as a wide range of chemicals that could potentially be used. This Knowledge Management System allows SC Johnson chemists to input data on the problems they are trying to solve, to propose specific formulas, and to receive instant feedback about both the chemicals that will best suit the purpose and those that are prohibited. Two years in development, the system also constantly updates all regulatory constraints on chemicals, providing assurance for SC Johnson that it will not produce products that violate any regulations worldwide. In addition, the system also tracks various 'grey list' chemicals, i.e. those on which there have been research findings questioning their environmental profile or which are on the alert lists of any of a wide range of environmental groups or regulatory bodies around the world. SC Johnson chemists are thus in a position to redesign new product formulas that will position them ahead of potential criticism.

This embedding of intellectual capital into organisational capability provides SC Johnson with strategic advantages in terms of time-to-market, brand equity, reduced liability, superior product performance and improved research productivity.

SC Johnson remains uncertain about whether it will be able to make the transition from a leader in eco-efficiency to a legitimate practitioner of sustainability. But it is systems such as this, and new approaches to product development, that will help pave the way.

c. Investing in people, partnerships and communities

Finally, it is impossible to examine SC Johnson's approach to sustainable development without examining its conviction about investing in its employees, in meaningful partnerships, and in the local communities within which it operates.

Virtually all major corporations participate in significant philanthropic endeavours. SC Johnson, however, invests a level of conviction and enthusiasm that is much more than simply money. The ethic of serving local communities runs as deep at SC Johnson as it does in any company in the world. It preaches that the vitality of its businesses depends on the vitality of its surrounding communities. Its commitment is to go beyond arm's-length financial assistance and to provide talent and people as much as or more than money. Sixty per cent of all SC Johnson employees are active community volunteers (twice the national average for large corporations).

At its headquarters, it has joined in a deep partnership with its local community of Racine, WI, to create the 'Sustainable Racine' initiative. A model for the nation,

Several 'lessons learned' stand out in examining what aspects of the SC Johnson experience may be generalisable to other firms:

Deeply embedded in the culture

A genuine commitment to people, planet and products has been a central part of the SC Johnson culture since its inception—and this cultural ethic pervades all levels: senior and middle management, and all employees.

Acting on beliefs

The high standards set in 'This We Believe' and the commitment to measurable goals foster a passion for action, for progress and for accountability.

Never satisfied

The company continually seeks to improve on its accomplishments. Each accomplishment viewed by itself appears to be relatively modest; the relentlessness of continuous improvement leads to dramatic improvements over time.

Specific practices

Each business and key function has considered and developed specific practices to deal with environmental and social responsibility issues, and to institutionalise sustainable development thinking into the decision-making processes.

Basing efforts on customer focus

Virtually all its sustainability-related efforts, although clearly emanating from its values platform, are specifically developed in direct relation to customer needs. SC Johnson's intensity of understanding customer needs, its focus on marketing and developing brand equity, and its methodical integration of customer requirements assure sustainability work that will be rewarded in the marketplace.

Extending influence to larger communities

SC Johnson has extended its efforts beyond the company and beyond customers to local communities, national and international communities, and its entire employee population. It has served as catalyst for social responsibility and thriving community development.

Integrity

Increasingly so in the Internet age, it is hard to deceive the worldwide community. SC Johnson has been leading with integrity for more than a century. It does not take 100 years to build integrity, but long-term success with employees, customers and communities requires it now more than ever.

Box 2: **The highlights of what SC Johnson has done**

'Sustainable Racine' has focused the entire community on creating its vision for the future and then developing the path for getting there. Hundreds of Racine residents, for example, participated in 23 different meetings to craft their vision. Specific goals emerged in ten major areas. Catalysed by SC Johnson people, sustainability is a central theme throughout the vision—sustainability in the fullest sense of the word. SC Johnson has helped the community to understand that traditional solutions and traditional visions will no longer be enough. Now, together with the community, SC Johnson people—leaders of traditional corporate success—are walking down a new path. They are focused on helping enrich the lives of the least privileged and on developing programmes for building community assets.

One major focus is on creating developmental advantages for Racine children through its 'Next Generation Now' initiative (a comprehensive programme designed to assure healthy development for all children aged 0–5). Further, it is evolving its efforts to allow for the development of comprehensive community sustainability indicators.

SC Johnson is now aligning all its local donations to support the Sustainable Racine initiatives and taking a more strategic view of its community partnerships, becoming increasingly committed to taking on the responsibility of leading its communities to clearer understandings of the sustainability imperative. In the end, it is committed to creating community competence, to investment in leadership development, and to the assurance that there is an integrated coherence to its community contributions and development.

Similarly, at locations around the globe, SC Johnson has been focused on building strong local communities: managers are appointed from local communities; philanthropic efforts are directed back to the host communities; and needs are prioritised based on the views of local-community members. Examples of support include: building and funding schools; sponsoring theatre groups that provide touring education; funding conservation programmes; leading habitat restoration; underwriting video productions; designing and leading local industrial ecology projects; building new water systems; and granting local scholarships. There is only one SC Johnson company-wide award, and that is for volunteerism.

Inside the company walls, the spirit of partnership and investment in people extends to all employees. Consistently, SC Johnson is cited by its employees as one of the '100 Best Places to Work' (*Fortune* 1999), 'Most Family Friendly', and '100 Best Companies for Working Mothers' (*Working Mother* 1999). The profit-sharing at the company is legendary, as are the annual profit-sharing meetings, where everyone turns out at Christmastime in Racine to celebrate, to sing, to reward and to share in the profitability of their efforts. Superlative childcare facilities, health and fitness facilities, holiday cottages, intramural programmes and comprehensive benefit packages all leave employees feeling respected, cared for, and included in a larger circle of support. This in turn creates a more truly sustainable social network, a vital (but, at this point in the debate, much overlooked) element of sustainable development.

4. *The journey continues*

The platform of principles on which SC Johnson was founded has grown over the past century. The spirit of respect for people and the planet, for communities and for customers, has pervaded everything about the company since its inception. This principled activism and moral leadership has resulted in an extraordinarily prosperous company, and one that exemplifies the best in caring for its people, its communities and its customers.

Beyond this, the principles have also provided the foundation for driving eco-efficiency as successfully as anywhere in the world. The challenge before SC Johnson now is to evolve its core business practices and major strategic models to more fully embrace a broader concept of sustainable development.

This is the target it has set. Traditional business pressures will not disappear. Some daunting challenges lie ahead: for example, how to deal with profitable yet fundamentally unsustainable product lines. However, if we are to see any North American corporations succeed in making the transition, SC Johnson is very likely to be among them. Sam Johnson summarises the company's view:

> No matter who you are—or what you do—your actions, or lack of action, will either help or hurt the planet . . . Clearly, then, when we set aside the obvious business benefits of being an environmentally responsible company, we are left with the simple human truth that we cannot lead lives of dignity and worth when the natural resources that sustain us are threatened or destroyed. We must act responsibly and we must act now (*100 Years Beyond* and *Environmental Leadership*).

We get the feeling they will indeed be leading the transition. After all, it's the right thing to do.

References

SC Johnson publications

http://www.scjohnson.com

100 Years Beyond (Racine, WI: SC Johnson).

Environmental Leadership (Racine, WI: SC Johnson).

Other

Fortune (1999) '100 Best Companies to Work For', *Fortune* 139.1 (11 January 1999).

Levering, R., and M. Moskowitz (1994) *The 100 Best Companies to Work for in America* (New York: Bantam Doubleday Dell, rev. edn).

Working Mother (1999) '100 Best Companies for Working Mothers', *Working Mother*, October 1999.

Organisational contacts

Ken Alston, Director of Sustainable Product Innovation

Greg Anderegg, Manager, Community Relations Worldwide

Tom Benson, Environmental Actions Manager, North America

F.H. 'Chip' Brewer, Director of Worldwide Government Relations

Armin Clobes, Platform Leader, Indoor Environmental Science

Ed Eeg, Senior Packaging Engineer (Retired)

Lew Falbo, Director, Worldwide Safety, Health and Environment Operations

Cynthia Georgeson, Director, Corporate Pubic Affairs Worldwide

Brenda Gieszler, Department Manager, Packaging Development

Patrick Guiney, PhD, Senior Section Manager, Product Safety

Reva Holmes, Vice-President, Secretary and Trustee of SC Johnson Wax Fund (Retired)

Jane Hutterly, Senior Vice-President, Worldwide Corporate Affairs

Robert Israel, PhD, Director, Regulatory Affairs and Product Safety, SC Johnson Professional

Darcy Massey, Senior Vice-President, Research, Development and Engineering

David Sanders, President and Chief Operating Officer, SC Johnson Polymer, Worldwide

Craig Shiesley, Senior Brand Manager, Home Cleaning

Judy Zaunbrecher, Director, Global Home Cleaning, Research, Development and Engineering

DAIMLERCHRYSLER

Redefining cost

Introduction

For DaimlerChrysler Corporation,[1] life-cycle management (LCM) is a business tool that helps the company identify and incorporate environmental, health, occupational safety and recycling (EHS&R) aspects with traditional business decisions using cost as a unit of measurement. This exposes the indirect or hidden costs and facilitates the integration of EHS&R in decision-making. Considering components of traditional life-cycle assessment with health, occupational safety and recycling tools, as part of an activity-based costing methodology, the LCM approach enables DaimlerChrysler to compare costs between different materials, products and manufacturing processes.

In the past, DaimlerChrysler dealt with EHS&R issues in a piecemeal fashion, dispersed throughout the product development process with the result that, in some cases, they were only considered after the product was built. Today Daimler-Chrysler is pursuing an integrated approach where EHS&R issues are systematically integrated into product development alongside issues such as quality, cost, performance and Just-in-Time delivery. The advantage of the LCM approach is that it provides full cost information and this enables DaimlerChrysler to integrate EHS&R information into business decisions.

1 DaimlerChrysler is the company formed from the merger of Daimler-Benz and Chrysler Corporation.

Drivers

The LCM programme is part of DaimlerChrysler's overall EHS&R strategy and includes:

▷ Ensuring that EHS&R is an integral part of the business decision-making process

▷ Targeting and screening of regulated substances for elimination, reformulation and/or reduction

▷ Using recycled content in materials

▷ Designing vehicles for ease of recovery/re-use at end-of-life

The main drivers for DaimlerChrysler's LCM programme are primarily related to reducing non-value-added costs that can be avoided through more informed decision-making. These costs arise from two broad categories. First, within the US there has been a steady increase in regulatory requirements, particularly since 1970. As a global company and an international exporter, it is also necessary for DaimlerChrysler to track and comply with regulations worldwide. These efforts incur significant costs, particularly if they are addressed only from a compliance or end-of-pipe management approach.

Secondly, DaimlerChrysler recognised that there is a number of other costs associated with EHS&R that impact the corporation. These costs include liability, training, medical testing, administrative costs, lost opportunities in recycling, disposal, and need for over-design of products. According to Robert Kainz, senior manager of DaimlerChrysler's pollution prevention and life-cycle programmes, these costs 'come at you in pennies, nickels and dimes'. By identifying and quantifying life-cycle costs, DaimlerChrysler has been able to optimise business decisions as well as reduce the number of restricted substances and increase the recycled content and recyclability of materials and parts within its supply chain.

Implementation

A simplified version of the LCM approach used at DaimlerChrysler is graphically illustrated in Figure 1. DaimlerChrysler has developed a hierarchy of substances of concern and recycling targets that it uses when screening supplier parts and products. Its list was developed by examining priority substance lists and substance specific information from leading jurisdictions around the world. It looks at international, national, regional and local regulations and also examines 'bellwether' or leading-edge jurisdictions to get a feel for future directions with

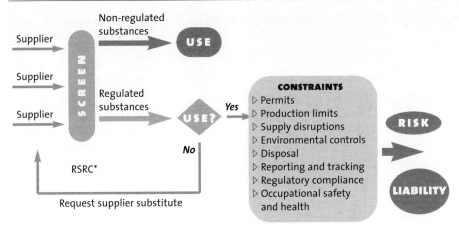

Figure 1: **Life-cycle management approach**

respect to restricted substances. Issues of concern in compiling the list included toxicity, exposure, regulatory controls, financial risk, potential for release and reporting requirements. Additionally, DaimlerChrysler reviewed proposed regulatory requirements for recycled content, recyclability and waste management to develop strategic targets for internal and external suppliers.

A major part of the LCM programme was deciding what to screen and track. DaimlerChrysler identified 1,700 restricted substances of concern in its products and operations. It has further classified these substances into a tier-2 level of concern (761 substances) and a tier-1 level of concern (103 substances). These 103 tier-1 compounds represent about 90% of risk and reporting requirements. Recycled content and recyclability targets are identified in proposed regulatory requirements. These requirements have been incorporated in the overall product development strategy.

The LCM programme is being used to select between different parts, materials or processes that involve the use of these tier-1 substances[2] while considering the recycled content, recyclability and material complexity targets. Franklin Associates, a US consulting firm who has worked with DaimlerChrysler on its LCM programme, described the comparison of options as involving the following steps.

---

2   In addition to comparing processes, materials or products, LCM has been used for applications such as policy development and the evaluation of design alternatives.

▷ **Identifying the environmental strategy**. The first step is to understand the strategic approach being undertaken. In DaimlerChrysler's case, this is outlined by the global policy and EHS&R strategy.

▷ **Defining the organisation**. To properly identify costs and evaluate alternatives, it is necessary to involve cross-functional teams made up of the various players involved with the particular options under consideration. This involves not only the traditional design and engineering personnel, but also those who can provide information on costs and environmental, health and safety issues and asset recovery. For example, in looking at lead-free alternatives for electrocoating,[3] it was necessary to involve personnel from procurement and supply, paint and energy management, occupational health and safety, product strategy and environmental affairs, materials engineering, manufacturing and the electrocoat suppliers (Franklin 1998).

▷ **Define the alternative designs/processes under consideration.** Alternatives must meet all the standard criteria such as function, quality and performance.

▷ **Map out the process**. The 'business' process for the current part or manufacturing process and the alternative(s) are mapped out. All relevant costs associated with the current part or process and the alternative(s) are calculated. Issues examined include acquisition costs, environmental issues, occupational health and safety, medical, and recycling. It also includes potential future liability and end-of-life scenarios that could become the responsibility of DaimlerChrysler (Franklin 1998). The process map is also an important tool for ensuring that the right individuals from the organisation are involved in the analysis.

▷ **Perform the LCM analysis.** The costs are added up and any relevant qualitative information is also reported. In general, the LCM cost data provides information that was not typically brought into an analysis of alternative parts or processes. Therefore, to properly identify all costs, it is important to correctly map out the business process and ensure that the right individuals and departments are involved.

In the case of the lead-free electrocoat, straight acquisition costs favoured the lead-containing option. The LCM analysis demonstrated that, when environmental (filter disposal, equipment salvage costs, reporting, regulatory trends) and health and safety (risk and training) costs were

---

3 Electrocoating is a method of organic finishing that uses electrical current to deposit the paint. The process works on the principle that opposite charges attract.

considered, the lead-free electrocoat was the clear cost winner. This was further supported by improvements in manufacturing efficiencies and improved product performance.

Results

Over the last four years, DaimlerChrysler has performed over 30 LCM analyses resulting in savings or cost avoidance of US$22 million and the reduction of 400 tonnes of waste to landfill. Additionally, through the LCM approach, the elimination or reduction of several regulated substances and the increase of recycled content occurred in plant processes and/or products.

The LCM programme has demonstrated that, when the full costs are considered, the environmentally preferable option is often the least-cost solution.

References

http://www1.daimlerchrysler.com

Franklin, William E. (1998) 'The Extended Enterprise: Life Cycle Cost Management of Environmental, Health, Safety and Recycling/End of Life as a Business Decision Process', SAE paper no. 982165; *SAE Total Life Cycle Conference*, 1–3 December 1998, Graz, Austria.

Organisational contacts

Robert Kainz, Senior Manager, Pollution Prevention and Life Cycle Programmes

CENTER FOR TECHNOLOGY ASSESSMENT (CTA)

Pursuing regional approaches to qualitative growth and sustainability

Baden-Württemberg, Germany

Deep in the heart of southern Germany lies its most powerful industrial region, Baden-Württemberg. In addition to being the headquarters for global giants such as Bosch (automotive, mobile phones), DaimlerChrysler, Hugo Boss AG (fashion and lifestyle products), Porsche and ZF Friedrichshafen AG (automotive components), it is also home to hundreds of small and medium-sized companies. Companies located in Baden-Württemberg, both large and small, are world leaders in a wide range of high-technology industries, including automotive engineering, electrical and electronics engineering, environmental engineering, biotechnology and genetic engineering, communications and information technology, automatic assembly systems, and large-scale industrial equipment.

Home to 10 million people (12% of the German population), Baden-Württemberg is the third-largest state in Germany, and consistently ranks as the nation's economic leader. Among all German states, it has the highest income, lowest unemployment, most direct foreign investment, and fewest bankruptcies. It is Germany's leading exporter, with exports of DM120 billion (over US$70 billion), larger than Spain, Sweden and Switzerland combined. It also boasts Germany's highest rate of R&D investment, spending 3.8% of state GDP on R&D, compared to

CTA's choice of structure illustrates one of the many lessons that may be learned from its overall effort. Specifically, CTA designed its structure to best facilitate its intentions:

▷ It leveraged networks of scientific expertise.

▷ It formally linked itself with all the many stakeholders who have a vested interest in its mission.

▷ It created an administrative structure that brings all the key players into the design and management process in a way that focuses day-to-day work on scientific expertise while providing both community vision and continuity over a significant time-period.

Box 1: Matching structure to the challenge

3.2% for Japan, 3.1% for Sweden, 3.0% for the US and 2.6% for the rest of Germany. Its technical base and intellectual capital is fuelled by nine universities, 39 technical colleges, 130 research institutes, and more than 240 technology transfer centres. It also has an excellent environmental record, with the highest rate of bottle recycling in Germany, the highest quality output from sewage treatment plants, the cleanest rivers, and lower greenhouse gas emissions per capita (by nearly 40%) than the rest of Germany.

In the centre of this industrial powerhouse, Stuttgart, the state of Baden-Württemberg has created a politically neutral public foundation to guide the region on a journey to sustainable development. Just six years old, the Center For Technology Assessment (CTA) now has a staff of 100, half funded by the state, half funded by third parties. Their mission is twofold: (1) to explore the consequences and impacts of scientific and technological developments; and (2) to initiate, organise and promote the evaluation of and decision-making about technology with and by society, through the use of sophisticated social dialogue and conflict resolution processes. In particular, it has been charged with designing the 'public process through which sustainable development can be both conceptualised and made practical for the . . . state of Baden-Württemberg'.[1]

1   This chapter is based on Renn and Goble 1996 and on meetings and follow-up interviews with Dr Ortwin Renn (Director of CTA Department of Technology, Society and Environmental Economics), Dr Diethard Schade (Executive Director of CTA) and Dr Hans Kastenholz (CTA Department of Technology, Society and Environmental Economics) in Stuttgart, June 1997, November 1997, April 1998 and January 1999.

One of the most important deductions to be made from the CTA experience is the critical importance of government-funded research that crosses sectors and disciplines. Baden-Württemberg is one of the most prosperous regions in the world. The foresight of the regional government and the scale of its investment (e.g. the funding of a hundred researchers) outlines the parameters of what other regions must do to even consider participating in the evolving global industrial game.

Box 2: For Regions or countries to compete globally, they must invest in publicly funded research

Organisationally, CTA is run by a small board of directors (four science directors and an administrative head), a working board of trustees (14 representatives of the state parliament, the state government and relevant outside stakeholder groups), and a 26-member advisory committee (with representatives from parliament, government, universities and outside 'social' groups, including industry, trade unions, churches and environmental groups.

In addition, it has created two types of network: an institutionalised 'scientific network' where CTA is formally and permanently linked with all the universities, technical colleges and research institutes throughout Baden-Württemberg; and numerous project-related networks, each lasting one to five years, consisting of companies, industrial associations, research institutes, trade unions and technical specialists who are involved in specific technology and research projects.

Although the story of CTA as an organisation is fascinating in its own right, of more direct interest are the breakthrough perspectives that have emerged from its projects, its social processes and its research analyses. Therefore, rather than portraying CTA's own organisational journey, this case study details the specific content that has formed the basis for its work throughout the Baden-Württemberg region—the content it believes will guide the region to achieve sustainable development, and the specific operational methods connected to sustainable development that it is using in the region. Throughout this case study, major management processes behind CTA's story are highlighted in boxes and generally applicable lessons are drawn out. The combination of sophisticated and competitive high-technology industrial activity, hand-in-hand with advanced conceptualisations about sustainable development, has produced a clarity of insight most applicable to the demanding challenges of the 21st century. This is the story of those insights, and of the path currently being walked by one of the leading industrial regions in the world.

Overall CTA project design for sustainable development in Baden-Württemberg

CTA is committed to a collaborative, democratic process in which it catalyses collective deliberation and action toward sustainable development. Given that, it is actively open to the dynamic evolution of its strategy. At the same time, it is proactive about pushing the region to explore the most advanced approaches to sustainable development. Thus, its overall design for sustainable development in the region currently consists of seven major phases. These phases have remained coherent for more than two years, but, because they are embedded in the collaborative deliberative process, they may evolve. They are:

▷ Inventory all existing economic structures: diagnosing and describing the current state of economic affairs in Baden-Württemberg and assessing the potential for probable transition processes to move toward sustainability.

▷ Conceptualise terms: develop understandings of sustainable development, 'qualitative growth', and the necessary elements of an implementation strategy.

▷ Assess and analyse renewable and non-renewable natural resources, energy needs and human resources.

▷ Quantitatively assess carrying capacity and appropriated carrying capacity: identify and quantify all the material flows into and out of Baden-Württemberg, and assess their impacts on sustainable development for the region.

Box 3: A comprehensive approach starts with intellectual rigour and extensive diagnosis

CTA illustrates the necessity of bringing comprehensive thinking to the challenge of sustainable development. To achieve system solutions to such a complex set of issues, simple superficial solutions will prove limited at best, and more likely be counterproductive. Thus CTA began with a thorough development of a definition of sustainable development (see below) that involved all stakeholders. It then anchored the project in extensive diagnostic activities and a wide range of assessments. The lesson seems clear: there can be no progress toward any management objective without thorough, collaboratively developed initial definitions and very solid assessments of the current state of affairs.

One of the most powerful tools CTA developed was its citizens' panels for resolving difficult environmental, economic and social issues. Wherever within this account of CTA's process for achieving sustainable development, a 'democratic process' or a 'collective deliberative process' is mentioned, it is a reference to this approach. CTA specifically calls its citizens' panels an 'analytic deliberative process' and is continually assessing and improving the approach as a vital tool in creating a sustainable society. This methodology is a quintessential example of how CTA views itself as playing a bridging role, connecting science and policy in the melting pot of well-informed democratic deliberation. It works as follows:

For difficult issues in the arena of sustainable development (e.g. siting a waste management facility, determining carrying capacity or regeneration rates, deciding when to use the precautionary principle), CTA randomly selects citizens and forms them into groups of 20–25 people per group. About ten such groups are created. Each group then spends six to seven evenings meeting and studying the issue, as well as one or two Saturdays. The citizens receive intensive education on the topic, participate in site visits, are given in-depth background information, and listen to experts presenting their viewpoints in the same way jurors would listen to evidence from expert witnesses. As they develop a fuller understanding of the issues, the citizens collectively develop the criteria by which they will make their decision. Then they are guided through ranking and selection processes, and together they come up with specific recommendations, policy choices and detailed input to the political decision-making processes. This same process is occurring simultaneously across the ten groups. Thus, in the end, ten different citizens' panels have addressed the same issue and have presented their recommendations. The aggregate recommendations carry enormous weight as indicators of the collective value judgements.

Typically, CTA gets up to a 30% response rate from the citizens it invites onto the panels. While participants are paid about DM1,000 to take part, most have a sense of legitimate empowerment and view themselves as partners in the commitment to explicit community determination of sustainable development choices. Citizens sign a contract, they deliberate and debate, they listen and reflect carefully, they write a full report, with options and arguments—and they pass on their recommendations with great fanfare to the mayor or other political body. CTA's head of environmental economics comments: 'Experience shows you can educate normal citizens on complex issues in around four days.' Ultimately, citizens bring three things that experts cannot:

▷ Anecdotal evidence of local knowledge

▷ A clear vision of how they want to live—their priorities and values

▷ Integration, holistic prudence, and a wisdom about making choices

Box 4: **Citizens' panels**

▷ Create a catalogue of indicators: to be used for ongoing assessment of the region of Baden-Württemberg *vis-à-vis* their movement toward (or away from) sustainability.

▷ Develop case studies in agriculture, forestry, trades, small and medium-sized companies, and waste management.

▷ Analyse and evaluate conversion strategies and instruments; design efficient, practical, cost-effective policy tools

CTA *Strategy*

CTA developed this overall research project through a systematic process. It began with a strategy linked to specific tactical steps, the specific implementation tools for which are outlined below. CTA's strategy, priorities and values are clear and straightforward. They are encapsulated as follows:

> furthering practical near-term steps toward sustainability within Baden-Württemberg and doing so by catalysing democratic processes.

This choice of strategy was based on three considerations:

▷ A conviction that the common elements inherent in the diversity of concepts and definitions of sustainable development have substantial political force

▷ A recognition that the great diversity in views and definitions of sustainable development is an asset to be nurtured and leveraged, as well as a potential cause of disagreement

Box 5: Practical case examples are critical

Along with the comprehensive intellectual approach, CTA also made a substantive commitment to supporting specific case studies. Managers learned that understanding and impact occur most effectively through action. This was not, however, the typical Western business approach to action. Instead, it pointed to a careful coupling of intellectual intensity with a pragmatic approach to pilots, case studies, parallel activities, learning loops and feedback based on practical applications.

▷ A focus on trying to develop a practical definition of sustainable development (see below) and to pursue it over a limited time-frame in a specific region

Specific steps to achieve the strategy

Given this clear strategic mandate, CTA specified and is systematically pursuing five major steps to make sustainable development a reality for Baden-Württemberg:

▷ Construct a broad working definition of sustainable development that is generally accepted throughout the region

▷ Develop a set of operational understandings about sustainable development that reflects the diversity of perspectives

▷ Develop the concept of 'qualitative growth'

▷ Describe how sustainability would work for a region, including links to the external world

▷ Develop operational principles to serve as practical guidance for bringing progress toward sustainability within the region of Baden-Württemberg

Step 1: *Working definition of sustainable development*

Historically, trying to define sustainable development has proven problematic. Definitions broad enough to engender widespread consensus fail to delineate specifics and risk being so inclusive as to be meaningless. Specific definitions fail to win broad support. Given this, CTA worked hard to develop its own working definition of sustainable development. In its deliberations and working groups, three major elements emerged as critical for inclusion:

▷ An increase in resource productivity

▷ A preservation of natural cycles (e.g. carbon, water, phosphorous, nitrogen)

▷ The preservation (or increase) of present levels of wellbeing for future generations

Integrating the work together, it has developed the following definition of sustainable development:

> Sustainability is achieved when the capital of natural resources is preserved to the extent that the quality of life available for future generations will not be inferior to the quality of life of the present generation.

This definition builds on the globally accepted Brundtland version from *Our Common Future* (WCED 1987). What is important is that there is a huge amount of dialogue and research being undertaken to understand the implications for Baden-Württemberg and to develop specific strategies and plans to operationalise this definition.

Step 2: *Operational understandings of sustainable development (which reflect and integrate a diversity of perspectives)*

While having such a definition of sustainable development may be at least theoretically useful, successful implementation would rely on a further elaboration of this definition into practical principles. Therefore, CTA sought out a wide range of views about operationalising the underlying principles behind the definition. Integrating a diversity of perspectives (e.g. chemistry, physics, biology, agriculture, ecology, economics, social and community sciences, ethics), four operational principles emerged as critical to sustainable development:

1. **Acknowledge absolute limits to the carrying capacity of the earth**. This will require increases in human-made capital and dramatic increases in resource productivity.

2. **Acknowledge limits of substitution between natural and artificial capital, and ensure natural cycles necessary for human survival are identified and appropriately protected by political measures.** For many natural-system services and natural-system cycles, it is difficult to determine true costs or value, although it is clear those externalities are extremely high, and imposing the externalities is impractical. Thus, developing sophisticated understandings of the natural cycles that are critical for survival, and consequently for sustainable development, and protecting those cycles through political interventions, seemed essential to CTA and its constituencies.

3. **Focus on the resilience of anthropogenic ecosystems**. Although renewable resources are theoretically available indefinitely, that is only true if the ecosystems that support those resources are resilient enough to sustain their productivity under dynamic conditions. Thus, for example, if humans manage their ecosystems for renewable materials and energy too intensively, or force them to be too monocultural, they undermine the resilience of those ecosystems and jeopardise their sustainability. From a practical perspective, achieving sustainable development will require a commitment to economic and societal decision-making that ensures resilient ecosystems.

4. **Incorporate social and cultural values into society's relationship to environment and nature**. Different societies (regions) will have different cultural and social perspectives on the intrinsic value of nature. To ensure sustainable development, those values will have to have a voice, consistent with local preferences.

Step 3: *Qualitative growth*

Given this definition of—and the practical understandings that can guide actual progress toward—sustainable development, CTA also confronted the issue of growth.

Because Western-style free-market capitalism is currently the dominant model for global commerce, and even societal organisation, trying to move toward sustainable development without addressing the issue of growth would leave an enormous structural problem unresolved. Free-market capitalism requires growth. Certainly, it is not practically tenable (nor morally defensible) for industrialised countries to try now to limit the growth of the not-yet-industrialised countries. Thus, the issue must be faced. The challenge is how to achieve increasing levels of sustainability while continuing to acknowledge growth as a central tenet for market economies. The resolution for CTA is not to exclude growth, nor strive for a change in the dominant economic model, nor advocate for the abandonment of human aspiration. Rather, it is to endorse growth, to encourage it. But that growth must be of a different nature—no longer tied to concomitant growth in material consumption, but instead growth of human-made capital. This includes all areas of human knowledge and all economic growth that can be achieved independently of increases in material throughput. CTA has developed the following definition of desirable or allowable growth under a scenario of sustainable development:

> Qualitative growth: economic development during which resource productivity increases continuously with economic welfare

So CTA anticipates a 'second event', parallel to the Industrial Revolution, during which an enormous increase in the productivity of human labour per hour was attained. This next revolution will be characterised by a rising productivity of natural resources (per unit of energy or raw materials). The key is to substitute knowledge and non-material services for material resources. The bottom line is that structured knowledge and software replace raw materials.

CTA postulates that there are three stages of such qualitative growth:

> Stage 1: continuous decrease in resource use per unit of GDP
> Stage 2: continuous decrease in resource use per capita
> Stage 3: continuous decrease in resource use per national economy

Growth, as a fundamental metaphor, is probably the most critical of all cornerstones for the Western economic system. Whether one agrees with the final approach to dealing with the issue of growth developed by CTA, coming to some definitive resolution about this issue is critical for any organisation dealing with sustainable development.

Box 6: Dealing with the issue of growth

CTA finds that much of the industrialised world has achieved Stage 1, where qualitative growth implies that products use fewer resources for the same functionality. An example of Stage 1 is found in the electronics industry with the miniaturisation of products, and is characteristic of many sectors and most industrialised countries. Stage 2, a continuous decrease in resource use per capita, means growth could occur wherever there is more added value than there is increase in production or consumption of materials and energy. Very few products or countries have reached this stage. However, the work of Ernst Ulrich von Weizsäcker, Amory Lovins and L. Hunter Lovins in *Factor Four* (von Weizsäcker *et al.* 1997) provides 50 examples of the successful achievement of a four-fold improvement in resource productivity. Others, such as Friedrich Schmidt-Bleek (like von Weizsäcker formerly of Germany's Wuppertal Institute) and his 'Factor 10 Club' believe a factor of four is insufficient given regional, national and global patterns of consumption and population growth and a ten-fold increase in resource productivity may be critical to both the global ecosystem and the social fabric of society (Factor 10 Club 1997). Stage 3 only differs from Stage 2 in that it assumes increased value per national economy while the population of that economy continues to grow, with an absolute utilisation of resources decreasing. This stage will be difficult to achieve and is likely to require consideration of the ever-increasing population in addition to vastly increased resource productivity.

Software, knowledge and innovation lay the foundation for bringing about Stage 2 and 3 qualitative growth. While these non-material elements cannot completely replace materials, nor do so indefinitely, they will move us in the right direction for sustainability. And they will lay a foundation for having time to address the more fundamental societal, cultural, economic and even spiritual issues associated with the overarching growth model. Therefore, growth in knowledge, non-material services, value-added, dematerialisation, and growth in resource productivity are all highly encouraged.

Step 4: *Sustainable development on a regional basis*

With well-developed strategies and fundamental concepts, CTA turned its attention to the issue of implementation approach. After careful analysis, it strongly advocates the pursuit of sustainable development on a regional basis. The rationale for choosing 'region' as the unit of focus is as follows:

▷ **Homogeneity**. Because of the complexity and diversity inherent in trying to achieve sustainable development, a regional level allows enough homogeneity to make the chance of resolving differences in perspective and managing complexity realistic. A global or national scale may be overwhelmed by the diversity of views and the complexity of issues inherent at that level of analysis and intervention.

▷ **Political institutions and regulatory mechanisms**. Unlike the international community, regional communities in general have long-standing political institutions capable of making effective decisions and pursuing regulatory mechanisms to support sustainable development.

▷ **Better chances of implementation success, without 'eco-imperialism'**. Emerging nations will resist the imposition of values on them by (already developed) industrialised nations. If regions can pursue sustainable development solely on their own level, they will serve as role models and catalysts for others.

▷ **Regions can experiment, adapt, compete and exchange ideas with other regions more easily than nations**. Even though nations have capable political institutions, they lack the flexibility of a region to capitalise on its homogeneity in order to collaborate quickly with similar regions around the world, share experiences candidly with others, learn and adapt.

▷ **Smaller entities, such as cities, although they may have homogeneity, do not have sufficient scale to influence the overall economy.** They are too dependent on outside flows of goods and services, and do not have enough control over the design of those flows.

▷ Finally, **smaller entities often lack enough basic diversity to develop robust mechanisms for resolving differences**. If sustainability is to succeed, it will require a political unit with experience and capability in resolving conflicting views. The regional level provides the most compelling case for sufficient diversity to develop those mechanisms, with sufficient homogeneity to ensure the efforts are not overwhelmed.

Given this argument, CTA is supporting the regional pursuit of sustainable development by Baden-Württemberg. **Specifically, it is working with the region**

to promote the demand and acceptance of only sustainable products from outside the region, and the export of only sustainable products from the region. To support this, it is analysing all major material flows for both exports and imports to assess the degree to which they are either in line with or inconsistent with the four operational understandings (Step 2), the definition of qualitative growth (Step 3) and the operational principles of practical sustainable development (described in Step 5).

To assist with this effort, CTA is helping the region to use a range of indicators, and a great deal of work has gone into selecting and refining those most appropriate for Baden-Württemberg. CTA suggests looking at basic indicators such as water consumption, land use, soil degradation, energy conversion, quantity of waste, NO_x emissions, water quality, air quality and 'settlement' (paving of green surfaces).

Clearly, there are issues to overcome with this specific kind of regional approach to sustainable development. The primary concern is that committing to sustainability will make businesses in the region less competitive. In addition, it is often difficult to trace material flows for many products given the complexity of modern global commerce. Additionally, it may also be difficult to persuade two regions to agree on what they mean by sustainability.

But all of these concerns have potential means of resolution. The challenge from CTA's perspective is developing creative solutions for these concerns within the context of a democratic process. Its view is that, as we make progress region by region, global progress (and thus the elimination of ever more barriers and challenges) will ensue.

Step 5: *Operational principles to guide practical progress toward sustainable development*

Finally, as CTA has attempted to support its region in designing and implementing a strategy of sustainable development, it has developed six pragmatic principles of sustainable development and has begun to articulate specific policy tools that can be used to operationalise sustainable development. Again, both these practical guidelines and the policy tools were derived from collective processes that incorporated a diversity of views—scientific, economic and social.

▷ Non-renewable energy resources can only be used until:

   a resources used in a given time-period exceed resources found in that period

   b resources used in a period exceed resources known to be available in economically utilisable form

   c increase in resource productivity is proportional to increase in energy used for the energy conversion.

▷ Non-renewable raw materials can only be used as long as they are recycled without exorbitant economic expense (i.e. in at least partially closed-loop systems).

▷ Renewable raw materials can only be used at a rate that allows a balance between consumption and regeneration, with limits on human intervention or energy inputs.

▷ Environmental damage must be avoided wherever it impairs human health or preservation of natural cycles. Determining what represents unacceptable risk is to be resolved through democratic collective discussion and deliberation.

▷ All other interventions in nature (not previously mentioned) can be left to market forces, provided, wherever there are external effects, collective strategies will be permitted to control prices (e.g. through taxation) or to restrict quantities of undesirable products (e.g. wastes, pollution) through means suitably aligned with market forces.

▷ Interventions in the environment, in general, should be justifiable on a cost–benefit analysis basis, but every society may also attach intrinsic values collectively derived (even if this creates a specific negative cost–benefit ratio).

Matching policy tools to implementation requirements

The next question is: if these practical guidelines are to be designed in specific form and enforced, how is that best done? CTA has coupled its six guidelines with packages of policy tools to help facilitate implementation. It has identified six major types of tool or method. It has also specified which type of implementation challenge can be best addressed by which tools. below is an overview of the policy tools, and how they might best be packaged to meet varying implementation situations.

Six basic policy tools

1. Governmental regulations (e.g. health standards, environmental standards, safety standards, technical guidelines, land use regulations, prohibitions)

2. Governmental planning

3. Private planning

4. Economic incentives (e.g. eco-taxes, credits, insurance, subsidies)

5. Negotiation and mediation—such as the citizens' panel process, product substitution, emergency plans, risk-avoidance strategies, voluntary agreements, collective agreements, and producer–consumer voluntary agreements

6. Education, information sharing and communication (e.g. personal protection guidelines, awareness campaigns, right-to-know legislation, emergency training, eco-labelling, education programmes, public information campaigns, information about product life-cycle)

Implementation situations

These policy tools are then packaged to address four basic types of implementation challenge:

1. **Where absolute limits are needed**, regulatory standards and prohibitions are required; economic approaches may sometimes also be used to help reduce levels beyond the threshold defined by regulatory standards. The decision-making here should, as much as is possible, be based on science—and is required to protect human health and critical cycles in the environment.

2. **Where stretching the resource base, closing loops or reducing pressure on ecosystems is needed**, economic and social incentives are seen as the best tools. Other interests should also be included here, where appropriate (e.g. general economic welfare, improved social conditions, cultural development). Unlike the first category, where science should be the primary driver of decision-making, the decision-making here should

---

Box 7: Deep scientific knowledge is required—in a way that is accessible for decision-making and policy development

Sustainable development in its fullest sense requires understandings at the nexus of virtually all the scientific disciplines, in conjunction with implementation approaches that are informed by many of the social and political science disciplines. The challenge, then, is to develop and communicate this deep scientific analysis in ways that are accessible for decision-making and policy development. The CTA experience illustrates methods for achieving this synthesis.

rely on an economic perspective combined with a stewardship approach to nature.

3. **Where there is possible damage and uncertainty,** categorise probabilities and severity. Catastrophic potentials should be subjected to the precautionary principle; low-probability, low-catastrophe events should be handled with communicative tools. In both cases, invest in further knowledge development. The decision-making here is ecologically based, and it is preferable to avoid regulatory approaches wherever possible.

4. **Where there is no likely environmental damage, but people have environmental values**, use legal, negotiation, mediation, communicative or economic tools. Make the costs clear to everyone. The decision-making here relies primarily on social and cultural sciences.

Conclusion

Beyond the specific content related to sustainable development, what are the key lessons from CTA experience that may be applied in other settings? Some of the highlights include:

▷ The integration of sophisticated theoretical models and practical results-oriented work

▷ An unwavering commitment to a comprehensive approach, implemented thoroughly

▷ Systematic development and then alignment of vision, strategy and project steps

▷ Explicit, thoughtful alignment of tools with specific actions and policies

▷ A commitment to intensive diagnosis as the first step in the effort

▷ A commitment to vigorous, but practically oriented, measurement

▷ An example of vitalised citizen participation as the fundamental linchpin of how we, as a society, may be able to deal with the growing crisis around the conflict between technology development and social, environmental and moral imperatives

▷ Candour and integrity in facing the full range of issues that will require resolution if we are serious about moving toward strategies for sustainable development that have a legitimate chance of genuine transformation

▷ Equivalent investment in simultaneously addressing sustainable development content and working on the social mechanisms and core processes to promote dialogue and decision-making about that content

▷ The deliberate and constructive use of networks

▷ A role model for how government may come to see itself helping society to proactively and explicitly shape itself

In the end, CTA illustrates the union of intellect and action. Organisations aspiring to develop strategies for sustainable development can take inspiration from their example of concept-driven, customised, comprehensive, collaborative action.

References

Factor 10 Club (1997) *The Carnoules Declaration* (Carnoules, France: The Factor 10 Club).
Renn, O., and R. Goble (1996) 'A Regional Concept of Qualitative Growth and Sustainability: Support for a Case Study in the German State of Baden-Württemberg', *International Journal of Sustainable Development and World Ecology* 3: 1-22.
von Weizsäcker, E.U., A.B. Lovins and L.H. Lovins (1997) *Factor Four: Doubling Wealth, Halving Resource Use* (The New Report to the Club of Rome; London: Earthscan).
WCED (World Commission on Environment and Development) (1987) *Our Common Future* ('The Brundtland Report'; Oxford: Oxford University Press).

Organisational contacts

Professor Ortwin Renn, PhD, Director and Professor of Environmental Sociology
Hans Kastenholz, PhD, Technology, Society, Environmental Economics
Diethard Schade, PhD, Director of CTA

HENKEL

*Traditional values and
ecological leadership*

1. *The lie of the land*

a. *Corporate overview*

Founded in 1876, Henkel is a family-owned global company that specialises in applied chemistry. The Henkel Group employees over 56,000 people and is comprised of 340 companies operating in more than 70 countries. Group sales for 1998 were DM 21.3 billion (US$11.6 billion). The Henkel Group manufactures almost 10,000 products through its six main product divisions or business sectors:

▷ **Cognis** (formerly Henkel Chemical Products). Cognis is the world's largest processor and manufacturer of oils and fats based on renewable raw materials such as coconut, palm, palm kernel and soybean. It produces and sells oleochemical base materials, feedstock products for the cosmetics, detergents and pharmaceutical industries, organic speciality chemicals, and water glass. Cognis has production facilities in all the major economic regions of the world.

▷ **Surface Technologies.** This business sector develops, produces and markets products and application systems (lubricants, cleaning agents, corrosion inhibitors, etc.) for the surface treatment of metals and metal substitutes. It also offers a comprehensive range of technical support services. Henkel's Surface Technologies business sector is the global

We are ready to meet the economic and ecological challenges of the 21st century. We assure Henkel's position as a top international company. This goal guides our actions. Through applied chemistry and expert service, we make people's lives easier, safer and better. We are dedicated to helping our customers improve their own performance and meet their requirements. We manage change and we are proud of our achievements.

Box 1: **Henkel mission statement**

Source: Henkel Annual Report 1998

market and technology leader in metal surface treatment. One of the major markets for surface technologies is the automotive sector.

▷ **Adhesives.** This includes products for craftsmen and end-consumers (wallpaper pastes, tile adhesives, contact adhesives, wood glues, etc.) as well as industrial and packaging adhesives, industrial reactive adhesives and high-performance sealants. Henkel is the global leader in the adhesives market.

▷ **Cosmetics/toiletries.** Henkel is a leading supplier of cosmetics and toiletries in Europe. The core segments of the business are hair cosmetics, toiletries, oral and skincare products and hair salon products.

▷ **Detergents/household cleansers.** Henkel is a leading provider of detergents and household cleansers in Europe. It is also exploiting its growth opportunities in the detergents and household cleansers sector in the Mediterranean and Asian markets.

▷ **Henkel–Ecolab: industrial and institutional hygiene.** Henkel-Ecolab was formed in 1991 as a 50–50 joint venture between Henkel (Germany) and the North American cleaning products and services company Ecolab Inc. (USA). The joint venture holds the leading market position in Europe and, together with Ecolab Inc., Henkel is the global leader in industrial and institutional hygiene products. It sells products, appliances, systems and services for cleaning, washing, maintenance, sanitising and disinfecting applications for institutional and industrial customers.

Henkel believes in a style of corporate management based on shareholder value aimed at meeting the expectations of shareholders, customers and employees. The keys to its environmental work are a strong leadership position and the integration of environmental considerations into overall management systems that also incorporate safety, health and quality.

b. *Business context*

Henkel operates in a highly competitive and volatile marketplace. Key competitors on the consumer product side of their operations include companies such as Unilever and Procter & Gamble. For many of its product lines (e.g. adhesives, cosmetics and household cleaners), Henkel deals directly with the consumer and has therefore faced a number of green consumer demands, particularly in the German and European marketplaces.

Henkel's industrial business lines, such as chemicals, adhesives, surface coatings and industrial hygiene products, are also increasingly being evaluated from an environmental perspective. This trend is growing as downstream customers such as the automotive sector strive to reduce their own environmental burdens and risks, and improve the environmental performance of their products. In many cases, this involves the evaluation of the environmental performance of materials and suppliers. This 'greening of the supply chain' affects both ends of Henkel's business and it is providing an opportunity for Henkel to differentiate itself. In this climate, the environmental attributes of Henkel's products are seen as a way of providing added value to its customers and to gain competitive advantage.

In addition to increasing customer demands about environmental issues, the regulatory situation is also changing. Product environmental labels (eco-labels) are proliferating and programmes that help manufacturers integrate environmental considerations into product design and material selection decisions are being developed in a number of countries. Governments are enacting green procurement initiatives, and product-focused environmental policies are being discussed at the European level. Rather than focusing on the environmental aspects of facilities or on priority toxic substances, these product policies focus on the product system and reducing the environmental impact throughout the life-cycle (raw materials, manufacturing, use and end-of-life). This shift to product-focused policies and tools such as eco-labels may ultimately favour companies who can demonstrate in a quantitative way the environmental attributes of their products in addition to meeting cost and performance demands. Consequently, a number of companies in this sector are actively involved in the development of data and tools such as life-cycle assessment to measure and report on a product's environmental performance.

These drivers and Henkel's own corporate philosophy have led the company to its stated objective to be a global leader in environmental and consumer protection. For Henkel, this is a competitive issue based in traditional company values. As a family-controlled but public-traded company, Henkel has a long history. The family has owned the company for six generations and they have maintained high expectations with respect to performance on all levels. Recently, these expectations have been challenged as Henkel expanded to become a truly global company (close to 80% of its business is now outside of its traditional German market). This expansion requires the integration of management systems into different countries and different cultures and the rate of expansion is straining the company's commitment to maintain its high standards throughout its worldwide operations.

c. Preview

At Henkel, sustainability is defined not only from a social and environmental viewpoint, but also from a business perspective. As Henkel is a family-owned corporation, the economic health of the company is directly linked to the owner's economic sustainability. Very early in its history, Henkel was faced with environmental pressures such as concern over phosphates in detergents. In the 1950s, the 'foam mountains' created by detergents in rivers became a serious environmental problem. By 1961, Henkel was producing biodegradable detergents three years ahead of German government legislation that forced all manufacturers to do the same. Marketplace pressure from consumers, particularly in Europe, to deal with environmental issues, and the potential economic consequences of not doing so, led to a serious consideration of environmental concerns. This in turn led to the integration of environmental concerns into the company's core business practices such as the product development process and marketing.

A key early success for the company was the development of phosphate-reduced detergents. In the mid-1960s, phosphates in detergents were identified as one of the main causes of eutrophication of bodies of water. Until the mid-1970s, close to 40% of all phosphates in rivers came from detergents and cleaning agents. However, Henkel had been working for some time on substitutes for phosphates in detergents and household cleaners. This led to the development of an ecologically and technically sound substitute called SASIL (sodium aluminium silicate). In 1976, with little fanfare, Henkel released Dixan, the first detergent to include SASIL. This was the first time that a detergent with reduced phosphate content was put on the market. This was a high-risk strategy, but a year and a half after its introduction, the company realised that the product was setting the market standard for environmentally sound detergents and capturing market share. This work ultimately led to Henkel producing in 1983 the first phosphate-free detergents. The success led to a flood of environmental activity within the company, although little of this could be said to be connected at a strategic or philosophical level. Gradually, these activities were brought together and co-ordinated.

This co-ordination took some time, however, as the lessons of the detergent business were not readily accepted by other product divisions. There was a certain level of uncertainty that environmental activity could be sustained and there were fears that proactive communication of environmental issues might be dangerous for what was essentially a speciality chemical company. Consequently, progress toward the current ecological leadership approach proceeded carefully, step by step. Product evaluations were conducted and markets were monitored closely; and, as confidence built, all of the product divisions embraced the ecological

The worldwide activities of Henkel in its business sectors Chemical Products, Institutional Hygiene/Industrial Cleaning, Industrial Adhesives, Cosmetics, Detergents/Household Cleaners share in common the fact that these activities result from a combination of research, product development, application technology, production, and marketing. With the tools and resources of chemistry, Henkel supplies innovative solutions to problems in numerous areas of life. Environmental and consumer protections are primary business objectives for Henkel.

With its principles on the subjects of environmental and consumer protection, Henkel accepts its responsibility. Environmentally compatible production processes and products are a key factor for Henkel's continued success in the marketplace, now and in future. In this context, environmental protection also preserves jobs.

Henkel has set itself the following goals:

▷ to satisfy the wishes of consumers;

▷ to aim for and achieve compatibility between production processes, products, on the one hand, and the environment, on the other;

▷ to ensure safety for customers and users, employees and the general public.

Henkel acknowledges the following principles: Responsibility to society, safety, quality, ecological responsibility, willingness to cooperate, willingness to communicate, responsibility of employees.

Box 2: 'Corporate Policy on Environmental and Consumer Protection in the Henkel Group'

Source: www.henkel.com

leadership position. In addition to the business units, employees were an important ingredient in Henkel's ecological leadership strategy. The company knew that, if it was going to take an ecological leadership position, the employees, who knew about Henkel's daily performance better that anyone, would need to be in favour of the strategy. Henkel views its employees not only as a mirror of society but also as an important link to the communities in which it operates. Henkel's German employees are very advanced with respect to environmental and ecological awareness and demand for high standards. For credibility and implementation purposes, it was necessary to ensure that the position the company took on environmental issues was consistent with the day-to-day experience of the employees.

The company conducted training seminars and formed working groups; and, only when it was convinced that the majority of employees would support the new strategy, did it define ecological leadership as part of its competitive toolbox and its core business strategy. The Henkel strategy embraces some simple but important concepts:

▷ Quality products sell better.

▷ A bad reputation harms business success.

▷ Only an economically healthy company is able to be socially and environmentally responsible.

▷ It is important to communicate with your neighbours.

▷ Workers and their families are also customers and the best marketing staff a company can get. If their working place is clean and healthy, they have a positive story to tell all their friends.

▷ Stakeholder involvement and communication is key to supporting the company as well as for the products in the market.

▷ Finally, energy- and resource-efficient manufacturing processes are not only environmentally sound, but also economically relevant.

In 1982 Henkel formulated the its 'Corporate Policy on Environmental and Consumer Protection in the Henkel Group', set out in Box 2. This statement illustrates that Henkel formulated its strategic aim to be an ecological leader, not only from the owners' and employees' sense of social and environmental responsibility, but also for good business reasons. Henkel has cultivated extremely positive name recognition in its major markets and has developed an outstanding image in the environmental field. It has effectively 'advertised' its environmental performance to key markets and other stakeholders and has systematically dealt with environmental issues it has faced. Henkel was one of first companies to sign the Business Charter for Sustainable Development and it is a member of the chemical sector's Responsible Care programme. With its environmental activities well in hand, the company is now focusing more attention on the third leg of sustainability: namely, the social aspects of production and consumption.

This case study describes some of the business practices that Henkel has undertaken to maintain its ecological leadership position and to develop a platform for integrating broader sustainability considerations into its products and services.

2. Trailblazing

a. Principles and objectives and management systems

The goals and objectives Henkel set in 1982 are still reflected in its current goals. Today the company identifies three primary areas in which it has set targets for itself. These can be summarised as follows:

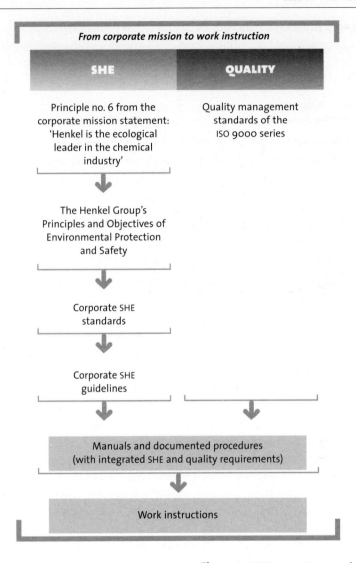

Figure 1: **SHEQ management system**

1. **Products and systems.** Supply products and systems that are recognised by acknowledged scientific criteria as environmentally compatible and ensure safe use through effective communication of information and advise to customers

2. **Production**
   ▷ Processes are designed so that proper operation will ensure that employees and neighbours are not exposed to any health hazard.

   ▷ Regular and systematic checks are conducted using group-wide criteria.

   ▷ A commitment to continuous improvement to reduce the potential for accidents and adverse impacts

   ▷ Integration of environmental protection, safety, resource conservation and pollution minimisation into the development of new production processes and the design and construction of new plants

3. **Occupational safety.** Integration of occupational safety into the organisation of work, safety management, safety technology, production processes, substances and occupational health precautions

A comprehensive safety, health, environment plus quality management system (SHEQ) backs up these goals. The SHEQ system defines Henkel's standards in the area of safety, environment, health and quality for all business sectors and sites. The system is designed for compatibility with all of the major requirements of Responsible Care, the European Union's Eco-Management and Audit Scheme (EMAS), the international environmental management standard ISO 14001, and the international quality management standard ISO 9001.

There are 15 safety, health and environment (SHE) standards and 55 associated guidelines that have been developed. These standards and the guidelines are binding for the entire Henkel Group. Figure 1 illustrates how the management system is structured. The standards cover a variety of areas, including: resource consumption and releases; manufacturing; products; workplace health and safety; distribution; acquisitions and divestment; suppliers and contractors; reporting on environmental performance; training; and regulatory and other external issues. For example, one standard addresses the development and implementation of programmes to avoid or minimise any harmful effects of emissions on the environment. The associated guidelines then specify how the standard is to be implemented. In this case, an inventory of hazardous materials must be compiled, emissions must be measured, an emissions inventory must be developed, ecological and toxicological tests must be conducted, and, if required, improvement programmes must be developed and applied.

For greater effectiveness, as well as to provide administrative ease and to reduce the reporting burden on employees, the SHE system and the quality system have been integrated. Both standards have a similar structure in that they are subject to a continuous improvement process. Henkel has been successful in integrating the two systems at a number of facilities, and implementation throughout the entire group is scheduled for 2000. Henkel also believes that the integrated system is 'less complex, easier for employees to apply, and thus more readily internalised'.[1]

The integrated management system is a combination of top-down control and support—the businesses are supplied with the standards and tools—and bottom-up tracking of data and measurement of performance.

b. Strategic and comprehensive communication of environmental messages

Although environmental improvements are typically good for business, it is often difficult to get market recognition for these efforts. This is due to a number of factors:

1. Even if there is a common societal understanding about the importance of protecting the environment, there is little evidence that industrial customers or individual consumers are willing to pay a premium for environmentally friendlier products.

2. Consumers are generally reluctant to change their behaviour.

3. Products, and especially consumer products, are sold as much by emotion and brand image as by quality and performance.

For Henkel, these realities led them to strive for an emotional advantage in the market by being proactive and being recognised as a leader. The foundation of this leadership is innovative products and processes, but, to affect market behaviour and build brand loyalty, product information must be effectively communicated. At Henkel, a systematic and open communication strategy was developed to achieve the best possible market impacts. This communication strategy targets not only the traditional consumers but also professionals, scientists, communicators in media and government, as well as the financial sector. The following communication tools are used:

▷ Company information programmes (e.g. newsletters) and extensive visitor programmes

▷ A website with detailed information on products, business units, research and technology information, environmental reports, as well as a customer dialogue function where individuals can ask direct questions of the various business units. Product-level information often begins by describ-

---

1   Personal communication with Michael Bahn, Corporate Safety, Health and Environmental Quality Manager, Henkel.

ing the environmental and economic benefits of the products, and detailed site-level environmental information is also available.

▷ Environmental reporting, mainly focusing on analysts, media and press, as well as the scientific community. In 1998 Henkel released its eighth annual corporate environmental report.

▷ Neighbourhood and community programmes at each plant—involving regular consultation with neighbours

▷ Open workshops, including those with stakeholders to discuss concerns and achievements

▷ Institutional advertising (e.g. in automotive journals)

▷ Press conferences and press releases

▷ Dialogue with governmental agencies to influence legislation and receive recognition for innovative approaches and programmes

▷ Dialogue and co-operation with scientific organisations

▷ Active participation in competitions: for example, in 1999 Henkel won the Institute for Management Development (IMD) Award for Distinguished Family Business and was ranked as the best company worldwide in the chemical sector with regard to environmental performance by the Hamburg Environment Institute.

▷ Monitoring programmes, and conducting market surveys to better understand customers' needs and the level of brand recognition

The content analysis and opinion research that Henkel conducts is actively disseminated through the company to ensure that the feedback from customers and other stakeholders is being heard. Such an active communication strategy is not without its challenges: for example, Henkel has had an almost overwhelming response to its website.

The 1998 corporate environmental report provides a good example of Henkel's open communication process. The report provides detailed information on Henkel's management system, information on each product division, including the objectives and status of its environmental programmes, production information from locations around the world, as well as company-level trend data. This company data includes key indicators such as energy consumption and emissions data for carbon dioxide, sulphur dioxide, nitrogen, dust, volatile organic compounds and chemical oxygen demand. In addition, water consumption and volume of wastewater is reported, along with emissions of heavy metals into surface waters, tonnes of waste sent for recycling and disposal, and consumption of chlorinated hydrocarbons. Importantly, the report also identifies where Henkel failed to meet its objectives (1997 was the first time site objectives were not achieved, primarily due to increases in production volume).

Henkel's communication work is focused and targeted and, through these efforts, the company is actively trying to increase stakeholder awareness of its ecological leadership and thereby increase its competitive advantage in key markets.

c. Product development process and policy

At Henkel, there are no speciality niche products: all products must be premium performers and meet internal and external criteria. The development process is distinguished by four steps:

1. Get permission for individual ingredients. Criteria: consumer safety, environmental compatibility, and worker safety.

2. Ongoing survey on scientific developments, concerning emerging issues on ingredients and products

3. Core technical product development process

4. Economic, social and environmental evaluation of products prior to market introduction. This evaluation includes the use of a variety of tools such as risk assessment, substance flow analysis, life-cycle assessment and full-cost accounting.

The development process is embedded into the SHEQ integrated management system described above. By relying on this one uniform system, which includes management training, Henkel is able to achieve a more consistent and effective approach to core business practices such as product development. For example, the integrated management system embraces a number of different tools such as Responsible Care procedures, risk assessment tools, life-cycle tools and product- or ingredient-specific data. Central toolbox managers supply access to information and keep the system updated. This leads to a dynamic and flexible working environment, with greatly reduced duplications, contradictions, misunderstandings and errors. For example, all developers have access to an ingredients database consisting of safety data sheets, toxicity data, information about the allowance for use within Henkel in general and for specific products.

In addition to its own data sets, Henkel also works with its suppliers to identify the relevant data required for evaluating its products. Environment, health and safety considerations have defined gate functions in the product development process. Unless these considerations are met, the product cannot move ahead in the process.

Examples of a few recent innovative products that Henkel has developed include:

▷ **Detergents:** vegetable-based surfactants for application in the cosmetic industry; these use renewable raw materials and require a reduced number of production processes, which saves time and energy.

▷ **Adhesives:** vegetable-based adhesives, solvent-free adhesives and low-emission floor-covering adhesives

▷ The development of a **water-recycling system** for industrial cleaning and washing which purifies the water so that it can be re-used. The remaining solids are sold to the agricultural sector as soil conditioners.

▷ The development of customised **cleaning products, technical equipment** and an **environmental review system** for a Scandinavian hotel chain that is a brand leader in green hotel rooms

▷ An **enzyme-based system** for cleaning containers and equipment used to transport, store or process milk. This system replaces conventional alkaline cleansers, works at a lower temperature, requires fewer rinsing stages and is almost pH-neutral. This results in less energy, less water consumption, and less waste-water.

▷ Solvent-free **glues** for the 'green shoe' project. Henkel's water-based glues are being used by Asian manufacturing sites with workers' exposure to solvents being drastically reduced.

d. New strategic directions: a shift from product to service

Henkel is developing a new sales strategy in some business areas, such as surface treatment and degreasing in the automotive industry. The goal of this strategy is to improve the client's processes by offering not only the product but also the service function. Henkel is not only successfully communicating the economic and environmental advantages of its products: in addition, process development support is offered, including in some cases an offer to run the clients' operations for them. The driving force behind this concept is to gain a better understanding of the real needs of the clients, which in turn can lead to superior product development, long-term contracts and supply security—advantages for both the client and the supplier.

One reason for this move from product to service is the growing trend within manufacturing operations for companies to operate with reduced personnel leading to a reduction in improvements and innovation, as it is difficult enough just to keep the system running. Henkel has therefore begun to offer system solutions, in which it is selling not only the products but also the complete service and client satisfaction. The service sales have turned out to be very effective, with revenues increasing by up to 200% within a year. Henkel is using this strategy in its strategic business units, offering tailored solutions to key clients in surface cleaning, adhesives and industrial hygiene. Henkel has achieved better product quality as well as reductions in the amount of adhesive used. The company has an incentive to perform the service function with less product, which in turn has led to a greater attention to detail and increased quality. Economic and environmental breakthroughs have been achieved.

. *Senior-level commitment: performance, targets and social aspects*

Senior managers interviewed express deep commitment to Henkel's environmental policy and strategy. The family ownership places special emphasis on this commitment, as well as the importance of taking a long-term perspective. After close to 125 years in operation, company executives now talk about ensuring Henkel is around for the next hundred years. There is also a high level of awareness within each business sector that they have a responsibility to maintain and not harm the brand image. It is the corporate image that has been fostered, not the sector's, and the market often associates the various consumer products with the group as a whole, not the specific business unit. This may change in the future as Cognis, the new chemicals group, carves out its own identity.

The company has set very challenging performance targets and, in order to provide incentives for reaching these targets, financial bonuses are linked to performance. This has the secondary effect of providing a very good vehicle for communicating ecological and environmental targets throughout the company. Failure to meet SHEQ targets often results in the operation drastically speeding up the improvement process.

As with the chemical sector in general, Henkel has not formalised social responsibility in the way it has with its environmental activities. However, the company is currently developing guidelines on business ethics and has an international committee comprised of senior managers who are examining the social aspects of the company in relation to sustainable development. It is hoped that this activity will give social issues a more prominent focus within the company. There are, however, a number of specific actions and projects that have been undertaken.

> ▷ Solvent abuse ('glue sniffing') is a major problem with adhesive products. In response, Henkel withdrew some of its products and developed solvent-free adhesives. When these products proved to be too expensive for the market, Henkel stepped in again and helped develop standards with major international companies. Unfortunately, some local producers still manufacture the cheaper and more dangerous solvent-based adhesives.

▷ In a statement to corporate management, in 1972 Dr Konrad Henkel first formulated his concern about a style of management that takes too little account of ecological aspects. This new way of thinking led to a strengthening of corporate management of activities related to environmental and consumer protection.

▷ In 1982 Henkel published the *Grundsätze zum Umwelt- und Verbraucherschutz in der Henkel-Gruppe* (*Principles of Environmental and Consumer Protection in the Henkel Group*). Henkel accepted its ecological responsibility. The document contains the statement: 'Environmentally responsible production and products are also a key condition for Henkel's future market success. In this respect, environmental protection safeguards jobs.'

▷ In 1987 Henkel published guidelines that included the statement: 'Henkel must take account of the environment.' Following the principles of environmental and consumer protection, the environmental aspect was now embedded in the corporate guidelines.

▷ In 1988 Henkel management and works (labour) council concluded a plant agreement to co-operate in matters of environmental protection. The agreement granted the works council far-reaching rights concerning information and participation.

▷ In 1989/90 Henkel carried out the first global eco-audit to register the actual environmental situation at all production facilities of the Henkel Group, and to register all products, on the basis of uniform, globally applicable criteria.

▷ In 1991 Henkel started an 'eco-programme' in response to the eco-audit. The programme provided for a stronger emphasis on environment-related research and development projects.

▷ In 1991 Henkel established the Cognis Gesellschaft für Bio- und Umwelttechnologie mbH with its head office in Düsseldorf. The new company carried out research, development and marketing in the fields of biotechnology and environmental technology. Priority was given to enzyme research for ecologically improved detergents, environmental consultancy, soil remediation and environmentally compatible production processes.

▷ In 1992 Henkel gave its support to the Business Charter for Sustainable Development. It agreed that future development must be organised in such a way that economic, ecological and social aims are given equal priority.

▷ In 1993 Henkel formulated the term 'eco leadership'. This expresses Henkel's aim to be the ecological leader in the chemical industry.

▷ In 1994 Henkel formulated a new corporate guideline. It started with the sentence: 'We are ready to meet the economic and ecological challenges of the 21st century.' At the same time one of the ten basic principles of the Henkel Group was: 'Henkel is the ecological leader in the chemical industry.'

▷ In 1994 Henkel switched from road to rail for the long-distance transport of detergents and household cleansers manufactured in Düsseldorf and Genthin to destinations in Germany. The distribution concept was singled out for an award in autumn 1995.

Box 3: **Milestones in strategy and management** *(continued opposite)*

▷ In 1994 the 'Verband der Chemischen Industrie in Deutschland' (VCI), with the participation of Henkel, developed a German version of the international 'Responsible Care' concept. Henkel committed itself to this programme.

▷ 1994: in connection with the wide variety of environmentally related improvements to processes and products, Henkel updated the concept of quality. Besides performance, reliability and service, Henkel quality includes a guarantee of the best ecological compatibility.

▷ In 1995 Henkel and other leading European manufacturers of surfactants presented the results of a study of 22 major detergent surfactants based on renewable raw materials and on petroleum. The conclusion was that both types of raw material have their advantages and disadvantages. In 1996, in the context of a life-cycle assessment, the ecological properties of solvent-free, water-based and solvent-containing polyurethane laminating adhesives were compared. These adhesives are used to make composite sheets from aluminium and plastic. The solvent-free adhesive came best out of the life-cycle assessments

▷ In 1995 Henkel updated its principles of environmental and consumer protection as an extension of international principles (e.g. signatory to the International Chamber of Commerce's Business Charter for Sustainable Development, support for the chemical industry's international Responsible Care initiative).

▷ Henkel Corporation was presented with an environment award by the US Environmental Protection Agency in recognition of its 'significant reduction in environmental pollution'. Together with 19 other leading American companies, Henkel Corp. voluntarily reduced its emissions by 30% in 1992 and 50% in 1995.

▷ Every two years the European Union presents the 'European Better Environment Awards for Industry' (EBEAFI). National winners are named first and Henkel Ireland gained two prizes at this level in 1996. The company proved successful at the European level, too. Henkel Ireland was the first Henkel subsidiary to win the European award.

▷ Every two years the Bundesverband deutscher Unternehmensberater (BDU)—the federation of German management consultants—presents an award for exemplary corporate strategy and methods. The winner in 1996 was Dietrich Winkhaus, President and Chief Executive Officer of the Henkel Group. Three factors played a decisive role in gaining him the award: his encouragement of innovation within the company; his successful personnel policies; and his consistent pursuit of the key corporate objective of eco leadership.

▷ In the late 1990s Henkel began its development of an integrated SHE (safety, health, environment) management system to facilitate the implementation of Responsible Care throughout the whole group.

▷ By 1997 numerous sites had already had their environmental management systems certified by accredited external verifiers in accordance with the European Union's Eco-Management and Audit Scheme (EMAS) or to the requirements of ISO 14001, the international standard for environmental management systems.

Box 3: Milestones in strategy and management *(continued from previous page)*

▷ In Argentina, Henkel is helping support a home for street children in the city of Avellaneda.

▷ In the Philippines, Henkel is providing economic support to a project that has helped coconut farmers develop their own co-operatives to improve their product quality and yields. The co-operatives are building copra (coconut meat) dryers, which allow the copra to dry without exposure to rain and dew, thereby reducing losses due to mould and mildew.

3. Conclusions

In many ways, Henkel still reflects the traditional values of a family-owned enterprise. It emphasises company loyalty, quality products and pride in work. Its strength is that it has married this traditional approach with thoroughly modern management systems, innovative product development processes, and sophisticated internal and external communications mechanisms. Periodically, the company asks the employees what they think with respect to the directions in which the company is heading, including the environment. Henkel also conducts external opinion research. The results have been very positive with employees endorsing the company approach and Henkel ranking as one of the top companies with regard to responsible management. In 1999 Henkel won the IMD Distinguished Family Business Award; was ranked top in the Hamburg Environment Institute's appraisal of environmental performance in the chemical sector; and was included in the Dow Jones Sustainability Index, which tracks the financial performance of 200 firms worldwide engaged with sustainability against like-for-like sector competitors perceived not to be engaged.

Maintaining this unusual approach is becoming a challenge as the company expands into new markets. With operations in 60 countries, maintaining a common vision and a top-down management system becomes difficult. As noted by a Henkel executive, trust and openness to new approaches and understanding of the realities and cultures of different countries becomes very important. For example, Henkel has approximately 18 joint ventures running in China. In many ways, industrial activity in China is more rooted in the 19th than the 21st century; consequently, the management systems it has developed for the rest of its operations may not be applicable there. Henkel is committed to following its approach while adapting to regional realities and it will be interesting to see how it balances these two needs.

Clearly, Henkel has firmly established a leadership position in its sector with respect to the integration of environmental and economic and health and safety issues into core decision-making processes. The social aspects of sustainability, however, are less developed and, until more sophisticated management and measurement systems are formalised (perhaps through the work of the Global Reporting Initiative), it will be a challenge for the company to move into a leadership position.

References

http://www.henkel.com
Annual Report 1998 (Düsseldorf: Henkel, 1999).

Organisational contacts

Michael Bahn, Corporate Safety, Health and Environmental Quality
Rüdifger Wagner, Environmental Protection and Safety
Hans-Jürgen Klüppel, Process and Environmental Management

SJ RAIL

Turnaround to sustainable transport for the 21st century

1. *The lie of the land*

a. *Corporate overview*

Ten years ago, before its privatisation in 1998, SJ Rail was an inefficient state-run railway, losing money, mired in 19th-century bureaucratic structures, and failing on almost every measure of quality, customer service and employee morale. Today, in terms of productivity, it stands as the leading rail company in Europe, having revolutionised transport in Sweden and transformed itself into a model of a 21st-century global competitor.

SJ Group is the traffic operator, building owner and service provider of the Swedish railway. SJ Group has two main entities: SJ Rail and its subsidiaries. SJ Rail operations comprise four business sectors: passenger transport, freight transport, rolling-stock maintenance and real estate management.

Railway traffic is the core business of the SJ Group's operations: SJ provides 97% of Sweden's passenger railway transport and 80% of freight rail transport (excluding ore on the Malmbanan line), but receives no subsidies from the Swedish government. Passenger and freight transport account for 90% of the Group's revenue and occupy almost 65% of employees. All but 5% of SJ's rail transportation is now electrically powered, using 1.1% of Sweden's total electricity production. In

1998, SJ Group employed 15,694 people and had an operating revenue of SEK 14,798 million (US$1.7 billion).

b. *Preview*

> Environmental issues are one of our core values. The purpose of our work in this area is to improve our profitability and ability to reach our overall goals and vision.

This was the response Daniel Johannesson, Director-General and Group CEO of SJ Rail, gave to the question of how environmental performance fitted with SJ Rail's business strategy. Johannesson describes three areas of focus for the company related to environment:

> (1) Increasing knowledge and understanding of our customers (and also of the general public, politicians and decision-making in SJ personnel) about the importance of environmental issues to SJ Rail, and SJ's efforts to create a 'Sustainable Transport System'; (2) excelling in our ability to be a good teacher explaining and creating very good arguments (about the rationale for 'Sustainable Transport' and the environmental advantages of rail)—not a 20-page thesis, but quick, good sentences to the point. We need to be good teachers, and [use our communication] as a vehicle to increase knowledge; and (3) being a good company ourselves— even if rail is inherently good for the environment, we need to be in the forefront. It is easy to take for granted the inherent goodness of rail.

Today in Sweden, companies such as IKEA are using rail as a primary mode of transport, in large part because of its superior environmental profile. SJ's branded door-to-door 'Green Cargo' service is winning contracts from companies that previously hadn't thought about rail. Companies that outsource transport are now recommending 'Green Cargo' to their suppliers. 'Green Cargo' is an integrated logistics system that determines optimum delivery options based on a sophisticated software analysis of least environmental impact and fastest, cheapest delivery. SJ Rail has had the system certified by the Swedish Society for the Conservation of Nature.

SJ Rail's progress toward integrating environment into its core strategy, product and service offerings, and operational processes is inextricably intertwined with its corporate turnaround more generally. SJ Rail's story includes changes in strategic direction, regulatory shifts, cultural transformation and the introduction of management systems that combined to reform this corporation into a customer-focused, competitive player, aimed at leading the way toward sustainable transport systems. Highlights of SJ Rail's accomplishments are summarised in Box 1.

▷ In less than a decade, SJ Rail was transformed from an inefficient, state-run bureaucracy to a customer-driven competitive leader, differentiating its services on the basis of sustainable transport.

▷ With its high-speed tilting trains, the company captured 60% of the market share from air traffic between Sweden's two largest cities, Stockholm and Gothenburg.

▷ In freight transport, SJ has introduced a branded transportation service called 'Green Cargo', bolstered by the fact that Sweden's trains are 98% electric.

▷ SJ offers corporate customers on-line software that allows for a comparative analysis of environmental costs of different transport modes and logistical arrangement.

▷ SJ's innovative communication plan galvanised the nation in participating in the company's turnaround and vision for promoting societal and environmental health in service of Sweden's national competitiveness.

▷ As of January 1999, in an effort to support both Swedish and EU goals of 'sustainable transport' and reflect the true societal costs of different modes of transport, Sweden passed a landmark bill lowering the infrastructure charges to rail. This promises to dramatically shift the competitive structure in the marketplace in favour of rail.

Box 1: SJ Rail's progress toward providing sustainable transport

c. A history: from quagmire to high speed

The Swedish Transport Act of 1988 marked the beginning of a completely new era in Swedish railway history. The act separated railway infrastructure from operations, transferring the infrastructure to the newly independent National Rail Administration (NRA). SJ was given authority to own and operate the trains and stations, while the NRA took over responsibility for running the tracks and signals, and providing the power supply. According to SJ, the company was 'as poorly perceived as is possible' as it began 1988. The state-run railway was viewed as bureaucratic, decrepit and anachronistic. The 140-year-old track bed had not been updated since it was laid. Across the nation, SJ was routinely and publicly criticised. There were poor relations with the union and employee morale was at an all-time low. Finances were deeply and chronically in the red, with a loss of more than SEK 1 billion (US$116.5 million) in 1987. To think that rail might be a viable competitor for air travel was laughable. Into this nightmare and this new structure, SJ hired its first non-politician CEO, Stig Larsson.

Over the course of the next six years, Larsson led a stirring turnaround. After replacing 35 of the top 50 managers, Larsson and the new management team led the development of a comprehensive strategic vision and pushed SJ into a creative, productive break from the past that rocketed it to the number one position among all European rail companies (UIC 1998). SJ invested SEK 8 billion (US$932 million) in new state-of-the-art high-speed tilting trains. It modernised over 100 train stations, created and brought on-line more than a dozen major new services, and joined arms with the union in reducing the workforce from 29,000 to 11,000. SJ specified a complete strategy, and then developed it in practical detail via 2,000 interlocking business plans.

The result? The SEK 8 billion high-speed train investment was fully financed from operating income—while simultaneously allowing the company to turn a profit. Nearly two-thirds of all air travellers on the major Swedish air route have now switched to rail. SJ's high-speed trains, sleeping coaches, family coaches, cinema coaches, business office coaches, central station restaurants, computerised ticket services and ticket programmes, breakthrough environmental programmes and performance are all receiving high praise from customers. Internally, SJ has introduced new gender equity programmes, designed creative employee involvement programmes, revamped the salary structure to reward entrepreneurial and performance accountability, and put union members on the board of directors. Currently, SJ is by far the most productive rail company in Europe (of 17 European rail companies, SJ has 1,117 passenger- and freight-km per employee; its closest competitor, VR in Finland, has 923 [UIC 1998]). Revenue, profit, passengers and freight volumes have increased annually for five years running.

The inside story of this turnaround involves powerful leaders, national commitment and a renewed workforce. But the most fundamental analysis of the turnaround revolves around SJ's choice of strategy. SJ's management team realised that sustainability was the core foundation on which the company would have to build its future—not just environmentally, but as an organisation, and as a nation. It was decided that, as a rail company in a nation of highly environmentally aware consumers, SJ should strive to link the railway with both environmental sustainability and the sustainability/competitiveness of Sweden as a country. Thus, sustainable development became central to the strategy: the driver of the innovations, new services, approach to employees, the rebuilding of its national role, and the transformation of its identity with the Swedish people.

Below are the key milestones of the journey that resulted. The journey focused simultaneously on sustainable rail traffic as a core target and the business turnaround of a bureaucratic, inefficient organisation.

2. The journey

As we studied SJ, we discerned a dozen major milestones, or highlights, of its turnaround. These 12 milestones are described in this section.

i. *Sustainable development was integral from the outset*

SJ's vision, from the outset of the 1988 reform, was to create a sustainable passenger and freight rail transport system. Larsson and other senior SJ managers understood the critical role of environmental sustainability for SJ in two areas: as a competitive differentiator for SJ, and as a critical factor for the future of Sweden as a nation. SJ developed its vision of sustainability as the driver for its own turnaround, and as the basis for a new rail system that could be a key player in preserving both environmental health and the 'sustainability' of Sweden's national competitiveness. Beyond environmental sustainability, Larsson and his colleagues were keenly aware of SJ's fractured internal culture: the low morale, the poor productivity. The social sustainability of SJ as an organisation was in jeopardy. Thus, from the beginning, SJ laid out sustainable development as the core platform for the turnaround—a definition of sustainability that included not only environmental considerations but social considerations for SJ as an organisation, and a role for SJ in sustaining the societal and environmental health, as well as international competitiveness, of Sweden as a nation. This expanded view garnered the enthusiasm and commitment of the nation, captivated employees, and drove radical innovation.

The 'sustainable transport' message became critical to SJ's image, work with employees, productivity initiatives, design of new services, development of long-term product and service strategies, and fundamental approach to competitive positioning.

ii. *Structural change focuses on serving the market*

The government's decision to split the railway into two entities began the structural change process. One of the most dramatic changes for SJ was the simple fact that it now had responsibility for the profit and loss of its operations. The organisation developed a tremendous commitment to being customer-oriented, accelerated its response to market pressures, and developed a profound new sense of urgency—all initially driven by its new structure. This new structure (with its emphasis on customers and operations) allowed SJ the opportunity to close or reform unprofitable services, and focus on modernising the trains, analysing customer needs and quickly creating a dozen major ancillary services to meet those needs. The most capital intensive investment was the introduction of the X2000 tilting trains which operate at speeds of up to 300 kmh. Between 1988 and 1994, SEK 8 billion was invested in the new X2000 trains and others. As a consequence, SJ's market share for all travel between Stockholm and Gothenburg (Sweden's two major cities) has increased to a remarkable 60%. SJ has introduced first-class service, unique and exciting amenities, sleeping cars, cinema coaches, family coaches, business services on board, and modern stations in city centres integrated with other transportation options. Thus, the first step in SJ's journey was to adapt to its new structure: this helped propel its orientation away from fixed assets and toward service, customers and operational breakthroughs.

iii. *Leadership: from vision to action*

If the new structure started the journey, then, clearly, new leadership provided the motivation to help SJ travel down the road so quickly. The first non-politician ever hired to run SJ, Stig Larsson, came from his previous position as President of Ericsson Data Systems with a grand vision, a world-class approach to aligning the organisation in pursuit of the vision, and a conviction about the kinds of people, management–employee relations, and action-oriented culture that would be necessary for success. Larsson's initial major effort was rationalisation, with 5,000 employees leaving (most through early retirement) and 35 out of the top 50 managers being replaced in the first year. Over the first six years, in collaboration with the union, the workforce was reduced from 29,000 to 11,000, mostly through early retirement and natural wastage. On top of employee downsizing and the push for labour productivity, Larsson and the new management team also added a new phase called 're-structuring' increasing the 'value-added' proportions of all jobs and reconfiguring routes and service provision. The leadership team articulated a vision of a high speed, sustainable passenger and freight rail network. They inspired the organisation to focus more intently on the market and on customers' needs, implemented massive investments and upgrading, and increased performance measurement and managerial accountability. They embarked on a public communications strategy that made every leader's improvement pledges public knowledge across the nation. The executive team captivated employees, radically improved relationships with the union (see section vi below), invested in mid-management and supervisory development, and committed all of them to a level of performance and service unprecedented in SJ's 140-year history.

In February 1998, the baton was passed to a new Director-General and Group CEO, Daniel Johannesson. He is carrying on the vision and strategy of SJ Rail, leading the way toward a more sustainable transportation system, as a key vehicle for competitive advantage, new services, and new business development.

iv. *Aligning with larger societal objectives*

With a new structure and new leadership, SJ began to consciously portray itself as a company capable of solving larger societal problems. With that mantle, it both garnered significant government investment and capitalised on national pride in its drive to modernise and increase market share. In addition, employees were encouraged to join with managers, who were given a context for changing their own management styles to be more inclusive and collaborative, and everyone developed a deepened sense of partnership with customers.

For example, SJ recognised that the integration of transport modes is one of the greatest challenges for both passenger and freight customers. SJ seized the opportunity to solve transport problems—with an eye to turning business transport into a seamless journey—by solving the logistics problems of the total transport chain. To date, SJ has integrated its service with the three main airports in the Nordic countries and established a 17 km bridge to the Copenhagen airport. SJ now provides service that co-ordinates rail traffic with airline, ferry, bus/coach and car traffic through the ongoing development of the travel centres. The train thus acts as the centrepiece for a nationwide Swedish passenger and freight transport system.

SJ has also developed a software analysis package that addresses Sweden's national goals to invest in clean transport and reduce air pollutants such as nitric oxides, SO_2, CO_2 and hydrocarbons. The software demonstrates for SJ customers, the media, authorities, politicians and public interest groups how rail contributes to achieving these goals. SJ achieves strategic advantage because it successfully positioned itself as supporting societal objectives.

v. *Business planning and management deployment system*

A new structure, a new leadership and a new mission—all now had to meet with everyday reality. What enabled SJ's vision and hopes to come to fruition was in large measure due to a sophisticated management goal-setting, planning and accountability system. SJ instituted the business planning process over a six-month period, starting with significant management training over a five-day programme. During this six-month period, managers took the major strategic vision, developed it more completely, and then created a comprehensive strategic and tactical plan broken down into 2,000 sub-business plans. All these plans had to include key success factors. Performance indicators were linked to those success factors, measurement methods for the indicators were established and specific action plans set. The five specific success factors that had to be included were: customer requirements; employees' competence and morale; process efficiency; profitability; and organisational renewal and development. The plans were then co-ordinated through a new, common business planning system. This final business plan became the internal marketing idea for change and led to work on cross-functional co-operation.

With the plan in place, SJ also installed a vigorous plan–do–check–act follow-up and reporting process. All business and support managers had to come to corporate headquarters and report directly to the CEO. Everyone was held to strict dates, formalised reporting procedures, and performance measures tightly integrated with costs and benefits.

Once this rigorous system was well established, SJ evolved it to include the '100 Points Programme' (see section vii below) and the 'STIL' system (key performance indicators in the management process). The STIL system involves all managers identifying their key success factors, developing measurable indicators, specifying their measurement reporting, and actively linking action plan items and follow-up activities. In all cases, specific goals combined with explicit measurement is the key. The aim is that all employees should be aware of their units' indicators and ratios, how they are related to one another, and how their own efforts contribute to achieving the objectives.

vi. *Involving and investing in people*

Without collaboration, competence and commitment, even the best management systems can fail. SJ moved in two directions to help ensure its people would bring life and capability to the system. First, SJ executives worked intensively on their management style. They got managers out of their offices—talking to people, walking through the operations, engaging in dialogue. They implemented a five-day training programme. A collaborative style became the new norm.

At the same time, the executive team and SJ reached out to the union. They created a joint programme for higher efficiency; put union members on the board of directors; and made the union a partner in increasing employee morale. They opened up financial records and shared them with the union as a mechanism to gain support in helping to solve the real problems that faced the organisation—extremely poor labour productivity, huge financial losses and gross inefficiency. Initially, 5,000 employees left. By 1998, the figure had risen to 18,000. The union participated in the planning of this reduction, achieved mostly via early retire-ments. A new salary system was put in place for employees, which rewarded entrepreneurial and performance accountability and was perceived as being fairer, particularly by younger workers and managers. Through openness and a sharing of financial information, employees' commitment to the rationalisation pro-gramme became possible. The unions were involved from the beginning, and felt truly responsible for the higher efficiency of the operation. They knew SJ could not survive if it did not increase labour productivity; hence they co-operated in decreasing resources by 60%. The early invitation to share knowledge and participate helped to encourage ideas on how to compete in a deregulated market. The union also recognised that management was doing its part to improve its own performance, so the sense of partnership ran deep. In the end, virtually everyone understood that the process that helped them become an efficient and competitive transport enterprise had created valuable intellectual capital. As competition increases, SJ has furthered its commitment to invest in the ongoing development of its people.

vii. *Communication as a strategic management tool*

The challenge that lay ahead was motivating employees to accomplish the enormous changes desired, and achieving the trust and confidence of consumers throughout Sweden. SJ assigned a top executive to implement both the internal and external communications strategy, which has been a 'cohesive, driving force behind SJ's change and development-related work'.[1] Press relations staff were now permanently available around the clock, the objective being to increase knowledge and commitment to the change programme. The change process itself was used as the communication vehicle. One hundred projects were selected from the business plans and listed for publication (see section x below). Booklets were distributed to all employees outlining the 100 specific areas in which SJ was going to improve over the next three years.

Another booklet was sent out as a newspaper insert to over four million house-holds—every household in Sweden—with the 100-point, three-year plan. Managers found their children reading about each of their specific individual goals and time-frames for completion in the newspaper. Accountability became very high with such a public process. Peer pressure also incited progress: work groups competed to accomplish goals. As projects were completed, they were 'checked off', and progress was frequently published in the newspaper. After the first year, 36 of the 100 points were completed and, throughout the nation, the Swedish people began ticking off points. This engendered pride among employees and spurred on their advancement, with the check mark becoming the symbol or icon for progress. Within two and a half years, all 100 points were successfully completed. The slogan of SJ's new communication programme, 'Post-100 Points', is: 'Success for the train is development for the environment.' The strategic linkage, across multiple fronts, is clear.

viii. *An image and reality of being ultra-modern and eco-efficient*

Beyond the management changes, there were core investments and specific new services that propelled the turnaround. Before SJ could invest in their 36 new X2000 trains, extensive R&D was required to ensure that these high-speed trains could negotiate existing rail beds—which, in Sweden, have a large number of curves. Trains in Sweden also need to perform in winters that can be as cold as −40°C, which brutally tests brakes, hydraulics, axles and heating, electrical and mechanical systems. Beyond particular trains, SJ also faced logistical hurdles: the option of building new rail beds was functionally out of the question, as distances throughout Sweden and the Nordic countries are prohibitive and ocean separates them from the rest of Europe. Also, single tracks pose planning dilemmas for

---

1   Personal communication with Anders Lundberg.

freight transport. To all these challenges, SJ responded with innovation, high technology and a spirit of problem-solving. For example, the solution to the problem of maintaining high speeds around curves was not to build expensive new track that ran straight, but to use trains that tilt—allowing them to race around existing, 140-year-old curves without disturbing passengers. SJ currently has over 50 major projects to link Sweden with the other Nordic countries and—via ferries and bridges—with the remainder of Europe. It has built a 200-person computer centre and installed sensors in all the tracks, which has enabled SJ to achieve breakthroughs in logistical planning and control, and to deliver computerised ticketing and travel planning services to customers. It has created new coupling systems, and developed rotating containers and loading equipment to achieve vast improvements in flexibility and logistical efficiency. It has also extensively modernised over 100 train stations, ending the campaign with a celebrated refurbishing of Stockholm Central Station (an intentional reversal of the common corporate priority of starting with headquarters).

ix. Rationalisation: productivity increases

Along with the modernisation, SJ's turnaround also included a strategic and carefully conducted rationalisation programme. The basic events and outcomes have already been highlighted above, but the point *vis-à-vis* the journey is that the choices on productivity increases were made from a strategic perspective, and then achieved in collaboration with the employees.

In addition to shedding jobs, SJ also restructured unprofitable routes, selling some off, redesigning and increasing revenue on others. Over four years, the organisation achieved a 50% increase in the productivity of mechanics through the redesign of maintenance work and the re-engineering of their spare parts flows and storage, as well the establishment of mobile repair patrols. Similar productivity increases were achieved in sales and administration through breakthroughs in information technology (IT) design and new system functionalities. SJ's broad view of sustainability included the assertion that the sustainability of SJ as a viable organisation was at risk without dramatic improvements in productivity. Seen in this context, employees (for the most part) embraced the changes that were required, and creatively addressed how to best design and implement them. Clearly, there were hard realities to face, but the partnership approach implied by a broadly defined sustainable development perspective led to strategic and collaborative solutions.

x. The '100 Points' programme

One of the most exciting and innovative elements of SJ's journey was its '100 Points' programme. As sketched briefly above, after a series of reviews and dialogue, SJ selected 100 areas for improvement from its strategic plan. Examples included direct freight trains, a new ticketing system, new exclusively family compartments, a new salary structure for employees, and business services in first class. SJ pledged to itself, internally, and to the entire Swedish nation, that it would improve in all 100 of these areas within three years. The specific goals and dates promised for completion were published in newspaper inserts, including individual managers' names and their specific implementation plans and targets. This was followed by advertising campaigns, throughout the trains as well as across Sweden, with the improvement areas and the target dates displayed. As projects were completed, the publicity material would be altered to include large red tick marks in boxes next to each success. By the end of the first year, 36 had been completed, all on time, and the tick mark had acquired public notoriety. Now the Swedes as a people were pulling for 'their' railway, applauding improvements, convinced that its success would increase Sweden's international competitiveness as well as improve the quality of life and the natural environment at home. The three years were characterised by an infectious enthusiasm both inside and outside SJ, and a sense of optimism that the efforts would be completed—in contrast to the cynicism with which corporate proclamations are typically met. The strategic ploy of aligning employees with the nation in a shared public commitment harnessed a positive intensity seen in few other corporate improvement efforts in recent times.

xi. *Quality, customer orientation, new services, and expansion*

Once productivity was increased, morale restored and modernisation well under way, SJ turned its attention to expanding its service and performance for customers. It doubled, then tripled the number of high-speed X2000 trains. It opened new routes, built a new computer centre, opened high-quality restaurants in the train stations, and added luxury shopping in first-class carriages.

Beyond 'hard' products, SJ has also pioneered new relationships. The organisation changed the core nature of value exchange with key freight customers by linking multiple parties together and planning end-to-end logistics. This has dramatically reduced total value-chain logistics costs while simultaneously increasing logistical, handling and environmental performance. For passengers, SJ has initiated totally seamless travel, with one ticket covering train, bus and underground.

Taken together, the structural and managerial changes have gone hand in hand with specific physical upgrades and product/service breakthroughs to produce a new reality and a new identity. SJ trained employees in customer service and created international alliances to make it significantly easier for both passengers and freight to travel to and from Europe. The organisation set explicit quality targets, and included them in the management planning, measurement and review system that had been so instrumental in supporting the turnaround. Employees now feel like they are part of a continuing effort to accelerate into the 21st century, achieving comparative levels of performance against their peer companies throughout Europe, such that they are now acknowledged European leaders. This confidence, vision and enthusiasm is apparent to customers, both passengers and freight customers, in terms of better service and a more vigorous problem-solving and creative orientation.

xii. *Enhancing environmental sustainability*

The commitment to sustainable development that guided the turnaround has led to a number of specific environmental initiatives and continues to play a key role in SJ's ongoing evolution.

Throughout 1988, alongside the new structure, new leadership, new management systems and new internal relationships, SJ also worked on the development of its environmental policy, which was adopted in 1989. It consists of six major goals or commitments:

▷ To increase electrically powered rail traffic by being customer-oriented and more efficient

▷ To continuously educate and inform about the environmental benefits of rail

▷ To deal with all environmental issues with integrity and consistency in order to enable SJ to legitimately project an environmentally friendly image

▷ To serve as a role model for other companies of what an environmentally aware company should be

▷ To use raw materials, resources and energy as efficiently and environmentally appropriately as possible

▷ To make demands of suppliers that lead them to produce products and use processes that are as environmentally friendly as possible

There has been a consistent programme of action to bring the policy to life. SJ began environmental surveys in 1989,[2] determining that the greatest environ-

---

2   SJ conducts both environmental surveys (begun in 1989) and environmental audits (begun in 1992). The surveys are undertaken to assess environmental impact and formed the basis of the company's prioritisation of environmental improvement programmes. The audits are conducted to assess whether its environmental actions conform to its environmental policy, its own internal standards and legal requirements. It also conducts what it calls 'eco-audits', by which it means environmental analyses for customers of various transport options, resulting in an assessment of the best way to transport goods for least environmental impact.

mental damage occurred in workshops and stations. It then established a two-year programme that produced nine major changes to dramatically improve environmental performance (these included new work routines, preventative actions, changes in stocking procedures and in choices of raw materials, retrofitting and upgrading physical facilities and buildings, eliminating a wide range of toxic and hazardous materials, as well as using new paints and painting methods: water-based paints where possible; low-solvent paints where it is not; and advanced filtering technologies at facilities where low-solvent paints cannot be used). SJ no longer purchases any materials containing freon, and is phasing out all existing equipment and products that contain freon because of its ozone-depleting properties.

SJ is open and honest about the negative environmental effects of its business. In the document, *The Railway and the Environment: SJ's Plan for Sustainable Road Traffic*, Stig Larsson states: '. . . the transportation sector is one of the prime causes of many of our most pressing environmental problems. We must take responsibility for the environmental problems our activities cause.' The document goes on to say: '[we are] absolutely one of the prime contributors to every one of the major large-scale threats to our future environment: environmental poisons, health problems, acidification, eutrophication, holes in the ozone layer and the greenhouse effect.' The organisation also has a rigorous environmental management system that combines elements of both EMAS and ISO 14001, including recycling programmes, environmental audits, soil and water pollution prevention programmes, energy-saving programmes, and demands on suppliers for superior environmental performance. In addition, SJ has also developed software using Excel 5.0 to help educate customers regarding the life-cycle of different modes of transport, comparing trucking, shipping, air and rail transport. As a consequence of these efforts, the Swedish Society for the Conservation of Nature has awarded SJ the 'Good Environmental Choice' eco-label symbol and Parliament has allowed rail greater potential to increase its capacity by granting planning expansion in favour of rail over roads and the airline industry.

3. *Management processes and best practices*

First and foremost, the SJ experience underscores the value of strong vision and strategy. The SJ strategy is particularly comprehensive, covering all aspects of SJ operations, customers' needs, competitors' capabilities, demographic trends and environmental issues. The vision is a grand one: creating a superior passenger and freight transportation system, revitalising the organisation, and providing Sweden with a sustainable transportation system for the 21st century. Such vision and strategy, when clearly communicated, deeply engage stakeholders—employees, customers, investors and government. It is a key part of the SJ story that others may want to understand more completely.

Linked to the strategic vision is a sophisticated management planning system, which incorporates accountability, performance measurement and extensive co-ordination across departments and management functions. The business planning system serves as the managerial infrastructure for cross-functional collaboration. More recently, it has evolved to the even more sophisticated 'STIL' system, which integrates the measurement system with daily action planning systems. Such comprehensive systems, beyond accelerating the quality and reliability of perfor-mance, also serve to provide meaning for everyone in the organisation, and to provide assurance about what role they and their colleagues are playing in the pursuit of the vision.

What brings reality to this management system is the intensity of the follow-up processes. Larsson's method of having all regional managers report to him with those managers' bosses in the room created a sense of linked accountability—a certainty in people's minds that the commitments they had made were real. There appears to be little limit to what people can do if they know it is being measured, that they will be held accountable for it, and that it matters.

At the same time, expectations and accountability without capability can be disastrous, and SJ's commitment to management development highlights another key step here. SJ made extensive investments in both improving relations with the union and in developing its managers. This commitment could not be 'faked'. The union really did have a major say in the productivity programmes and staff reduction plans, and really was active on the board of directors. The management development effort and the management culture change were sincere and vigor-ous. But not everyone will perform well or be comfortable in a new culture, and many staff opted for early retirement rather than embrace radical change. Those who want to try need training, structures and cultural norms to enable them to succeed in meeting the new expectations. The turnaround relied, in a significant way, on legitimate management–labour collaboration.

We cannot conclude without at least touching on the rationalisation effort. There are two major elements of the SJ experience. First, productivity improvements, often at the breakthrough level, are a critical part of any sustainable development effort. SJ's integration of the productivity requirements into its strategic plan, and its vision of what it means to be sustainable, made that vision credible and the strategy intelligent. Those realities cannot be avoided if one is to face the sus-tainable development challenge honestly. Second, the approach to the productivity improvements put 'all the cards on the table'. SJ shared facts fully with employees and the union. They articulated a vision and outlined how the productivity improvements fitted into that vision. By carrying out the rationalisation effort with integrity and meaning, it became an effort employees could share in, even co-own.

As such, the rationalisation was a comprehensive and inclusive effort endorsed by virtually all, whose outcome provided the intended results. Not all of those things can be said about more typical corporate rationalisation programmes.

Finally, SJ's socioeconomic approach to funding may be worthy of emulation. SJ highlighted for the Swedish government the socioeconomic costs of car, air and truck transport: the costs to Swedish society of carbon emissions and reduction of green space, and the healthcare consequences of fossil fuel use. It then made the case for government investment in rail as a way of mitigating these societal costs. As we move into the 21st century, this kind of government–industry collaboration is likely to be more and more necessary.

SJ today

SJ's years of work educating politicians and the public about the need to internalise the societal costs of different modes of transport into the cost of goods and services has paid off. As of January 1999, Sweden passed a landmark bill lowering the infrastructure charges to rail, which sidesteps the more controversial strategy of 'carbon taxes' or some other form of revenue-neutral tax shift to internalise negative environmental, health and social costs, yet supports both Swedish and EU goals of 'sustainable transport'. It introduces an adjustment to more closely reflect the true societal costs of different modes of transport and promises to shift the competitive structure in the marketplace dramatically in favour of rail. In the words of SJ CEO Daniel Johannesson, 'It makes rail the only possible solution to reach the European Union target of sustainable mobility. It is a very important milestone.'

SJ's educational campaign sought to raise the visibility of the externalised costs of transportation such as traffic accidents, air pollution, noise and congestion. It clarified for policy-makers, passengers and transport operators the fact that prices do not reflect the full social cost of transport, so demand is artificially high. These costs were then quantified, and SJ demonstrated that a socioeconomic evaluation shows that social costs for environment, traffic accidents and maintenance of infrastructure in Sweden would increase by about SEK 2 billion (US$240 million) annually, according to internal company analyses, if rail transport was abandoned. SJ worked in alliance with operators and train construction suppliers (ABB) to promote the train as the best environmental choice.

Almost as important is the deregulation of the rail industry, passed by the Swedish parliament in December 1995, which SJ has decided to support. Although some contracts will be lost in a competitive playing field, SJ's position is that deregulation will provide more freedom and opportunity to grow.

Customers, both corporate and individual, are increasingly concerned with reducing the negative environmental impact of transport. Johannesson commented that 'More and more companies are publicising corporate environmental reports, and transport is a big part of the environmental liability. They can calculate how much they can win and report as improvements using our computer programme'. SJ's branded 'Green Cargo' service, which delivers door to door, overnight, to any destination, is the first major branded transportation service endorsed by the Swedish Society for the Conservation of Nature as environmentally friendly (other than the bicycle). This service is being marketed very aggressively, using modern technology.

In fact, SJ's marketing overall appears very sophisticated. Its slogan, aimed at converting the air passenger to rail, states: 'Rail is not a way of travel, it is a way of thinking.' SJ underlines the point that rail travel time is 100% useful, and backs it up with technology hook-ups and amenities to meet both business and leisure customers, supported by city centre-to-city centre connections. The overall angle of SJ's current marketing is very unusual for a transportation company, and builds on the company's belief that people are fundamental to everything they do—marketing material depicts not trains and pallets but people in everyday situations. Daniel Johannesson provides insight into the motivation behind this: 'Cargo and freight are normally thought of as dirty, low-skilled. We want to lift it: we are using environmental issues as a crane to lift it out of a hole.'

SJ Rail is integrating environmental and social sustainability considerations into the total product/service package. For example, in its redesign of the train station as a travel centre, it is supporting a return to the time when train stations functioned as the centre of the community. Also, as a final touch to passenger service, SJ serves ecologically grown coffee!

4. Conclusions and themes

With the changes to the rail system introduced in 1988, sustainable development became essential to the overhaul of SJ Rail. Sustainability was the goal from the outset. It is also clear that the SJ Group could not become 'sustainable' without a commitment to becoming a world-class competitor. In achieving its dramatic turnaround, these two pursuits have become interlinked. Also, each short-term action taken to improve performance, quality and service has been guided by SJ's longer-term plan and vision. All of this has taken place within a context of openness and integrity: a transformation would not have been possible if the organisation had not been extremely open and clear about the realities it was facing.

The depth and clarity of the communications strategy is also striking. From the beginning, Larsson recognised that he could not 'turn a supertanker' without very skilled internal and external communications. SJ used the business planning process itself as the communications vehicle. Although much of what SJ was doing was image building, that image was not hollow or 'greenwash'. It was a careful reflection of the changing reality.

The effect of integrity on the actions of your workforce is leveraged if you are operating with vision and integrity. The financial performance for shareholders is short-term; but you must also have a parallel vision of where things need to be because of the strategic advantage of a long-term perspective. These paths are parallel but separate and the long-term perspective must derive from a visioning process. The value it creates is what makes stakeholders feel good when they read the annual report and what makes employees feel good about their company.

References

SJ Rail publications

http://www.sj.se

The Development of High-Speed Tilting Trains (Stockholm: SJ Rail).
On the Tracks to Sweden (Stockholm: SJ Freight International).
Annual Report 1995 (Stockholm: SJ Rail, 1996).
Annual Report 1996 (Stockholm: SJ Rail, 1997).
The Railway and the Environment: SJ's Plan for Sustainable Rail Traffic (Stockholm: SJ Information Staff, 1994).

Other

UIC (International Union of Railways) (1998) *International Railway Statistics 1997* (Paris: UIC).

Organisational contacts

Daniel Johannesson, Director General and Group CEO of SJ Rail
Karin Jansson, SJ Communications
Anders Lundberg, Senior Vice-President, Director of Corporate Planning and Strategic Development
Gunnel Sundbom, Senior Vice-President, Director of Communications
Johan Trouve, MSc, Policy Officer Environment/R&D

Tell us where you want your goods to go and we'll find a fast, green way to get there.

GreenCargo
Ecological and economical transport

The green arrow is a symbol for GreenCargo, our new cargo transport service for Swedish business and industry. For complete terms and conditions, regulations re time guarantees, etc., please order our GreenCargo Concept Manual (tel. +46 771 65 20 20, 020-65 20 20 if you are in Sweden) or read it on www.greencargo.com

➡ Times change

GreenCargo

Ecological and economical transport solutions

www.greencargo.com

Service Centre +46 771 65 20 20

GreenCargo
Ekologiska och ekonomiska transportlösningar

www.greencargo.com

Servicecenter 020-65 20 20

At last: ecological and economical transport. From door to door.

GreenCargo
Ecological and economical transport

Some examples of SJ Rail's marketing for its 'Green Cargo' service

TransAlta

New terrain: reducing greenhouse gas emissions

1. The lie of the land

a. Corporate overview

TransAlta Corporation is an electric utility based in Calgary, Canada, that owns and operates thermal and hydroelectric power plants, and electric transmission and distribution systems, servicing 1.7 million people directly and indirectly. The company's asset base is approximately C$5 billion (US$3.2 billion). In 1998, the corporation restructured into five profit-and-loss centres: 'Generation', 'Transmission and Distribution', 'Independent Power Projects', 'New Zealand', and 'Energy Marketing'. This altered the previous structure, adding the latter three divisions to the organisation. TransAlta Utilities, the original name for the Transmission business unit, has been operating in the province of Alberta since 1911 and is the largest investor-owned electric utility in Canada. In 1998 three coal-fired plants accounted for 95% of TransAlta's Alberta electrical generation, supported by 13 hydroelectric plants.

Moving from its traditional role as a power company for the province of Alberta, the company now operates in Ontario, New Zealand, Australia and the US—with interests in electricity generation, gas and electricity distribution, energy services and energy marketing. It provides energy-generation services in Alberta, Ontario,

Washington state, New Zealand, Australia and Argentina, plus energy marketing in New Zealand and North America. TransAlta New Zealand is New Zealand's largest energy retailer. TransAlta Corporation employs about 2,200 people throughout its operations.

The good news is that TransAlta supplies low-cost energy to its commercial and independent customers—a 1995 survey by the UK's Electricity Association indicated that TransAlta Utilities' domestic and industrial rates are among the lowest internationally. The bad news is that TransAlta is Canada's second-largest source point emitter of greenhouse gas emissions. The silver lining, and the basis of this chapter, is that the risks associated with this emissions profile have stimulated TransAlta toward proactively integrating sustainable development considerations into all business decisions. In full recognition that TransAlta is not a 'green company', TransAlta management has been working diligently over the past ten years to integrate sustainable development as a core element of TransAlta's business strategy. As a result, TransAlta has gained international recognition as an energy company actively pursuing environmental initiatives. These efforts are now bearing fruit beyond risk reduction, and the corporation is winning international bids, gaining competitive advantage, and generating new revenues as a direct result of its environmental initiatives and competences. TransAlta's journey, past, present and future, is particularly illustrative for other companies and industries facing the need to be more sustainable when they have huge 'sunk' costs in assets and infrastructure.

b. *The business context*

TransAlta has had to adapt to fundamental shifts in the context of its business, driven by a diversification of its operations and the following dramatic changes in the electric utility industry:

1. Increasing competition in a deregulated power market—and the inherent challenges of preparing the company for a competitive environment where they must earn customers' business. Deregulation means that the 'rules' of business conduct must be rewritten, which is particularly difficult in the transition stage due to uncertainty in the timing and outcomes of the restructuring process.

2. Technological change—from large coal-fired generation toward new gas turbine technology capable of cogeneration on a smaller, more decentralised scale

3. Opportunities emerging from utility privatisation

4. The challenge for sustainable development as concern increases regarding greenhouse gas emissions, ecosystem degradation and loss of biodiversity

▷ Sustainable development is, and will continue to be, a major challenge for TransAlta, with its legacy of major investments in coal-fired generation with significant greenhouse gas emissions, and in hydro facilities facing increasing land and resource use pressures. TransAlta recognises the challenge and it has responded with improvements and innovative projects.

▷ Environmental issues have moved from a narrow, regulatory, compliance-oriented concern at local level to a corporate issue that is part of the overall company positioning with a global reach.

▷ A Senior Vice-President, Sustainable Development, was appointed in June 1994. Following the retirement of the incumbent, a Vice-President of Sustainable Development position was staffed in 1998 by an external expert in ecology.

▷ Commitment and performance in sustainable development is providing new business opportunities. For example, TransAlta won bids in New Zealand and Australia partially on the merits of its demonstrated environmental stewardship record.

▷ TransAlta is meeting, ahead of schedule, its 'Greenhouse Gas Action Plan' for stabilising net emissions of greenhouse gases to the atmosphere at 1990 levels by 2000 (*Sustainable Development: Economy–Environment–Society* [1995 Progress Report])— through contributions from improved efficiency of internal operations, promotion of customer efficiencies, purchase of renewable energy, acquiring offset projects, joint implementation internationally, and displacement from cogeneration.

▷ Nine out of ten employees have been educated in 'Environmental Citizenship Initiative' sessions.

▷ TransAlta has participated actively and played a leadership role in provincial, national and international projects, research efforts, and forums focused on sustainable development.

Box 1: **Sustainable development at TransAlta**

c. *Preview*

The changes in business climate stimulated an intensive analysis and repositioning of TransAlta's corporate development strategy during the late 1980s and early 1990s. Sustainable development emerged as one critical component of TransAlta's strategy for succeeding in the new world of an emerging deregulated market concerned about the environmental and social impacts of energy production and consumption.

The sections below describe the continuing journey of TransAlta, the coal-based electric power company, as it has discovered and defined its meaning of sustainable development.

d. *Drivers toward sustainability*

There were several **key drivers** toward sustainability strategies in TransAlta:

▷ The early acknowledgement of global climate change as a substantial business issue

▷ Continued customer demand, in all its markets, for both low prices and environmental protection

▷ The development of a clear strategic rationale to maintain as much flexibility as possible, through proactivity and participation in policy development forums both locally, in Alberta, and at national level

▷ The adoption of market-based approaches for service development and distribution

More than any other, it is the climate change issue that has driven TransAlta's most ambitious actions through the 1990s. Health, and particularly safety, are important internal values, and have been taken seriously for decades. Environmental management, too, stands on its own legs as an internal driver for the organisation.

More recently, in the deregulated market, some corporate customers are choosing green power—and are even willing to pay a premium—as projecting a green image has become an increasingly important part of their competitive positioning and advertising. TransAlta is forming strategic alliances with these big industrial customers to achieve energy savings, thus generating revenues from advice and consultation as well as power generation. There is also increasing awareness of and demand for green power at the consumer level, and TransAlta's competitors are developing product packages and marketing campaigns to capitalise on this.

2. *The journey*

a. *Starting a little beyond compliance*

Environmental activities at TransAlta Corporation during the 1960s and '70s are best characterised by limited compliance-motivated responses at the local facility level. Even in those early days, however, TransAlta had strong philosophical values regarding the environment embedded in its leadership: CEO Marshall Williams advocated a responsible approach, saying, 'We won't wait for regulators; we will anticipate, be proactive.' During those years, TransAlta established the objective of remediating its mine sites to a state of 'equal to or better than' original condition. Well in advance of legislative guidelines, TransAlta began land reclamation with seeding and restoring mined-out sections to reinstate land to productive use.

b. *Toward environmental management and risk management*

In 1988, the same year Ken McCready became CEO, the environment was increasingly being perceived as a key issue by Canadians. Given that TransAlta was one of the largest greenhouse gas emitters in Canada, and concerned that TransAlta was receiving increasing exposure, McCready began to address this complex issue. TransAlta subsequently developed an environmental policy statement, thus making a public declaration about its commitment to the environment.

c. *Stakeholders identify two strategic requirements*

At that point, in the late 1980s, TransAlta was also in the process of re-examining its corporate vision, stimulated in large part by the quality movement. TransAlta's implementation of a quality programme not only generated the intended increases in quality, but provided a fertile ground for its future sustainable development strategy. The 'Quality of Service' programme at TransAlta contributed to a fundamental shift in the corporate mind-set, replacing the company's internal focus with an external focus, emphasising the objective of satisfying customer needs. As a result, TransAlta began thinking about customers and other stakeholders in a wholly different way, an insight that has led to its competence in stakeholder management today.

As the world prepared for the 1992 Rio conference, McCready realised that the environment had to be a major part of TransAlta's position. He brought together the key stakeholder groups—customers and NGOs—expecting fireworks to ensue as a result of the conflicting views. The surprise was that TransAlta's customers didn't simply say they needed low prices, while environmentalists pleaded for environmental protection. What the customers did say was that they wanted *both low prices and to protect the environment*.

The upshot of this was that, by the late 1980s and early '90s, TransAlta recognised that it wanted and needed to be proactive on sustainable development—on the issue of global climate change in particular. It was felt that, by adopting an advanced position, the company would reduce risks and retain flexibility for growth and change.

d. *Taking a broader perspective leads to sustainable development*

In the early 1990s, TransAlta executives participated in a series of national and international activities related to sustainable development: the publication *Changing Course* (Schmidheiny and the Business Council for Sustainable Development 1992, prepared for the Rio Conference); its project on 'Internalising Environmental Costs to Promote Eco-efficiency' and two projects on joint implementation; the

Canadian National Roundtable on Environment and Economy; and the Alberta Clean Air Strategic Alliance. In these roles, TransAlta became an early developer of concepts and tools for sustainable development and a conceptual leader in the world business community.

In hindsight, these activities have played a significant role in contributing to networking and in increasing the knowledge, understanding and conviction of the management team about the issues. In particular, McCready's involvement as chair of the Alberta Roundtable on Environment and Economy (a collaborative multi-stakeholder process involving government, NGOs, academics and industry to develop economic instruments) laid the groundwork for similar processes at TransAlta. Now TransAlta's goal is to solve 80% of the issues ahead of potential conflict with various stakeholder groups, since this saves money otherwise spent on time and lawyers. Prevention is better than cure.

e. Clear measurable goals and internal costing programmes drive improvement

In 1994, TransAlta set a **stabilisation goal** to return greenhouse gas emissions to 1990 levels by 2000, in parallel with the target agreed in the Rio conference. **This was extremely instrumental in operationalising the commitment to sustainable development**, as it required action by all TransAlta business units. In an effort to convert this policy to action, TransAlta began working both internally and with customers. What is significant here is the lesson that a clear, measurable policy or goal provided the major catalyst for change.

One particularly advanced practice at TransAlta was a programme **for costing CO_2 emissions internally** as a signal and incentive for action. This involved creating an internal market for CO_2 emissions, whereby the generation side of the company would pay other business units for any emissions reductions they were given as offsets. Internally, TransAlta began charging C$2/tonne for CO_2 as a way of: (1) changing people's thinking (to understand that CO_2 emissions have value); (2) stimulating creativity; and (3) providing an internal incentive to reduce. This internal emissions trading programme was characterised symbolically as a 'helping hand' across business functions. This programme provides one example of how the clear goal of stabilisation was supported, as performance improvements were tied to incentives.

As a result, people began to look at operations in a different way. In some cases, they found it was possible to reduce CO_2 emissions at no cost (they found ways of making operational changes that didn't require the $2/tonne). The greatest benefits TransAlta reports from this programme are that it 'helps to get people thinking about sustainable development issues in a business way, and it drives action'.[1] Once

1 Personal communication with Jim Leslie.

people were mobilised, paying attention and looking at their operations in a different way, then the programme was phased out as it was no longer needed. This programme was instrumental in helping the company overcome the initial reaction that environmental changes are 'hard, expensive and will cripple us all'[2] and develop an understanding that environmental initiatives can stimulate innovation and improve performance at a lower cost than expected.

In 1995, TransAlta submitted its 'Greenhouse Gas Action Plan' in response to the Voluntary Climate Change and Registry (VCR) programme. It provided a five-point plan for achieving its goal of returning its net contribution of greenhouse gases to the atmosphere to 1990 levels by 2000. The plan includes:

▷ Improving the efficiency of TransAlta's operations

▷ Promoting energy efficiency initiatives in customer operations

▷ Purchasing renewable energy

▷ Developing greenhouse gas offset projects, both domestically and internationally

▷ Developing cogeneration facilities to supply high-efficiency energy with lower overall emissions

Currently, with the emissions stabilisation plan in implementation, TransAlta is focusing on the following priorities:

▷ Strengthening the voluntary approach through an enhanced VCR

▷ Harnessing flexible market mechanisms by exploiting offsets credits and trading (in fact, by creating its own marketplace to purchase offsets)

▷ Promoting technological innovation, especially in coal technology

▷ Enhancing competitive opportunities through incentives

▷ Participating in the public policy of climate, through the Canadian National Climate Change Tables, and, more regionally by building an Alberta partnership through public/private-sector co-operation

f. Implementation supported by frameworks, metrics and communication

TransAlta has guided implementation of its strategy for sustainable development through the use of a framework of five 'Strategic Cornerstones', each an arena for continual improvement, and each with set objectives for operationalisation (see

2   *Ibid.*

1. Environment, health and safety management

In 1996, TransAlta adopted revised environment, health and safety policies. A management system framework and detailed 'Expectations and Standards' were put in place. These ensure compliance with regulations and operating licences, assist in managing environment, health and safety risks, and help TransAlta protect the environment and ensure a safe workplace—all while contributing to continual improvement in key areas of corporate performance.

The firm has acted to bring its operations to ISO 14001 compliance. This has been done for business reasons, with a strong emphasis on systems process design and a tremendous level of detail.

2. Sustainable business initiatives

In existing operations, and in its development of new opportunities, TransAlta is pursuing business practices that provide both economic and environmental benefits. As part of this pursuit, TransAlta is focusing on eco-efficiency—producing greater value with fewer resources while reducing environmental impact.

The Edmonton, Alberta, Composting Center is, at first glance, a somewhat surprising project for an energy company. When complete in 1999, the centre will process Edmonton's municipal solid waste, waste- water treatment sludge and lime sludge into compost for use in the reclamation of TransAlta's mine sites immediately west of the city. The facility will be the largest of its kind in North America. True to the company's strategy, the project will also divert organic waste from traditional landfills, offsetting methane emissions and substantially contributing to TransAlta's greenhouse gas stabilisation goals.

3. External issues, relationships and opportunities

Sustainable development includes working with communities and addressing stakeholder concerns. As has been emphasised elsewhere, TransAlta's networking and partnership skills are a continuing corporate strong point.

4. Improved decision-making

Through new business processes, TransAlta encourages business decision-making that supports sustainable development. It is company policy to include sustainable development considerations in all capital decisions over C$200,000. This is enforced via major project approval by the sustainable development department.

The significant tool for enhancing decision-making has been life-cycle value assessment (LCVA), which brings economic and environmental criteria onto a common platform for evaluations (e.g. transmission line formats, transformer station construction). Although the tool is still being developed in the organisation, it is credited with providing a discipline for more effective financial decision-making at the employee level. Particularly for capital projects, LCVA forces consideration of multiple economic and environmental factors in the context of the total life-cycle. The effect of LCVA has been to define the often vague line at which environmental benefits can be promoted even where incremental financial cost is incurred.

5. Sustainable development infrastructure

TransAlta supports more sustainable business practices through employee incentives, funding, education and standards. In 1997, the company discontinued the internal CO_2 emission trading system because it had achieved its objective of encouraging operations staff to look for ways of improving energy efficiencies in generation, transmission and buildings. An employee incentive pay programme also encourages energy efficiency.

Box 2: **TransAlta's five strategic cornerstones**

Sustainable development indicators at TransAlta have been tracked back to 1991. They include various reviewable measures covering numerous categories: greenhouse gases, other emissions, ash disposal, water flows, land use patterns, health and safety, and societal parameters (e.g. financial donations). In fact, TransAlta commented that the list of metrics currently employed is too long and too complex. To improve the management and reporting system, the list would benefit from some aggregation. Both internally and externally, a concise yet meaningful set of indicators would provide focus and greater clarity.

Heat rate (a measure of thermal efficiency for electric power production) was introduced as one of the indicators specific to sustainable development. It was thus distinct from more traditional measures of environment or health and safety. In its implementation, there were significant beneficial side-effects that generated a 'win–win' effect on cost and emissions. Previously, in the coal-fired generation plants, heat rate was an area of 'operational drift'—it was traditionally not an area of designated responsibility or importance. With the request for measurement coming from the sustainable development department, the heat rate metric actually focused overall accountability for plant performance. This resulted in a production yields increase, improved eco-efficiencies and, ultimately, increased profit margins.

Box 3: **TransAlta's metrics**

Box 2). Box 3 summarises TransAlta's metrics and Box 4 outlines the communication and reporting systems.

g. *Management procedures and best practices*

TransAlta implemented its sustainable development strategy with a solid understanding of the difficulties of institutional change. A top-down approach was taken, with initial conceptual development taking place in the CEO's office. In 1993–95, the groundwork was laid for the implementation of sustainable development activities. This work was co-ordinated centrally by the corporate sustainable development group, which at its peak included about 20 individuals.

During this time, what Jim Leslie, Vice-President of Sustainable Development, defined as the three essential underpinnings of implementation were established— **knowledge, networks and action**. Any one or two of these without the others is ineffectual.

i. *Knowledge: educating for change*
Through a variety of mechanisms, knowledge was generated—providing an understanding of the issues, identifying principles and establishing conceptual frameworks and models. In 1994–95, TransAlta implemented extensive employee training under the 'Environmental Citizenship Initiative'. With assistance from the

TransAlta has developed excellent internal communications and reporting systems. Consistent with the rigours of ISO 9000 and 14000, documentation of management processes is thorough throughout all operations and functions. These practices extend to sustainable development—whether as procedures reporting, or in the *Sustainable Development Dashboard*, the quarterly progress newsletter for management and other employees.

At the annual technical excellence conference, 20%–30% of presentations could be categorised under the banner of sustainable development. The 'Environmental Citizenship Initiative' has been key in TransAlta's internal communications on sustainable development. Through this initiative, nine out of ten employees have been educated in sessions that provide awareness and understanding of environmental issues and pressures.

TransAlta has internalised the notion that making sustainable development work optimally requires deep and ongoing recognition and integration.

Box 4: TransAlta's communication and reporting systems

Pembina Institute for Appropriate Development, an external, non-profit institute, all of the firm's employees were immersed in a four-day grass-roots programme on environmental awareness, tools and activities. The programme was used early in the process to prepare fertile ground across the organisation, particularly at the employee level. These sessions were treated seriously at set-up, execution and results levels. Consequently, early buy-in was gained across the company, leading to a good general understanding of environmental issues and pressures facing the company.

Also important in building widespread internal knowledge and creating the required infrastructure for change management, the Corporate Sustainable Development Group was at this time growing and attracting individuals from the different business units and regions of operation. Then, in 1995, specialists from the corporate group were sent back to the business units in order to put into practice the plans and policies that had been developed.

ii. *Networks: engaging stakeholders*
A **network** was developed with a variety of stakeholders, outside and inside the corporation. TransAlta's participation in national and international activities was leveraged and fostered. This ongoing engagement of stakeholders provided a perspective of what and whose needs would have to be satisfied in order to accomplish change, and participation in planning helped to build the necessary acceptance and commitment (see Box 5).

iii. *Action: moving the company towards sustainability*
Building on its knowledge, with extensive involvement of stakeholders, TransAlta implemented a series of **actions** in the 1990s to move the organisation toward

In 1995, TransAlta completed an upgrade in its transmission service to the Banff area of Canada. As part of the project, the company relied on a collaborative public process to achieve environmental and economic benefits while satisfying multiple stakeholder concerns and attaining service reliability within an environmentally sensitive area.

The public collaborative process, begun in 1992, allowed the company to gain a better appreciation for stakeholder concerns and to address them within its proposal. Consequently, the project received straightforward federal and provincial approval.

In the project, no easy solutions emerged. In fact, it took several iterations by the project team and with the stakeholders before a multifaceted and unique set of solutions was eventually found. An energy efficiency programme was launched in 1994 to reduce local electricity, gas and water consumption. In 1995, the electrical service capacity doubled using local hydro power. Segments of hydro lines were built underground or around old-growth forest areas to minimise impacts. An existing distribution line was also removed; alleviating standing concerns, components were salvaged, and land was returned to its original state.

In the end, through collaborative processes, multidisciplinary teams and well-considered synergies, the project cost roughly half that of an earlier estimate.

Box 5: Stakeholder engagement: think globally; act locally

sustainability. Together with the two elements outlined above, this formed the basis for a sustained, workable, strategic implementation.

In this top-down bottom-up change process, middle managers were, in effect, motivated from both above and below, yet were still described by Jim Leslie as 'the hole in the doughnut'. Middle managers were initially hesitant participants. They were the ones responsible for the tangible production results and operational performance, so their initial difficulties with respect to modifications to old processes were entirely understandable.

3. *Reflections on TransAlta's journey toward implementation*

TransAlta's vision is 'to become the premier supplier of electric and thermal energy, satisfying customers' individual needs for competitive energy services, while building a sustainable future' (*Sustainable Development: Economy–Environment–Society* [1995 Progress Report, p. 2]). As such, sustainable development for TransAlta Corporation is positioned to be 'the guiding context for the company's business, now and in the future' (*ibid.*).

Key milestones in TransAlta's journey are: the involvement of TransAlta leadership in international work on business and sustainable development; the shift in vision from internal to external—a focus on the customer which contributed to stakeholder involvement; the establishment of measurable goals, with attention to and incentives tied to their accomplishment; and the education of management and employees in sustainable development issues.

Two long-standing keys to TransAlta's approach are:

1.   Effective networking: broadly engaging stakeholders, and, in more focused formats, business partners, to understand needs, gain knowledge about the issues, and develop and test new concepts

2.   Development and use of economic instruments: for example, costing of CO_2 in-house

Sustainable development in TransAlta has been consistently led by the President and CEO, with a high degree of company-wide involvement. TransAlta's vision, and its operationalisation, is largely a story of people and strong management: CEO Ken McCready, a visionary leader; Vice-President of Sustainable Development Jim Leslie, a strategist; employees, motivated into action; senior managers, committed to implementing, and provided with incentives and tools for change.

For managers, the sustainable development programme became more firmly operationalised when clear targets for performance were implemented. Incentive/recognition/reward schemes were incorporated to include sustainable development targets, the CO_2 costing programme being the best-known incentive programme. Additionally, connection with the middle managers improved when leadership shifted to the business units, away from the corporate group. With tangible, measurable goals and objectives, and decision latitude, middle managers could perform in their own territory.

The greatest issue for TransAlta remains global climate change. TransAlta is now at a critical point with the regulatory path post-Kyoto still very uncertain. Although TransAlta stabilised greenhouse gas emissions at 1990 levels in 1997, the company continues to prepare for and influence the next phase of changes, whether they be tradable greenhouse gas permits, more offsets and joint implementation, or breakthrough technologies.

A second challenge, this time from outside the organisation, is the ever-changing cast of actors in government. With no sustaining government backdrop, the effectiveness of the company's plans are often undermined in the face of shifting policy priorities and fragile relationships.

A third challenge will be to build on existing knowledge. No systematic education efforts have been undertaken to upgrade or advance the organisational learning in sustainable development for a number of years, for management, specialists, or the company at large.

4. *Maturing towards 2000*

In early 1996, CEO Ken McCready retired, followed within 14 months by Jim Leslie, the key strategist and co-ordinator of policy implementation (Mr Leslie continues to be involved as Consultant, Sustainable Development). In 1997, Stephen Snyder took the reigns as the new President and CEO and TransAlta hired Dr Bob Page, an external ecology expert, as the new Vice-President of Sustainable Development. This sends at least two signals: that the firm continues to reach out to stakeholder networks and that TransAlta will continue to strive to be proactive with respect to sustainability.

The integration of sustainable development into business strategy appears to have withstood, and even flourished under, this change in leadership. The groundwork that was laid in building the commitment and competence within line management has proven critical in maintaining the momentum during the transition. Bob Page was given a clear mandate from the CEO, and the rest of the leadership team, to move TransAlta into the next phase on its journey toward sustainable industrial practices. His position on the senior management team ensures that environment and sustainable development are part of the equation in all decisions at the executive level. Further, sustainable development is a permanent agenda item at board meetings. Page reports that, at TransAlta, sustainable development is integrated into decision-making just like other strategic considerations such as fiscal management or technology development. All new business development planning includes an environmental component, whether it involves mergers, licensing or new power plant construction. Staff from the sustainable development department are on teams for new development and planning processes. This approach is in stark contrast to the all-too-common situation in which the environment department is marginalised or invited in only at the end of a process.

a. 'There are no trade-offs when it comes to sustainable development.'

The dynamic tension for sustainable development is apparent even in the company's own publications. On its 1999 website, introducing its sustainable development initiative is the paragraph:

> TransAlta has earned its reputation as a company that is taking on the challenges of sustainable development. We take responsible and effective actions to help balance the demands of environmental protection and our economic growth. Our view is straightforward—that there are no trade-offs when it comes to sustainable development.

TransAlta has indeed earned its reputation, but can it, in its own words, continue to *balance* the demands of environmental protection and economic growth *without trade-offs*?

With respect to sustainable development, TransAlta faces a difficult strategic dilemma, as the mainstay of its current business is three coal-fired plants. Given present technological capability, this implies a myriad of environmental consequences: it generates high levels of greenhouse gases, raises issues of land use and reclamation, and, with consumer and commercial demand growing stronger, is perceived more and more as 'dirty' power.

TransAlta hasn't built a major generating plant in Alberta since the late 1980s, as, until recently, overcapacity in generation was able to absorb demand growth. However, recently several sizeable cogeneration projects have been undertaken by TransAlta, including facilities at Suncor, Dow and Huskey. Nonetheless, most growth has primarily occurred outside of Alberta (in Ontario, New Zealand and Australia). Today, gas turbine technology with cogeneration capability—reducing greenhouse gas emissions by 50%–60% compared to coal—is the company's preferred power generation option. As Jim Leslie points out, one strength of gas turbines is that 'the economic and environmental arrows are pointing in the same direction'. Since gas turbines do not have to be large to achieve economies of scale, this allows for small, distributed plants, with faster construction rates and vastly improved economics.

Even gas turbine technology, however, is understood to be part of a greater transition. TransAlta's current path is to attempt to harvest the optimum value prior to the retirement of coal. Its projections imply that greenhouse gas emissions will be reduced, even presuming 2%–3% economic growth, with the retirement of coal plants. However, investments in R&D include a number of ambitious technological fixes that may make coal more sustainable. One project with international partners is the development of a combustion technology that would burn coal in oxygen, to allow cost-effective recovery of CO_2 which could then be permanently stored underground. Another research project is considering pumping CO_2 into deep unmineable coal beds to force out the natural gas, which would then be used as fuel in a power plant. If the overall scheme is successful, it could result in the development of a power plant with zero net greenhouse gas emissions.

Box 6: TransAlta and Suncor

In early 1999, TransAlta and Suncor jointly announced a new project at Suncor's Oil Sands operation in Fort McMurray, Alberta. A cogeneration facility will generate 220 megawatts of electricity by the fall of 1999. Any excess power not used by Suncor will be available for sale directly to the provincial power grid, taking advantage of the now deregulated industry, and helping to alleviate the tight supply situation in Alberta.

At the 1999 AGM, CEO Steve Snyder proclaimed that 'coal is becoming a cleaner fuel'. Given that, the question is whether TransAlta's generation will increasingly stem from natural gas and renewables, supported by a continuing base of hydro electric power—or remain with coal.

One development in the company's rethinking of service delivery has been seeing its function in a clearer customer context. New customer partnership opportunities are developing where, for example, the old boundary to which power is delivered (the meter) is no longer the limit of service. Instead, the utility—in a climate of deregulation—is providing on-site service satisfaction: assisting in demand-side management, providing price transparency, and developing cogeneration partnerships. These and other new business initiatives hold the greatest promise for reaching TransAlta's goal of 'creating eco-efficient business practices and opportunities that provide long-term economic, environmental, and community benefits' (*Sustainable Development: Economy–Environment–Society* [1995 Progress Report]).

TransAlta is bringing business value to customers based on environmental competences. Drawing on its competences with emissions management, TransAlta has added novel services, such as '**LightSWITCH**', an energy services lighting retrofit programme that has had an excellent response from commercial and institutional customers. The aim is to create more economical, energy-efficient and effective workplaces by replacing existing lighting. TransAlta provides the demand management service, which includes lighting audits, retrofit evaluation, installation of new equipment, and an option for financing.

For TransAlta, the radical character of its rethinking cannot be overemphasised. Starting from the vision of sustainable development, the company has undertaken a conceptual reorientation: sustainability is not a barrier to doing business, but is rather the fundamental context within which business operates. The environmental, social and economic dimensions of that context are explored, tested and acted on. Concept leads to principles and subsequently to practices. The dichotomy of 'environment or economy' is tackled at a higher, more integrative level where solutions are found that achieve both environmental protection and economic prosperity simultaneously.

TransAlta continues to make structural and strategic shifts that reinforce its commitment to integrating sustainable development into business operations and offerings. Two of these are described in Boxes 7 and 8.

b. Climate change

The contradiction is apparent but was never voiced internally: TransAlta is one of Canada's largest emitters of climate change gases, yet it is also one of the most progressive companies in the area—in 1994 it was one of the first companies in Canada to commit to achieving greenhouse gas stabilisation to 1990 levels by 2000.

Exploring this tension allows a deeper understanding of the corporation and an appreciation of the long-term strategic approach it has taken so successfully.

The key to TransAlta's success in managing greenhouse gases (GHGs) has been its long-range approach to the issue. Actions were initiated in the early 1990s, long before most other power producers (and coal companies!) had even started to contemplate responses. As a founding member of what is now the World Business Council for Sustainable Development (WBCSD), early strategic sustainable development approaches were being formulated and tested. For TransAlta, the economic dimensions of GHG management soon became just as important (both as a cost and a driver) as its environmental aspects. Over the years, new business services and products have developed to complement TransAlta's approaches to achieve emission reductions.

In its 1998 *Sustainable Development Report*, TransAlta reported its accomplishments as follows:

> the following are cumulative tonnes of carbon dioxide (CO_2) equivalent emission reductions as of year end 1997:
>
> - improving the efficiency in our own operations—reductions of more than four million tonnes;
> - developing cogeneration facilities using leading-edge technology to efficiently supply energy with lower overall emissions—reductions of more than five million tonnes;

Box 7: 'Manager of Business Integration, Sustainable Development'

My shift from Marketing to the Sustainable Development Department is a forward move: it is a very interesting career opportunity.

In 1998 a notable new position was formed under the Vice-President, Sustainable Development: this was 'Manager of Business Integration'. The role was explicitly one of 'integrating sustainable development with the company's business interests'. When assigned this position, Don Wharton saw the move as a very interesting and important career opportunity, in support of TransAlta's leadership, commitment and successes in sustainable development in Canada and internationally.

The position involves responsibility for supporting key functions: independent power, conventional regulated power (in its transition to a deregulated structure), and transmission and distribution. The principal objective is to create new business value from the application of sustainable development practices by generating cost reductions or new revenue streams. The creation of this post demonstrates the scope and importance afforded to sustainable development in TransAlta. The manager has access to, and some influence over, a large cross-section of the firm, including both operating and revenue sides of the company.

TransAlta produces significant amounts of CO_2 from the generation of electricity in Alberta and cogeneration facilities in Eastern Canada.

It is the company's (now achieved) goal 'to return its net contribution of greenhouse gases to the atmosphere to 1990 levels in the year 2000' (*Sustainable Development: Economy–Environment–Society* [1995 Progress Report]). One of the elements is to pursue greenhouse gas offsets to reduce or absorb greenhouse gases. More sustainable agricultural practices, such as direct seeding, result in increased sequestration of atmospheric carbon in soils.

The 'Saskatchewan Soil Enhancement Project' promotes the adoption of direct seeding to conserve soil and increase soil carbon content. Direct seeding is seeding that occurs through crop residue (stubble), substantially reducing the amount of tillage and summer fallow required, compared with conventional tillage methods. The project provides the potential to improve productivity for farmers and lower input costs, while offsetting the effects of greenhouse gas emissions.

The project is a partnership involving TransAlta, the government of Canada, the government of Saskatchewan, the Saskatchewan Soil Conservation Association (SSCA) and Monsanto Canada. Together there was a commitment to invest C$1.6 million on direct seeding over the period 1993–97.

This programme has been extremely successful, with approximately three million hectares converted from traditional practices to direct seeding. TransAlta continues to support the education efforts of the SSCA to ensure that hectares transferred to direct seeding are maintained. In addition, TransAlta has continued work with Agriculture Canada and the SSCA to implement a monitoring programme to verify the number of tonnes of carbon stored as a result of the Saskatchewan Soil Enhancement Project.

The Saskatchewan project was the company's first domestic greenhouse gas offset. The project aims to store a minimum of 200,000–300,000 tonnes of carbon equivalent in our soils annually (733,000–1,100,000 tonnes of CO_2).

Box 8: Saskatchewan Soil Enhancement Project: TransAlta's first domestic greenhouse gas offset

- acquiring a diverse portfolio of greenhouse gas offset projects—reductions of nearly 5.5 million tonnes;
- purchasing renewable energy, such as wind, hydro and biomass from independent generators—reductions of more than 1.8 million tonnes; and
- promoting energy efficiency initiatives in customer operations—reductions of about 300,000 tonnes (*Sustainable Development Report, 1998*).

When speaking to the managers, the two stages of TransAlta's climate change strategy become apparent. First, there was the early, ground-breaking work in understanding the issues, experimenting internally, and moving on immediate actions for emissions reductions. The in-company emissions trading programme and the corporation's involvement in the WBCSD through the early 1990s are typical of this stage of development. TransAlta embarked on a variety of activities to reduce CO_2 emissions from its own operations. In addition, projects were inaugurated involving customers as well as joint implementation projects with international partners.

But, by 1998, it was apparent that most of the 'low-hanging fruit' had been picked. Rather than a diverse portfolio of actions, a new, more pragmatic strategy would be necessary. What were needed were dependable cost-effective climate change projects that reduce GHG emissions. For this, TransAlta's primary approach was to move to purchase offset projects from other parties. Offsets are actions outside of a company's normal operations that result in reduced GHG emissions or the removal of GHGs from the atmosphere. Because climate change is a global issue, reductions anywhere in the world are equally effective. TransAlta's interest in offsets is that, despite the fact that flexible mechanisms under the Kyoto Protocol have still to be approved, by demonstrating the effectiveness of offsets, TransAlta hopes its actions will become a model for framework development.

In autumn 1998, TransAlta launched advertisements to gather innovative submissions for new GHG offset projects. This creative approach involved the Request for Proposal (RFP) and the accompanying editorial appearing in airline magazines and other high-profile media (see Box 9). The advertisements asked 'the world for novel solutions'. By the end of 1998, more than 100 proposals had been submitted, with costs ranging from C$2 to C$50 per tonne of CO_2-equivalent. C$1 million had already been spent during that time on purchasing credits from third parties.

It is clear that TransAlta is taking radical measures to achieve its GHG targets—but the results are apparent. In 1997, the firm estimates it would have been responsible for about 32 million tonnes of CO_2 emissions for the year, but, with the action plans in place, that number is reduced by 21%; in 2000, it estimates the reductions attributable to its actions will be in the order of 30%—which amounts to 4.4 million tonnes under its 27.5 million tonne 1990 baseline.

c. 'Grow the business without increasing environmental risk.'

TransAlta is the largest independent power producer (IPP) in Canada. Recently, it has developed its overseas business, particularly to Australia, New Zealand and the USA. In fact, given the established infrastructure investment in its home territory of Alberta, the IPP business is the principal growth engine for the company. Of course, with the deregulation of power production and supply around the world, the market is fast-moving and growing tremendously. The key to TransAlta's success in this business are two advantages that its competitors may not be aware of: management of emissions risks and competitive differentiation on environmental performance.

To every new project TransAlta brings with it a wealth of knowledge in environmental management and sustainable development. Going into a new project, or assessing mergers and acquisitions, the sustainable development depart-

ADVERTISEMENT COPY

FYI -

This is an RFP for GHG offset projects. If your ideas are A-OK because of your IQ RSVP PDQ to our site on the www.

These acronyms are a short way to long term thinking. TransAlta is looking for innovative thinkers to rise to the challenge posed by greenhouse gas emissions.

At TransAlta, we have been recognised for our actions regarding the reduction of greenhouse gases. And as part of our continuing commitment to meaningful environmental programmes, we are now seeking help in further reducing greenhouse gas emissions here at home and around the earth. If you have a proposal that corresponds with our initiatives and makes good business sense, we would love to see your plans.

P.S. For details and more information, fax our SD department at (403) 267-7372 or visit our URL at www.transalta.com

EDITORIAL COPY

Energy today for a better tomorrow

For the Alberta-based energy company, TransAlta, sustainable development is more than just a buzzword—it is an integral part of doing business. "Keeping the environment high on our priority list helps us balance the demands of environmental protection and economic growth," says Bob Page, vice-president of Sustainable Development. "This means looking at everything we do and doing it better—and trying to help our customers do the same."

Leading-edge thinking assists TransAlta lessen its impact on the environment while lowering costs. "We balance cost against benefits over the lifetime of our projects," Page says in describing a process called life cycle assessment. For example, a compact fluorescent light bulb may cost three times as much as a regular light bulb, but it will last seven times as long. "By considering long-term impacts in all our decisions, we benefit today and tomorrow. We also think it's important to make sure the public is aware of the advantages in this type of environmentally-responsible approach."

Sometimes the best environmental approach is found in unlikely places. This is especially true when addressing global issues such as climate change. Companies and countries are working to offset effects of greenhouse gases. TransAlta's goal is to return its net contributions of greenhouse gases to the atmosphere to 1990 levels in the year 2000. The company is seeking innovative solutions to the challenge—solutions called greenhouse gas offset projects.

An example of such a project is TransAlta's involvement in reducing methane emissions from municipal solid waste disposal at the Edmonton Region Co-composting Facility. Changing traditional practices of managing municipal solid waste generates both environmental and business benefits. The Co-composter will significantly reduce greenhouse gas emissions because solid waste is diverted from landfill sites. The process also generates compost, in itself a valuable commodity.

Sustainable development can't be accomplished alone. TransAlta works with government and industry partners on long-term strategies, policy development and research, including the Greenhouse Emissions Management Consortium and the World Business Council on Sustainable Development.

"We work hard to stay at the forefront of sustainable energy developments because it makes sense for the environment, our employees and our business," says Page. "Every time someone comes up with a new technology, a new approach that lowers humanity's impact on the environment, we all gain. We're in this together—and TransAlta is here for the long haul."

Source: www.transalta.com

Box 9: Advertisement copy for the greenhouse gas Request for Proposal (RFP) and editorial

ment supports business objectives in an integrated, business-like fashion. This approach is one of the clearest examples of where sustainable development translates far beyond operational management into other functions of the company. In environmental management, the company promises to 'ensure that the environmental component of the EH&S Management System for newly built or acquired operations meets the ISO 14001 standard within two years of operation/acquisition' (*Sustainable Development Report, 1998*). Similarly, in safety and GHG emissions, the position of a new project is mapped out and integrated into the overall assessment. TransAlta's goal is to grow the business without increasing environmental risk.

Differentiation on environmental performance

Inside the company, TransAlta operates ISO 14001-compliant environmental management systems (although sees no business case for certification at the moment), diligently pursues improvement (using audits as a device for continual improvement), continues to minimise pollution, and pursues progressive gains in health and safety performance. This is an admirable track record and a sellable quality for a company that is transforming itself from a sleepy utility in southern Alberta into a player in independent power projects across North America and the world. Experience translates into bids for new projects. In New Zealand, Australia and Canada, TransAlta has repeatedly drawn on its environmental track record to demonstrate capability and commitment in environmental stewardship.

On the climate change issue, TransAlta's experience pays as well. The management of emissions risks represents TransAlta's recognition that new power projects assume constraints and requirements associated with its GHG emissions, present and future. In the purchase of gas fields and a pipeline system in Western Australia in 1997, TransAlta could discuss the climate change issue with the authorities constructively and progressively: 'Not only can we manage the facility well, we can bring greenhouse gas offsets that have been gathered internationally'.

Whether the project is a new cogeneration plant, as with Suncor in northern Alberta, or a major acquisition, such as the 1999 C$554 million purchase of the Centralia coal-fired generating plant in Washington state, TransAlta brings value that others cannot.

5. Critical conclusion

In the final analysis, we were left with the feeling that, despite TransAlta's tremendous accomplishments to date, there's still much more ahead. They still need to address what is ultimately necessary in a more sustainable world. In spite of their policies and actions to date, 95% of TransAlta remains reliant on coal-fired power: the forthcoming Centralia purchase in Washington state will actually increase this reliance. Is TransAlta's continued ownership and operation of coal generating plants inherently non-sustainable? It could be argued that the company's sustainable development strategy simply forestalls the future; its activities have extended its licence to operate—basically business as usual, coal to carbon. It has indeed done an excellent job in what it has set out to do: but switching from concrete to fibreglass transmission pads to save a few tonnes of CO_2 does not compensate for 32 million tonnes of greenhouse gases emitted per year.

However, consider that 52% of North America's electricity is generated from coal, and that this is unlikely to change in the foreseeable future, given the continued growth in demand for electricity and the current asset base. While renewables can, will and should continue to increase in market share (and TransAlta will be part of that business), the next few decades will still require existing coal plants to operate. TransAlta argues that this part of the energy sustainability debate is not about 'fuel' such as coal, but about 'emissions'. There may very well be huge environmental benefits in reducing emissions from coal plants—through clean coal technology, capture and sequestration of carbon gases, recycling, or plant efficiency improvements. In the recent Centralia plant purchase, C$300 million will be invested in air pollution control equipment. And if ways are discovered of making coal low- or zero-emission energy, then it could well remain the preferred fuel for centuries.

In 1999, the focus of TransAlta's efforts to reduce greenhouse gas emissions is, notably, becoming more *external*—perhaps because internal changes are exhausted, or the company is too restricted within its current paradigm. Somehow, this road seems to be a diversion from the real path. The firm that has done so much itself will now rely on others, outside the organisation, for creativity. Two thrusts are apparent: (1) the firm will purchase reductions credits from third parties— 'TransAlta is looking for innovative thinkers to rise to the challenge posed by greenhouse gas emissions' (according to the climate change RFP); (2) the firm will press forward, in search of the breakthrough technologies necessary to produce 'emissions-neutral coal power'.

The company's current stance is enunciated clearly from the top:

> Through technology development and greenhouse gas offsets, coal is becoming a cleaner fuel (Steve Snyder, President and CEO, speaking at the TransAlta annual meeting of shareholders, 28 April 1999, Edmonton, Alberta).

However, organisationally, in its development of human resources, on key issues such as emissions and land use, in the development of management systems and refinement of business processes, TransAlta provides an exemplary case study in strategy and action on the journey toward sustainable energy.

References

TransAlta publications

http://www.transalta.com

Environmental Performance Report: The Journey towards Sustainable Development (Calgary: TransAlta Corporation, September 1994).

Sustainable Development: Economy–Environment–Society (1995 Progress Report; Calgary: TransAlta Corporation, 1996)

TransAlta's Action Plan in Support of Canada's Climate Change Voluntary Challenge and Registry Programme (Calgary: TransAlta Corporation, September 1995).

1996 Annual Report (Calgary: TransAlta Corporation, 1997)

1997 Annual Report (Calgary: TransAlta Corporation, 1998)

Sustainable Development Report, 1998 (Calgary: TransAlta Corporation, 1999)

Committed to Building a Sustainable Future: Sustainable Development Strategy (Calgary: TransAlta Corporation, March 1996).

First Progress Report: TransAlta's Action Plan in Support of Canada's Climate Change Voluntary Challenge and Registry Programme (Calgary: TransAlta Corporation, August 1996).

Second Progress Report: TransAlta's Action Plan in Support of Canada's Climate Change Voluntary Challenge and Registry Programme (Calgary: TransAlta Corporation, August 1997).

Environment Health and Safety Management System: Expectations and Standards Handbook (Calgary: TransAlta Corporation, May 1997).

Greenhouse Gas *Request for Proposal (RFP)* and Editorial (Calgary: TransAlta Corporation, 1998).

'Suncor Energy and TransAlta sign long-term power agreement' (Press release; Calgary: TransAlta Corporation, 31 March 1999).

Steve Snyder, President and CEO, address to TransAlta's annual meeting of shareholders, 28 April 1999, Edmonton, Alberta, Canada; transcript).

'TransAlta successful bidder for Centralia' (Press release; Calgary: TransAlta Corporation, 10 May 1999).

Others

Electricity Association (UK) (1995) *International Electricity Prices: Issue 22* (London: The Electricity Association).

Schmidheiny, S., with the Business Council for Sustainable Development (1992) *Changing Course: A Global Perspective on Development and the Environment* (Cambridge, MA: MIT Press).

Organisational contacts

Jim Leslie, Consultant (former Senior Vice-President), Sustainable Development

Robert Page, PhD, Vice-President, Sustainable Development

John A. Tapics, PEng, Vice-President, Generation, TransAlta Utilities Corporation

Paul Vickers, PEng, Manager Sustainable Development Operations

Don Wharton, Manager of Business Integration, Sustainable Development

THE NETHERLANDS NATIONAL ENVIRONMENTAL POLICY PLAN

Developing sustainable industrial strategy

1. *The lie of the land*

The Netherlands is a small, densely populated, highly urbanised country of 15 million people, with a gross national product of approximately US$350 billion. It is heavily industrialised (chemicals, oil refining) with strong agricultural, horti-cultural and transport sectors (it is a transportation hub for northern Europe). It also has strong electronics, food-processing and financial services industries. This combination of industrialisation, small size and relative affluence has resulted in the Netherlands having one of the highest environmental impacts per square kilometre in Europe.

The Netherlands is a constitutional monarchy with a parliamentary system. The parliament has two chambers, both of which have an environmental committee. Over the past decade there has been a significant shift of power from the national government to provincial (12 provinces) and municipal authorities. Environmental policy, although developed at the national level, is designed to be implemented on a regional scale by provinces, municipalities and water boards.

Through a combination of history and geography, the Netherlands has evolved a consensus-based approach to decision-making, which was instrumental in its overcoming acute land use and water management problems associated with being a heavily populated low-lying coastal nation. The co-operative nature of the

Lessons learned from NEPP1 and NEPP2 have led the government to conclude that environmental policy is entering the phase of 'environmental management'. The previous period focused on the clean-up of existing problems, but, in NEPP3, the main focus has shifted to ensuring 'absolute decoupling' of economic growth and environmental pressure, and the sustainable use of natural resources (*NEPP3: The Summary*, p. 11). The main strands of policy, and the measures outlined in NEPP3, address the key issues identified by The Environmental Programme 1997–2000. They include:

▷ Greater integration of the environment into provincial, regional and municipal land use planning

▷ Further internationalisation of environmental policy through the Organisation for Economic Co-operation and Development (OECD), the European Union (EU), the United Nations Environment Programme (UNEP), the United Nations Conference on Sustainable Development (UNCSD), and others

▷ Continued attention to the biodiversity issue

▷ Sustainable economic development: greater attention to policies and programmes that foster appropriate economic development (e.g. green taxation)

▷ Sustainable consumption and production: environmental management systems implementation in companies, corporate environmental reporting, the development of cleaner production practices, particularly in the small and medium-sized enterprise (SME) sector, and sustainable technology development

▷ Further enhancement of self-regulation and involvement of key target groups in policy

Enormous success has been achieved through the integration of environmental considerations into national government decision-making and industrial activity. With the exception of greenhouse gases and NO_x, all indicators are heading in the right direction.

A staggering array of ongoing activity includes: grant schemes for provincial and local environmental policy; renewal of clean-up of contaminated sites; environmental monitoring by municipalities; international promotion of environmental indicators as a tool for policy-making and monitoring; the development of social policy instruments to help change attitudes and behaviours; the greening of the tax system; and the development of product-based environmental policies and tools.

* 'Absolute decoupling' occurs when the environmental pressure reduces or at least remains constant while economic growth increases (*NEPP3: The Summary*, p. 8).

Box 1: **Sustainable development in the Netherlands today**

Netherlands has also been a key to the development and implementation of its National Environmental Policy Plan (NEPP).

2. *The journey*

The sustainable development journey in the Netherlands began with the planning and development of NEPP in 1989, prior to which environmental policy was largely focused on toxic substance management and the sectoral regulation of processes that posed a threat to human health. Scientific and policy analysis indicated that this approach was failing because: it did not slow environmental degradation; solutions developed for one problem often caused other environmental problems; it was administratively burdensome; and it led to contradictory policies which were inefficient and costly. At this time a number of high-profile incidents (toxic waste dumps and industrial pollution) also focused the country's attention on environmental issues.

Throughout the journey, certain key stages can be discerned:

▷ Coping: pre-1985

▷ Strategic planning stage: 1985–89. Getting the science right, understanding stakeholder concerns, preparing the bureaucracy, policy formation

▷ Negotiation stage: between 1989 and when the first covenants were being signed in 1992. Cabinet discussions on financing of NEPP, public awareness campaign to share the 'credible story', continued discussions with target groups, CEO-to-minister discussions on covenants.

▷ Implementation stage: 1993 to the present. Revision of the Environmental Management Act, a proliferation of policy measures and programmes to enable target groups to meet objectives set out in NEPP 1, NEPP + and NEPP 3, and continuous monitoring of progress and revision of approach as necessary.

a. *Strategic planning*

In the middle-to-late 1980s, the need to address immediate problems and the failure of past environmental policy led to a new more strategic and integrated approach. This effort was lead by Peter Winsemius, then Minister of the Environment, who had a background in management consulting with the firm McKinsey & Co. He understood industry concerns and he recognised that there was a policy life-cycle (recognition, policy formation, solving and control) for environmental issues that required a managerial approach.

Under NEPP, environmental themes replaced sectors and environmental media (air, land and water) as the focus of environmental policy in the Netherlands. The themes reflect a scientific analysis of the core issues of concern in the Netherlands. They are:

▷ **Climate change (and ozone depletion)**: caused by greenhouse gases and chlorinated compounds

▷ **Acidification**: degradation of soils, water and buildings due to acid gases

▷ **Eutrophication**: degradation of marine and fresh-water habitat due to excessive nutrients

▷ **Toxic and hazardous pollutants**: continued release of toxic chemicals and metals

▷ **Contaminated land**: xenobiotic pollutants in soil that threaten human health or ecosystems

▷ **Waste disposal:** pollution and inefficient resource use caused by inappropriate management of wastes

▷ **Groundwater depletion** disturbed water cycles and effects on water supply caused by overuse

▷ **Resource dissipation**: depletion and pollution caused by inefficiency and over-consumption

▷ **Disturbance**: disturbance of people caused by noise, odour, local air pollution, and litter

Box 2: Environmental themes

At the same time it was recognised that the diffuse responsibility for environmental matters throughout central government would not easily allow the centralisation of authority in a single department. A decision was taken to transform the Environment Department and give it a process management role. To do this effectively, new skills such as project management, negotiation training and consensus-building were introduced. Staff were also trained in the 'principles and tools for the management of politically risky decisions' in order to better advise the minister (de Jongh 1996). This transformation and professionalisation of the Environment Department was instrumental in fostering co-operation within central government and with stakeholders during the development and implementation of NEPP.

A further strategic component of this approach was the grouping of environmental concerns into key 'themes' (see Box 2),[1] which had clearly identifiable target

1   Environmental policy is classified according to nine themes. An environmental theme is a label used to refer to closely interrelated environmental problems. Classifying by theme makes 'passing the buck' from one environmental medium (soil, water or air) to another visible.

groups (industrial sectors and other groups who were responsible for the development of solutions). In addition, policy-makers began to think about solutions in
terms of measures directed at the sources or causes of pollution as well as
measures directed at improving environmental quality (effects measures).

In 1989 a landmark national environmental report entitled *Concern for Tomorrow*
was released (Langeweg 1989). The report was organised on the basis of themes
and target groups and it used scientific models and scenario analysis to project
needed environmental improvements to achieve 'sustainable' levels of pollution. It
was used as the basis for the first NEPP in 1989.[2]

The NEPP is described as a national strategy for the environment, which has the
ambitious goal of 'achieving sustainable development in the Netherlands within
one generation'. NEPP sets out a **strategic environmental management approach**
which provides a vision, identifies problems, sets objectives and targets, identifies
roles and responsibilities and outlines how progress will be monitored. The policy
aims to integrate environmental considerations throughout society by:

▷   Adopting an integrated approach based on themes and targets

▷   Fostering the internalisation of environment issues, including self-regu-
    lation, by the target groups within an overall framework set out by
    government

▷   Developing an integrated long-term planning approach based on scien-
    tific quantitative objectives under each theme

b. *Implementing NEPP*

The history of sustainable development activity in the Netherlands over the past
ten years can be characterised as the continual implementation and refinement of
the strategic approach set out in NEPP. Some of the core processes that have
facilitated the implementation of NEPP include:

▷   The appointment of target group managers within the Environment
    Ministry to co-ordinate all work relating the themes (environmental
    quality, standards) to the target group (policy instruments directed at
    economic activity)

▷   The development of a sound scientific base in *Concern for Tomorrow* and
    the continued further enhancement of the scientific analysis with data on
    specific economic sectors

2   Shortly after the launch of NEPP, an election was held. The new government released a
    slightly modified document entitled NEPP+.

▷ The restructuring of the Environment Directorate along the lines of sources of environmental pollution and effects (economic activity), and the simplification of Dutch environmental law in the 1993 Environmental Management Act. The act allows for industrial facilities to operate under a single overall permit and it promotes integrated environmental management and pollution prevention.

▷ Integration of environmental policy with other federal ministries through joint responsibility.[3] For example, in the second iteration of the policy, NEPP 2, the Ministry for Economic Affairs developed the policy strategy for industry, energy, refineries, consumers and products. Cabinet is advised on environmental and resource policy proposals by a national environment commission made up of senior officials from most ministries.

▷ Integration of environmental policy with other levels of government through regionally based policies and programmes

▷ Intense and open negotiations among central and local government and representatives from major target groups to define responsibilities and outline action plans. Many of these action plans have been formalised in covenants. Covenants are agreements between government and industry that provide long-range (5–10 years) directions for where industry needs to improve environmental performance, and they provide more flexibility than regulations. They have been so well received that some industrial players have become champions of the implementation of their own covenants.

▷ The continued refinement and elaboration of key conceptual approaches such as **integrated life-cycle management** (reducing emissions and waste flows throughout the product life-cycle), **energy savings** (demand-side management, increased use of renewables and improved efficiency), and **quality improvement** (products and processes that are less wasteful or defective)

▷ A clear strategic plan to promote the Netherlands' approach in international organisations such as the United Nations Environment Programme (UNEP), United Nations Conference on Sustainable Development (UNCSD), the Organisation for Economic Co-operation and Development (OECD) and the European Union (EU)

In 1993 NEPP 2 was released. NEPP 2 reiterated the government's commitment to the themes and targets and to self-regulation through negotiated agreements. It

---

3 The NEPP itself is the responsibility of four federal ministries (Economic Affairs, the Ministry of Transport and Public Works, the Ministry of Agriculture, Nature Protection and Fisheries and the Ministry for Housing, Spatial Planning and the Environment).

also recognised that certain target groups, such as small and medium-sized enterprises (SMEs) and consumers, represented a difficult challenge for the self-regulation approach. To engage these target groups, NEPP 2 proposed a range of policy instruments including regulations, financial incentives and social action such as education and awareness-raising.

Another feature of NEPP 2 was greater recognition of the growing international nature of environmental issues. International policy was set out under three main headings:

▷ Fostering new environmental policy initiatives for sustainable development

▷ Promotion of international environmental agreements with concrete objectives, implementation plans and financing mechanisms

▷ Further development of EU environmental policy

The influence of the Netherlands in international environmental policy has been significant over the last decade. It has seeded the development of sustainable production and consumption discussions at the OECD; it has extended the vision of the UNEP Cleaner Production programme beyond looking at industrial processes to an examination of the environmental impacts of products; and it has greatly influenced EU environmental policies. This influence has been achieved by strategic placement of senior Dutch individuals within these organisations and by taking advantage of any chair (e.g. of the OECD Pollution Prevention and Control Group) it has held.

With the release of NEPP 3 in 1997, the core of the Netherlands approach (**an integrated environmental planning system based on long-term analyses and implementation via negotiations with stakeholders**) is still evident. As with NEPP 2, this new document will refer to scientific analysis and indicators to rationalise the introduction of new policies and programmes required to address areas in which the Netherlands is lagging, such as reducing greenhouse gas emissions.

c. *Vision*

There have been a number of key steps in the creation of the Netherlands' vision of sustainable development. They included:

▷ Planning a 20-year time-horizon, which forced the government to look beyond traditional regulatory approaches. For example, no regulatory mechanism could be envisioned that would enable a 70% reduction in SO_2 emissions. A new way of thinking was required.

▷ Translating the somewhat vague definition of sustainable development from the Brundtland Commission (WCED 1987) into tangible environmental themes with well-defined targets. Backed by a strong scientific effort, the themes were translated into real numbers (e.g. the required reductions of SO_2 emissions by 2000 and beyond). The targets developed under each theme provided a tangible focal point for discussion with the target groups on the actions required.

▷ Developing emissions and cost scenarios, which in one case demonstrated potential GDP growth over that of standard economic policies. This led to the conclusion that relatively strict environmental policies, implemented consistently and gradually with no big surprises for industry, in co-operation with the other EU countries, would not adversely affect—and might even improve—the overall economic position of the Netherlands.[4]

▷ Creating and disseminating a 'credible story' on sustainable development. Once the scientific and economic analyses were completed, a public aware-ness campaign (commercials, newspaper and magazine advertisements) was launched. Using Dutch television and sports stars and the motto 'A better environment begins at home', the campaign began by conveying the importance of the environment and then changed the focus to what could be done. This second action-oriented phase was often co-ordinated with policy measures (e.g. the introduction of recycling programmes).

d. *Planning and implementation*

The planning and implementation stages of NEPP are difficult to separate. A number of key planning steps were conducted in advance but, through continuous monitoring and feedback, the planning process is constantly being revised. Some of the important early steps included:

▷ The early unspoken agreement between the Minister of the Environment and certain CEOs that, if industry took environmental issues seriously, government would take a more long-term view of environmental policy. For industry, this reduced uncertainty and allowed a longer and smoother transition to environmentally sound behaviour.

▷ The open planning process, which involved all levels of government and all relevant target groups. This turned potential adversaries into engaged stakeholders.

▷ The decision to revisit NEPP every four years and to prepare annual updates on environmental progress. This created accountability.

---

4   This last aspect illustrates why the international focus of NEPP is so strong.

▷ The focus on developing and using project management skills. In the negotiations on the Dutch Energy Conservation Covenants, 62% of managers from Dutch industry believed that government support, through the financing of specialised project management experts, was more important than direct subsidies in making the agreement come about (Winsemius and Merkl 1996).

▷ A willingness to be truly flexible in the implementation of policies and programmes (based on successes or failures and on results reported through the annual updates)

An illustration of this last point is the flexibility the government has shown in the implementation of the Dutch policy on products and the environment. The aim of the policy is 'to bring about a situation whereby all market actors—producers, traders and consumers—are involved in an ongoing effort to reduce the impact products have on the environment' (Ministry of Housing, Spatial Planning and the Environment 1995). In implementing this policy, the government originally tried to identify good 'green' products versus bad products. This strategy was found to be scientifically and economically unsound, so the government shifted to an approach that targeted key product categories (automotive, appliances and electronics) and tried to draw environmental information into the marketplace about the materials, manufacturing, use and disposal of these products. This approach proved too data-intensive and unmanageable, so it shifted yet again and developed a programme that directly supports industry in the reduction of environmental releases and improvements in resource and energy efficiency.

This ability to adjust policies and programmes mid-stream has earned the government much respect from industry, supported a flexible planning framework in which the ends are more important than the means, and resulted in a better return on investment with respect to environmental expenditures.

Another key to the successful implementation of NEPP was the establishment of a training programme for 400 government officials. Under this training programme, conducted by the Massachusetts Institute of Technology (MIT), senior staff were trained to be trainers and exercises were conducted that simulated possible implementation issues around NEPP. The principles for this training are outlined in Box 3.

e. *Performance measurement and indicators*

As stated previously, under NEPP, the Dutch government has established a clear set of objectives and targets related to each environmental theme. It believes that, by achieving these targets, the overall goal of NEPP—sustainability by 2010—will be met. In addition to providing a long-term perspective, the targets help focus activity on environmental outcomes and on decision-making (how to achieve those

Take initiative

▷ Don't delay until you are in a defensive position

▷ Try to shape perceptions of problems and solutions

▷ Minimise the extent to which others dictate your moves

Emphasise outcomes

▷ Devise realistic options early

▷ Focus on solutions not analysis

▷ Link actions to results

Seek consensus

▷ Develop mechanisms to build trust

▷ Design options to satisfy interests

▷ Listen carefully and try to see other viewpoints

Act justifiably

▷ Behave as you would expect others to behave

▷ Strive for consistency with your mandate

▷ Explicitly justify actions

Maintain credibility

▷ Always consult before deciding

▷ Make realistic commitments

▷ Minimise secrecy

Box 3: Principles for the implementation challenge

Source: de Jongh 1996

outcomes). The Netherlands also uses the targets to focus the Dutch position during international negotiations on global environmental issues.

The level of consensus on the targets and their acceptance by Dutch society was clearly helped by the process under which they were developed. In the late 1980s, prior to the formal establishment of the themes in NEPP, senior-level co-ordinators were assigned the responsibility of analysing each theme and addressing the following questions:

▷ What is the nature of the problem in terms of causes and effects— described quantitatively? What is the level of (un)certainty in terms of the cause–effect relationship?

▷ When could the problem be solved? At what environmental quality standard?

▷ Which economic sectors are the largest contributors to the problem? What is their share of the overall problem? What possible measures can they take and at what cost?

▷ Which specific reductions in causes (emissions, wastes . . .) are necessary to achieve the desired standard of environmental quality?

▷ Of the measures defined, which are the most cost-effective and over what time-frame should they be implemented (de Jongh 1996)?

In addition, target group managers were assigned the task of establishing working relationships with industrial sectors (e.g. transport) responsible for contributing to the environmental problems associated with each theme. These managers not only co-ordinated negotiations and policy development with the target group, they also:

▷ Analysed each group, identified key individuals and organisations, particularly the progressive companies in each sector

▷ Quantified emissions and effluents

▷ Looked at desired and possible reductions

▷ Looked at costs and time-frames for implementing reductions

▷ Examined technological developments, national and international economic implications, and their relevance to the environment

These analyses were undertaken in conjunction with the government ministries who were responsible for economic considerations of the sectors. This not only broadened the knowledge of the environmental policy-makers, it broadened the network in which environmental policy-making took place.

The establishment of objectives and targets was facilitated by an overall analysis of the state of the environment. Conducted by independent scientific institutes, the report (Langeweg 1989) included scenario analysis with 10–25-year time-horizons. The scenarios or forecasts were used to calculate the emissions/discharge reductions needed to achieve sustainable levels.

The overall co-ordination of this activity is undertaken by the State Institute for Public Health and Environmental Protection which is under clear direction from the Department of the Environment to achieve scientific consensus and to report on any lack of consensus. This common, well-respected knowledge base is instrumental in the broader acceptance by government and society of the objectives and targets developed. In addition, environmental indicators, to track progress toward the targets, were developed.

Through all this work—scenario analysis, state of environment reporting, theme analysis and target group consultations—generally accepted quality objectives, reduction targets and indicators were developed under each NEPP theme. These objectives, targets and indicators, with some minor revisions, still comprise the measurement system used to track Dutch progress toward sustainability.

Indicators are reported in two ways. First, overall national progress—on issues such as Dutch CO_2 emissions—under each of the themes in NEPP is reported. These national figures are also put into regional or global contexts as appropriate. For example, the 1997–2000 Environmental Programme report also reports OECD figures for CO_2 equivalents and EU figures for deposition of acidifying substances (a more regional problem). The second way in which indicators are reported is on a target group basis. This shows the progress, or lack thereof, within each target group on achieving the results for which they are responsible. This adds accountability and enables the government to target follow-up policies and programmes.

f. Review and monitoring

As stated above, the Netherlands has developed an extensive capacity for tracking performance indicators, with periodic *National Environmental Outlook* reports monitoring progress on the targets established in NEPP. Overall progress on targets has been significant. CFCs have been virtually eliminated and SO_2 and NH_3 (ammonia) emissions are in steady decline. Greenhouse gas and NO_x emissions, however, are rising, primarily due to structural changes in the economy. These results are used to adjust policies and implementation strategies.

The government has continually demonstrated its flexibility in terms of achieving the targets and objectives, with dispute resolution mechanisms built into many

Box 4: Five challenges for the NEPP 3 plan period

Source: Ministry of Housing, Spatial Planning and the Environment 1998

1. To ensure the continued decoupling of economic growth and pressure on the environment, and to prevent any recoupling
2. To safeguard the good results achieved at the local and regional level, and to extend them into the longer term
3. To reduce the environmental impact of agriculture and traffic
4. To reduce the emission associated with fossil energy use (particularly CO_2) through, for example, energy conservation and greater use of renewable energy as provided in the action programme 'Renewable Energy on the Rise'.
5. To tackle noise, contaminated land and groundwater depletion

1. Continuous improvement in the efficiency with which environment is used
2. The judicious use of science and technology
3. A focus on quality of overall living environment
4. Increasing integration, customisation and flexibility
5. Internalising environmental costs in prices
6. Improving enforcement
7. Stepping up international activity

Box 5: **Seven main policy areas for NEPP 3**

covenants. An example is the covenant signed by the Dutch Paper and Board Industry in 1991. In 1995 the industry proposed a superior implementation plan which would result in greater economic and environmental results. The covenant was renegotiated and the industry is gaining competitive advantage in Europe.

NEPP 3 continues to emphasise 'external integration: the integration of environmental policies into other policy areas' (Ministry of Housing, Spatial Planning and the Environment 1998). External integration ensures other departments give consideration to the environment, and that the Ministry of Housing, Spatial Planning and the Environment gives consideration to social and economic issues. To promote external integration, the government has made extending and developing the Environmental Management Act a priority, such that it 'becomes a comprehensive and transparent law permitting an integrated approach to environmental problems' (Ministry of Housing, Spatial Planning and the Environment 1998: 17). NEPP 3 outlines five major challenges for the plan period, and describes seven main areas of policy. These are illustrated in Boxes 4 and 5 respectively.

In early 1998, expectations for economic growth suggested NEPP objectives would be met with the help of measures outlined in NEPP 3, although later than originally anticipated in some cases. In December 1998, the Dutch National Institute for Health and the Environment announced that its goals would not be met by 2000. Several years of high economic growth are blamed for counteracting the gains made from the environmental improvement measures set out in NEPP (*Tomorrow* 1998).

NEPP 3 developed specific environmental improvement measures for each of the 11 target groups. These range in scope from continuing to apply existing policy to developing new approaches such as joint agreements between more than one sector. For example:

▷ **The public.** Continued use of information and education to change the environmental behaviour of citizens, and lowering the barriers to changing behaviour, e.g. by ensuring prices reflect environmental costs.

▷ **Industry.** NO_x, climate change and products are the major issues, and the government combines agreements with regulations in order to meet agreed objectives.

▷ **Waste disposal industry.** A tax shift in January 1998 made the cost of landfilling combustible waste equal to incineration costs.

In order to meet the various objectives, the NEPP approach considers policy in terms of 'environmental themes': from a local policy dimension; from an international angle; in terms of policy instruments; in terms of science and technology; and in terms of the policy's spatial, financial and economic consequences.

g. Barriers and opportunities

Incorporation of environment into economic policy has been slow due to uncertainty over the calculation of environmental costs and benefits and the appropriate use of economic instruments. A policy document, *Environment and Economy* (Ministry of Housing, Spatial Planning and the Environment *et al.* 1998), has been prepared to examine policies and tools that can combine growth, increased competitiveness and employment with better local management, conservation of wildlife and reduced environmental impacts.

However, Dutch experimentation with radical approaches could jeopardise the trust developed between industry and government through the covenant approach. Eco-Indicators '95 and '97 are projects that attempt to assign an environmental value to materials and industrial processes. The indicators (e.g. primary aluminium 18, secondary steel 4.3, etc.) are being used by product designers and manufacturers to select between materials. This intrusion of government into the business of industry, through the ranking of products and materials, is not viewed favourably by some industry players.

The economic success of the country together with increases in population are making it difficult to achieve some of the targets set: for example, greenhouse gas emissions will certainly not be at 1990 levels by 2000. This may begin to create a credibility gap, which could undermine the effectiveness of the Netherlands' international strategy. On the opportunity front, the Netherlands has clearly positioned its industry to take advantage of the anticipated global shift to more environmentally sound products and technologies. In a recent policy statement, Dutch industry stated: 'the Netherlands' pioneering role can give Dutch industry a competitive edge in environmental know-how' (Ministry of Housing, Spatial Planning and the Environment *et al.* 1998). This must, however, be balanced with sound science, economic analysis and consideration of the measures being taken in other countries.

3. Conclusion

The Netherlands' journey toward sustainable development has been characterised as smart people making good decisions. **A management-oriented Environment Minister set in motion a clear strategic plan that has been systematically implemented over the last ten years.** The direction of environmental policy was mapped out in detail in the early stages, and the co-operative nature inherent in Dutch decision-making processes helped ensure a general societal consensus on the direction chosen. The three core steps discussed earlier have proven vital in the development of the NEPP: thorough strategic planning (involving both science and stakeholders), extensive negotiations (among all groups), and solid implementation (with vigorous action and extensive review and revision).

Throughout the last decade, the government of the Netherlands has shown a clear understanding of the planning groundwork required to implement the policies and programmes necessary for sustainable development. Just as importantly, it has demonstrated great flexibility in allowing the various actors, or target groups, in Dutch society to choose their own path to achieving the overall objectives set out in NEPP.

References

Dutch government publications

Ministry of Housing, Spatial Planning and the Environment (1995) *Policy on Products and the Environment* (The Hague: Ministry of Housing, Spatial Planning and the Environment).

Ministry of Housing, Spatial Planning and the Environment (1998) *NEPP 3: The Summary* (VROM 97672/b/3-98//13093/168; The Hague: Ministry of Housing, Spatial Planning and the Environment).

Ministry of Housing, Spatial Planning and the Environment, Ministry of Economic Affairs and Ministry of Agriculture, Nature Management and Fisheries (1998) *Policy Document on Environment and Economy: Towards a Sustainable Economy* (The Hague: Ministry of Housing, Spatial Planning and the Environment, Ministry of Economic Affairs and Ministry of Agriculture, Nature Management and Fisheries).

Others

de Jongh, A.E. (1996) *Netherlands' Approach on Environmental Policies: Integrated Environmental Policy Planning as a Step toward Sustainable Development* (Washington, DC: Center for strategic and International Studies).

Langeweg, F. (ed.) (1989) *Concern for Tomorrow: A National Environmental Survey 1985–2010* (Bilthoven, Netherlands: National Institute for Public Health and Environmental Protection [RIVM]).

Tomorrow (1998) 'Dutch retreat', *Tomorrow* 8.6 (December 1998): 32.

WCED (World Commission on Environment and Development) (1987) *Our Common Future* ('The Brundtland Report'; Oxford, UK: Oxford University Press).

Winsemius, P., and A. Merkl (1996) 'Towards Win–Win Partnerships in Environmental Management' (unpublished paper).

Organisational contacts

Jans Suurland, Directorate General for Environmental Protection, Ministry of Housing, Spatial Planning and the Environment

Henk Wijens, Directorate General for Environmental Protection, Ministry of Housing, Spatial Planning and the Environment

CLOSING COMMENTS

A strategic inflection point is when the balance of forces shifts from the old structure, from the old ways of doing business and the old ways of competing, to the new . . . Of all the changes in the forces of competition, the most difficult one to deal with is when one of the forces becomes so strong that it transforms the very essence of how business is conducted in an industry.

> Andy Grove, President and CEO, Intel, *Only the Paranoid Survive*

If redesign of the system is one side of the challenge facing us, ignition of the spirit is the other.

> Andrew Bard Schmooker, *The Parable of the Tribes*

With its almost overwhelming silence and depth, the Canyon shakes us, at least briefly, of our egocentric self-importance and persuades us to remember our place in the natural world.

> Larry Stevens, *The Colorado River in Grand Canyon: A Guide*

Andy Grove lived first-hand the 'morphing' of the computer industry, from vertical to horizontal integration, changing not only the industry but the basis of competition. In *Only the Paranoid Survive*, he describes the radical shift that occurred, and the challenges of developing the new language, perspectives, worldview and relationships that were critical for the success of his company (Intel) in the radically changing computer industry. This openness to seeing the world in alternative ways is an essential prerequisite for developing the strategies, technologies and competences needed to succeed in the new economy. Grove also underlined the importance, when in the midst of a strategic inflection point, of building the platform for the new framework before reaching the peak of the old:

> Given the amorphous nature of an inflection point, how do you know the right moment to take appropriate action, to make the changes that will save your company? Unfortunately, you don't. But you can't wait until you know: Timing is everything. If you undertake these changes while your company is still healthy, while your ongoing business forms a protective bubble in which you can experiment with the new ways of doing business, you can save much more of your company's strength, your employees and your strategic position. But that means acting when not everything is known, when the data aren't yet in . . . But the good news is that even though your judgment got you into this tough position, it can also get you out. It's just a question of training your instincts to pick up a different set of signals. These signals may have been out there all along but you may have ignored them. The strategic inflection point is the time to wake up and listen.

What power would accrue to the person, or organisation, that could look into a crystal ball and see the future? Who would refuse? The companies and their managers featured here represent a growing cadre worldwide of those no longer ignoring the fragmented 'signals' that a new industrial paradigm is emerging—that the requirement for sustainable development is an unavoidable strategic inflection point facing all corporations, industry segments, governments and society as a whole.

This book is a compendium of intent and action toward sustainability. It describes tangible solutions to achieving more sustainable development—new ways of gaining competitive advantage and increasing market share, innovative approaches to product and process design, radical alternatives to relationships with stakeholders. It summarises the drivers, internal and external, stimulating this visionary leadership. Further, it documents the breakthroughs and real benefits resulting from the synergistic integration of sustainability into multiple elements of core organisational strategy and operations. Clearly, these organisations are not 'stepping off a cliff'. But they are making a threshold commitment to using sustainability to gain competitive advantage and build brand equity. They are adopting a new design ethic, proactively assuming responsibility for the environmental and social impacts of their products throughout the life-cycle, linking metrics and compensation to progress toward more sustainable products and processes, and launching full-scale sustainability education for managers, employees, board members, suppliers and customers. Sustainability is clearly on senior management's agenda, and leaders are instilling the passion and vigour needed to create commitment and momentum. Throughout, people are embracing the learning requirement, bringing innovation and creativity to finding breakthrough solutions. They are igniting the spirit of us all.

Like travellers of former times, who astounded their contemporaries by bringing back tales of adventure and artefacts shaped by different assumptions, constraints, resources and competences, the companies documented in *Mapping the Journey*, aware of the constraints of our existing system, are beginning to design and operate in the emerging system and allow us glimpses of our own new worlds.

References

Grove, A. (1996) *Only the Paranoid Survive* (New York: Currency Doubleday).
Schmooker, A.S. (1984) *The Parable of the Tribes: The Problem of Power in Social Evolution* (Boston, MA: Houghton-Mifflin).
Stevens, L. (1983) *The Colorado River in Grand Canyon: A Guide* (Flagstaff, AZ: Red Lake Books).

ABOUT THE AUTHORS

Lorinda R. Rowledge PhD, Co-founder of EKOS International, has provided strategic consulting and implementation methodologies and support to management teams of *Fortune* 50–500 companies including Boeing, CPC, Nortel, SmithKline Beecham, Telus, US West and Weyerhäuser. She has led global benchmarking studies and developed models and methodologies for world-class excellence in Business-Driven Sustainability, Value Stream Management, Total Quality, Customer Loyalty, New Product Development, Business Process ReDesign, Lean Production, Design for Environment, and Urban and Regional Sustainability. Dr Rowledge's current work focuses on Sustainable Value Creation, Innovation and Knowledge Creation, Social Sustainability, and Enterprise Agility. She holds a PhD, specialising in Organisational and Community Psychology, from the University of Oregon.

Russell S. Barton PhD is Co-founder of EKOS International. Since 1982, Dr Barton has been a leading consultant to the senior management teams at many of North America's most well-known companies, helping them understand best practices worldwide, design comprehensive strategies, and execute successful multi-year transformations. Currently, his primary consulting is assisting vanguard managers in designing and implementing strategies that combine world-class management technology and strategic sustainability. He has led 12 in-depth Executive Study Missions, benchmarking Total Quality Management in Japan and Strategic Sustainability in Europe, and has shared his breakthrough perspectives with hundreds of audiences throughout North America, Europe and Japan. He holds a PhD in organisational psychology from the University of Oregon.

Kevin S. Brady is a Director of Five Winds International. He has been active in environmental work for the past ten years, primarily at the business and environment interface. Mr Brady has worked in areas such as product-focused environmental policy, life-cycle assessment, eco-efficiency indicators, sustainable consumption and production, state-of-environment reporting, packaging and pollution prevention. He is currently Canada's Head of Delegation to the International Organisation for Standardization's (ISO) sub-committee on Life Cycle Assessment and he also represents Canada on ISO's Climate Technology Task Force. Mr Brady provided technical support to Canada's National Round Table on Environment and Economy in their recent work on eco-efficiency indicators. He holds a Masters of Environmental Studies from York University in Toronto.

Cynthia L. Figge, the third co-founder of EKOS International, holds an MBA from Harvard Business School. Over the past 20 years, Ms Figge has been a leading new venture and technology executive in the US, most recently as an officer responsible for the pioneering effort at broadband wireless data broadcasting for McCaw Cellular (now AT&T Wireless).

James A. Fava, **Konrad Saur** and **Steven B. Young** are Directors of Five Winds International.

Dr Fava has 25 years' experience integrating product sustainability into organisations' strategic planning processes and practices. Dr Fava co-chairs the design for environment ad hoc group under the International Organisation for Standardization and chairs the Society of Environmental Toxicology and Chemistry (SETAC) LCA Advisory Group.

Dr Young is an international expert in evaluating and improving the performance of product systems. He serves as an expert to ISO 14000 standards committees, and chairs the LCA committee of the Canadian Standards Association. He has a PhD in materials and environmental engineering from the University of Toronto.

Dr Saur, an international expert in decision-making, environmental analysis and product engineering, has worked with a wide variety of clients including Ford, Daimler-Benz, Alcoa, Thyssen, Dow, DuPont, BASF, Motorola, Siemens, Magna, ABB, Bosch, LG Electronics and German Rail. He holds a PhD in decision theory from the University of Stuttgart.

EKOS International is a strategic consulting firm helping clients to create vision, strategies and competences required for pre-eminence and prosperity in the new economy. EKOS provides strategic consulting, executive and management education, technologies, tools and web-based content and services on the integration of sustainability into business strategy, brand, product and process design, customer and stakeholder relations, production and operations, and supply chain management.

Five Winds International advises private- and public-sector organisations on the integration of environmental and social considerations into the design, manufacture, use, and end-of-life of their products and services. Utilising tools such as Design for Environment, Life-Cycle Engineering and Environmental Supply Chain Management, Five Winds International helps clients integrate product sustainability into the core business practices of their organisations. Five Winds International has offices in Canada, Germany and the US.

EKOS International
http://www.EKOSi.com

Five Winds International
http://www.fivewinds.com

100 Points programme (SJ
    Rail)   226-29

ABB   63
Absolute decoupling   260
Acidification   262
Adhesives   202, 212, 215
Adidas   103
Agriculture Canada   253
Alberta Clean Air Strategic
    Alliance   242
Alberta Roundtable on
    Environment and
    Economy   242
Allen, Will   101, 102
Alternative fuels   46
Anderson, Ray   20, 123
Antimony   124, 127, 130
ASG   32, 46, 63, 151-64
    corporate overview of
        151
    and customers   159
    environmental aspects of
        155-56
    environmental manage-
        ment system of
        154
    and the Internet   160
    mission statement of
        161-62

AssiDomän   30, 31, 87-93
    corporate overview of
        87
Axford, Eric   82
Automobile industry
    competitive pressures on
        44, 180
    environmental pressures
        on   44, 46-47

Baden-Württemberg,
    Germany   185-88
    and systematic develop-
        ment   195-96
Ballard Power Systems Inc.
    40
Barium   127
Baxter   46, 151, 152, 158
Biodiversity   87
Biofuels   70
Biomass   73
Bosch   185
BP-Amoco   70
Brand image
    of ASG   154
    of Henkel   206, 209-10
    of IFS   125
    of Patagonia   109-10, 119
    of SJ Rail   221
    of Suncor   82
    of Volvo   42, 65
Brown, Mike   107

Brundtland Report   21,
    192, 241, 265
Business Charter for Sus-
    tainable Development
    134, 206, 214, 215

Cadmium   127
California
    2003 zero emissions law
        46
Canadian Lung Association
    125
Canadian National Climate
    Change Tables   243
Canadian National
    Roundtable on
    Environment and
    Economy   242
CARE Vision 2000   144,
    145
Case studies
    importance of   190
Catalytic converters   44,
    168
Center for Technology
    Assessment (CTA), Ger-
    many   20, 32, 185-200
    government support for
        187
    strategy of   190-91
Centralia   256-57

CFCs (chlorofluorocarbons)
phase-out at SC Johnson
168
phase-out at Sony 134
Chalmers University of
Technology 55, 63
Changing Course
see Brundtland Report
Chiyoda Corporation 75
Chlorofluorocarbons
see CFCs
Chouinard, Yvon 95, 99,
104, 107
Chouinard Equipment 95
Citizens' panels 189
Clean climbing 104
Clean coal technology 251,
257
Climate change 26, 69,
70, 73, 77-78, 248, 251,
254, 262
and the Netherlands
265, 270, 272
and Suncor 72-73
and TransAlta 239-43,
248, 250, 251-54
Cline, Geoff 114
CO_2 emissions
costing at TransAlta
242
Cogeneration 243, 250-51
Cognis 201, 214
Computer industry 275
Concern for Tomorrow 263
Contaminated land 262
Corporate communications
and Henkel 209-10
and SJ Rail 227
Corporate culture
at ASG 161
at Henkel 203
at Patagonia 96, 105,
120
at SC Johnson 167
at SJ Rail 223, 226
at Suncor 83-84
Corporate philanthropy
166
at SC Johnson 167, 174-
76

Corporate social respon-
sibility 79
at Henkel 213, 216
Cosmetics/toiletries 202
Cost accounting
at DaimlerChrysler 179-
84
Cotton production
negative environmental
impacts of 100-101
Covenants 261, 264, 267,
272
and dispute mechanisms
271-72
Covey, Steven 74, 85
Cross Functional Manage-
ment system 146
CTA
see Center for Technol-
ogy Assessment
Curitiba, Brazil 50, 52

Dahlberg, Torsten 51-52
Daily, Gretchen 27
Daily Management system
146
DaimlerChrysler 30, 32,
37, 40, 179-83, 185
and recycling 181
Daly, Herman 21
DBDPO (decabromo-
diphenyloxide) 127
Dell Computer 151
Dematerialisation 160, 194
Design for assembly/
disassembly 140, 141
Design for the Environment
(DfE) 53, 55
Detergents 202, 204, 212,
215
phosphate-free 204
Dialogue on the Environ-
ment (Volvo) 56, 64
Disassembly 130
Dow 250
Dow Europe 152
Dow Jones Sustainability
Group Index 86, 216
Driving Eco-Innovation 28

Earth Tax (Patagonia) 97,
105
Eastman Kodak 46, 151-52
Eckwortzel, Gary 117
ECMA (European Computer
Manufacturers'
Association) 145
Eco TV (Sony Europe)
130-33
Eco-efficiency 27
at SC Johnson 173
benefits of 172
at SJ Rail 170-73
at TransAlta 244
Eco-Efficiency in the
Electronics Industry
(WBCSD) 145
Eco-indicators
in the Netherlands 272
Eco-labels 133, 220, 231
Eco-taxes 272
Ecolab Inc. 202
Ecological Balance Sheet
(AssiDomän) 89-90
Edmonton, Alberta 244
Ekberg, Jörgen 153
Electricity Association, UK
238
Electric power generation
70
Electric utility industry
and deregulation 238
environmental pressures
on 238
Electrocoating 182
Electrolux 27, 63
Electronics industry
environmental pressures
on 133
EMAS (EU Eco-Management
and Audit Scheme) 19,
57, 132, 208, 215, 231
and Sony 141
Emissions standards 40
Emissions trading 70, 77,
83
internal systems of at
TransAlta 242, 244
Employees
at Henkel 205
at IFS 125

at SC Johnson 167, 174-76
at SJ Rail 221, 226
commitment of
  at Patagonia 111-12
education of
  at AssiDomän 89
  at Sony 143-44
  at Suncor 80-81
  at TransAlta 245-46
  at Volvo 44, 53, 56
End-of-Life Vehicle (ELV)
  legislation 46
Energy efficiency 70, 110
Energy-efficient lighting
  251
Energy sector 69-70
Enviro-Box (SC Johnson)
  172
Environmental action plans
  136-37
Environmental awards
  at SC Johnson 171
  at Sony 131, 147-48
Environmental awareness
  in the Netherlands 266
Environmental Calculation
  Programme (Volvo) 65
Environmental Choice™
  (Canada) 125
Environmental Citizenship
  Initiative (TransAlta)
  245-46
Environmental Conserva-
  tion Committees (ECCs)
  (Sony) 134, 136
Environmental indicators
  196, 210, 260
  in the Netherlands 267-70
  at TransAlta 245
Environmental load units
  (ELUs) 55, 64
Environmental manage-
  ment systems (EMSs)
  19, 61
Environmental perfor-
  mance evaluation
  at ASG 155, 157
  at Sony 135-37
  at Volvo 64-65

Environmental planning
  20
Environmental Priority
  Strategies (Volvo *et al.*)
  55, 63
Environmental reporting
  at ASG 152
  in the electricity sector
  145
  at Henkel 210-11
  and NEPP 270
  at Sony 147
  at TransAlta 252-53
Environmental Require-
  ments for All Major
  Suppliers and
  Contractors (Volvo) 57
Environmental and social
  performance
  and employees 27
  and shareholder value
  26-27
Environmental surveys
  of SJ Rail 230-31
Environmental target-
  setting
  at ASG 155, 157
  at Henkel 206, 208
  in the Netherlands 265-70
  at SC Johnson 173
  at Sony 136-38
  at TransAlta 242
  at Volvo 60-61
Ericsson Data Systems
  224
European Union (EU)
  260, 264
  and environmental policy
  265
  Packaging Directive 142
Extended Producer
  Responsibility 142

Fabric-dyeing techniques
  116
Factor Four 194
Factor 10 Club 194
Failure Mode and Effect
  Analysis (FMEA) 55
Federation of Swedish
  Industries 55
Flame-retardants 124

Flexible mechanisms 70,
  73, 77, 242-44, 248,
  253-55
Forbes 97
Ford 151, 158
Ford, William Clay, Jr 40
Forest Stewardship Council
  (FSC) 91
Formaldehyde 127
Fortune 123
Franklin Associates 181
Fuel cells 70
Fuel-efficient trucks 46
Full-cost accounting 211
  of transport 233
Fussler, Claude 28

George, Rick 70, 78, 82
Global Reporting Initiative
  217
Goodale, Ralph 84
Gore, Al 84
Gothenburg Board of Trade
  and Industry
  Development 63
'Green Cargo' (SJ Rail)
  220-21, 234
Green Management 2000
  (Sony) 136, 137
Green Management 2002
  (Sony) 138
Green marketing
  at SJ Rail 234
Green power 240
Green purchasing 81
Green Return (ASG) 152,
  158
Greenhouse Gas Action
  Plan (TransAlta) 239,
  243
Greenhouse gas emissions
  in the Netherlands 265,
  270, 272
Greenhouse effect 69
Greenplus 2000
  programme (Sony)
  131, 137
Grove, Andy 275
Günther, J. 130, 142

Hahn, Sieglinde   148
Hamburg Environment
   Institute   210, 216
Harward, Randy   109, 112,
   114, 120
Henkel   20, 32, 201-17
   corporate environmental
      policy of   205, 206
   corporate overview of
      201-202
   environmental pressures
      on   203-204
   mission statement of
      202
Henkel–Ecolab   202
Henkel, Dr Konrad   214
High-speed tilting trains
   see X2000 tilting trains
Hoshin Kanri   146
Hugo Boss AG   185
Huskey   250
Hutterly, Jane   171

Ibuka, Masaru   129
Idei, Nobuyuki   145
IKEA   220
Institute for Management
   Development (IMD)
   210, 216
Integrated transport sys-
   tems   50-52, 225, 229
Intel   275
Interface Flooring Systems
   (IFS)   20, 30, 31, 123-28
   corporate overview of
      123-24
   and supply chain man-
      agement   125
   and toxic substances man-
      agement   124-28
International Energy
   Agency   69
Internet
   and implications for the
      environment   160
ISO 14000 series   63, 246
   and development of LCA
      standard   63
ISO 14001   19, 26, 40, 57,
   78, 132, 208, 215, 231,
   244, 256

at ASG   154
   at Sony   134, 136, 141
ISO 9000 series   246
ISO 9001   208

Johannesson, Daniel   220,
   224, 233, 234
Johansson, Leif   42, 50, 58
Johnson, H.F., Jr   167
Johnson, Sam   166, 168, 177
Johnson & Johnson   151
Joint implementation   241,
   254
*Journal of Industrial
   Ecology*   107
Juran, Joseph   35
Just-in-Time (JIT)   41-42,
   158, 179

Kainz, Robert   180
Knowledge Management
   System (SC Johnson)
   174
Koeppel, Rob   103
Kyoto Protocol to the UN
   Framework Convention
   on Climate Change
   69, 70, 73, 78, 254

Lambert, Gordon   80
Larsson, Stig   221, 223,
   224, 234, 231, 232
LCA
   see Life-cycle analysis
LCVA
   see Life-cycle value
      assessment
Lead   127
Leslie, Jim   245, 247-250
Levi's   103
Life-cycle analysis (LCA)
   203, 211
   at Patagonia   100-101
   at Sony   137-41, 144
   at Volvo   47, 55-56
Life-cycle management
   (LCM)
   at DaimlerChrysler   179-
      83

Life-cycle value assessment
   (LCVA)   81-82
   at TransAlta   244
LightSWITCH (TransAlta)
   251
Lightweighting   172
Lovins, Amory   194
Lovins, L. Hunter   194
Lloyd Wright, Frank   167

Management by Policy
   system   146
Marikkar, Rahumathulla
   128
Massachusetts Institute of
   Technology (MIT)   267
Material flow analysis
   188, 196, 211
Mazda   151
McCready, Ken   241-42,
   248-49
McDivitt, Roger   113, 117
McKinsey & Co.   261
Molybdenum trioxide   127
Monsanto Canada   253

Nasser, Jac   40
National Environment
   Policy Plan (NEPP),
   Netherlands   20, 33,
   259-74
   aims of   262-63, 268-70
   environmental themes of
      272
   implementation of   263-
      70
   planning and develop-
      ment of   261
Natural gas   70
Netherlands   20
   socioeconomic overview
      of   259-60
Netherlands Environmental
   Management Act 1993
   261, 264
Netherlands Environment
   Ministry
   transformation of   262
Netherlands government
   37

Netherlands Ministry for
    Economic Affairs   264
Netherlands Ministry of
    Housing, Spatial
    Planning and the
    Environment   271
Netherlands National
    Institute for Health and
    the Environment,   271
Netherlands Paper and
    Board Industry   271
Netherlands State Institute
    for Public Health and
    Environmental
    Protection   269
Niagara Mohawk Power
    Corporation   83
Nike   103, 151

OECD
    see Organisation for
        Economic Co-
        operation and
        Development
Offsets   70, 243, 253, 254,
    255
Ohga, Norio   145
Oil Sands Environmental
    Coalition   74
Oil Sands operation
    (Suncor)   67-68, 70-73,
    250
    description of   74
Olsen, Dave   104, 106-108,
    112
Only the Paranoid Survive
    275
Organic cotton   20, 96,
    100-103
Organisation for Economic
    Co-operation and
    Development (OECD)
    260, 264, 265
    Pollution Prevention and
        Control Group of
        265
Organisational change
    at ASG   160-62
    at SJ Rail   222-27, 232
    at Sony   146-47
Our Common Future
    see Brundtland Report

Outdoor clothing and
    equipment sector   98

Packaging   142
    at SC Johnson   172
Page, Bob   249, 255
Partnerships and alliances
    62-63, 79
Patagonia   19, 31, 37, 95-122
    and brand image   109-10
    and conversion to organic
        cotton   100-103, 113
        problems with   104
    and corporate communi-
        cations   103
    corporate overview of
        95-96
    core values of   105-106
    and environmental
        activism   105
    environmental principles
        of   118-19
    new businesses of   110-11
    and product design
        environmental
        impacts of   115-17
    and renewable energy
        104, 108
    and supply chain man-
        agement   102-103,
        117-18
    values-driven culture of
        120
Pembina Institute for
    Appropriate Develop-
    ment   79, 80-81, 246
Pesticides   101
Porsche   185
President's Council for
    Sustainable Develop-
    ment   166
Procter & Gamble   203
Procurement standards   19
Producer responsibility   46
Product assessment process
    of Sony   139-42
Product design   19, 203
    at Henkel   211-12
    at Patagonia   112-18
    at SC Johnson   172-74
    at Sony   137-41, 146
    at Volvo   42, 44, 52-55
        holistic view of   53-54

Product development   19
Product-related environ-
    mental policy   203
    in the Netherlands   267
Product stewardship
    at IFS   125
Product take-back   133, 142
    in the EU   133
    and Sony   132
PVC   104, 117, 130

Qualitative growth   193-94,
    196
Quality of Service
    programme (TransAlta)
    241
QUEST Zero Waste initiative
    (IFS)   123-24

Recycling   133
    and the electricity
        industry   142
    at Sony   132
Rees, W.   26
Renewable energy   20, 70,
    73, 79, 243
    and Patagonia   97, 108
Reno Customer Service
    Center (Patagonia)
    97, 110
Request for Proposal (RFP)
    (TransAlta)   254, 255
Resource-Based Manage-
    ment
    at ASG   154
Resource productivity   191,
    193-94, 196
Responsible Care   206,
    208, 215
Reverse logistics   158

S80   44, 57-58
    Environmental Product
        Declaration of   57-58,
        59, 65
Safety, health, environment
    plus quality manage-
    ment system (SHEQ)
    (Henkel)   207, 208, 211
San Joaquin Valley   101
Sasagawa, Y.   133

SASIL 204

Saskatchewan Soil Enhancement Project 253

SC Johnson 32, 165-78
corporate overview of 165-66
and eco-efficiency 170-73
history of 167-68
mission statement of 168-69
and stakeholder relations 170, 176

Scenario planning
in the transport sector 153

Scenarios
and NEPP 265, 269-70
at Volvo 60

Schenker-BTL 159

Schmidt-Bleek, Friedrich 194

Schmooker, Andrew Bard 275

Servicisation
and Volvo 50
at Henkel 212

'Seven Habits of Highly Effective People' 74

Shaw, Mark 74-75

Shell 70, 151

SHEQ
see Safety, health, environment plus quality management system

Shewchuk, Ron 83

Silica 127

SJ Rail 33, 37, 219-36
business planning system of 225, 232
corporate overview of 219-20
environmental management system of 231
environmental policy of 230-31
and relations with government 233
and relations with trade unions 222, 226, 232

SKS 63

Small and medium-sized enterprises (SMEs) 260

Snyder, Stephen 249, 251, 257

SO_2 emissions 75

Solar energy 70, 73

Solvent-based adhesives 127

Sony 19, 31, 37, 129-50
corporate overview of 129-30
and educational programmes 143-44
and environmental management systems 141
and environmental product design 137-41
organisational infrastructure of 134-35
and packaging 142
and phase-out of CFCs 134
and recycling 142-43

Sony Eco Plaza 144

Sony Environmental Center Europe 142, 144, 148

Stakeholder relations 20, 73-76
at TransAlta 246-47

StatOil 70

Stevens, Larry 275

Stewart, Christine 84

STIL system (SJ Rail) 226, 232

Strategic Cornerstones (TransAlta) 243, 244

Strategies for change management 63-64

Stuart Oil Shale Project, 68, 72, 73

Substance flow analysis 211

Suncor 20, 31, 37, 67-86, 250, 256
'big six' value drivers of 71, 72
climate change strategy of 72-73, 77-78
corporate overview of 67

mission statement of 83
Oil Sands operation of
and stakeholder relations 74-76
and Steepbank Mine 76
problems faced by 70-71
and product development 75
and 'Project Millennium' 72, 76
Sarnia refinery of 78
and stakeholder relations 72-76
principles of 76
and top management support 71
values and beliefs of 84-85

Supply chain management
at Henkel 203
at IFS 125
at Patagonia 102-103
at Volvo 56-57, 60

Surface Technologies 201

Sustainability
business benefits of 37-38, 108-14
and business strategy 23-24, 26-27
at ASG 153-54, 159
components of 35
at Henkel 204-205
at Patagonia 107-108, 120
at SJ Rail 222-23
at Suncor 78-80
at TransAlta 247-48, 250
at Volvo 45-46, 48-49
drivers for
at SC Johnson 166
at TransAlta 240
the nexus model of 29

The Sustainable Business Challenge 144

Sustainable development
definition(s) of 21-22, 191-92, 265
operational principles of 192-93, 196-97
policy tools for 197-98
on a regional basis 195-96

Sustainable forest
management 87
economics of 91-92
Sustainable logistics 151-64
Sustainable mobility 48, 62
see also Volvo Mobility Systems
Sustainable production and consumption 260, 265
Sustainable Racine (SC Johnson) 166, 174, 176
Sustainable Transport 220-21, 223, 233
Swahn, Magnus 153, 160
Sweden 46
and environmental legislation 46
Swedish Environmental Research Institute 55
Swedish National Rail Administration (NRA) 221
Swedish National Road Administration 63
Swedish Society for the Conservation of Nature 220, 231
Swedish Transport Act 1988 221
Sweeney, Kevin 99-100, 102, 121

Teams
at Volvo 41
Thai Alliance Textiles, 113
Third-party logistics 158, 160
'This We Believe' (SC Johnson) 168-69
Top management support 58, 63, 71, 134, 145-46
at Henkel 213
at TransAlta 248
Total Quality Management (TQM) 35, 135, 139, 229, 241
at Patagonia 99

Toxic substances
management 20, 262
at DaimlerChrysler 181
at IFS 124-28
drivers for 124-26
TQM
see Total Quality Management
Trade unions
and SJ Rail 221, 222, 226, 232
Training
and NEPP 267
Transport sector
environmental pressures on 152-53
TransAlta 33, 37, 237-58
and climate change 240-42
climate change strategy of 248, 250, 251-54
corporate overview of 237
and environmental management systems 256
and greenhouse gas emissions 238
internal operations of 237-38, 254, 256-57
and stakeholder dialogue 241-42
Treacy, M. 120

Unilever 203
United Nations Conference on Environment and Development (UNCED) 21
United Nations Conference on Sustainable Development (UNCSD) 260, 264
United Nations Environment Programme (UNEP) 260, 264
Cleaner Production programme of 265
US Environmental Defense Fund 79
US Environmental Protection Agency 215

Volatile organic compound (VOC) emissions 170, 172
Voluntary Climate Change and Registry (VCR) programme 243
Volvo 19, 30, 37, 40-66
corporate overview of 41-42
corporate values of 42-43
and Curitiba, Brazil 50
and employee education 56
and environmental investment 62
and environmental policy infrastructure 61
mission statement of 48
and reorganisation of the board 45-46
and supply chain management 56-57, 60
truck operations of 49
Volvo agreements 264-65
Volvo Mobility Systems 19, 40, 44, 48, 50-52
see also Sustainable mobility
Volvo Truck Corporation 45

Wackernagel, M. 26
Waste-water treatment 170
WBCSD
see World Business Council for Sustainable Development
Weizsäcker, Ernst Ulrich von 194
Wendel, Agneta 52
Wharton, Don 252
Wiersema, F. 120
Williams, Marshall 240
Wind energy 20, 70, 73
and Patagonia 97
Winkhaus, Dietrich 215
Winsemius, Peter 261
Wolfe, Terri 111
Working Mother 97

The World Bank   21, 70

World Business Council for Sustainable Development (WBCSD)   22, 26, 79, 85, 144, 145, 252, 253, 255

World Wide Fund for Nature (WWF)   158

Worldwatch Institute's *State of the World: 1998*   25

X2000 tilting trains   221-23, 227, 229

Yeung, Johnny   113

Zero emissions   146

ZF Friedrichshafen AG   185

Zinc borate   127